FIRE BY NIGHT

FIRE BY NIGHT

The Story of One Pathfinder Crew
& Black Thursday,
16th/17th December 1943

JENNIE GRAY

GRUB STREET · LONDON

Published by
Grub Street
The Basement
10 Chivalry Road
London SW11 1HT

British Library Cataloguing in Publication Data
Gray, Jennie
 The fire by night: the dramatic story of one pathfinder
 crew and Black Thursday, 16/17 December 1943
 1. Great Britain. Royal Air Force. Bomber Command – History
 2. World War, 1939-1945 – Aerial operations, British
 3. Survival after airplane accidents, shipwrecks, etc.
 I. Title
 940.5'44'941

ISBN 1-902304-63-2

Typeset by Pearl Graphics, Hemel Hempstead

Printed and bound in Great Britain by
Biddles Ltd, Guildford and King's Lynn

This book is dedicated to the memory of

Ted Thackway, George Grundy, Jack Powell,
Tony Lawrence, Sandy Grant, Leslie Laver,
& Joe Mack who survived them by 50 years

"Bomber Command's first and everlasting enemy
– the weather . . ."

John Terraine, *The Right of the Line*

Contents

Acknowledgements

First and foremost, my eternal gratitude to Ken Basham, who took me to see the reputed crash site of K-King, and later permitted a detailed investigation with the Lincolnshire Aircraft Recovery Group. I also owe Ken a huge debt of gratitude for collecting and passing on local stories about the crash, and in particular for putting me in touch with Bob Plane, who very sadly died of cancer shortly after I spoke to him.

I would also particularly like to thank Michael Bowyer, the well-known aviation writer, for putting me in touch with Ken Basham in the first place, and for being the person who first confirmed we really were dealing with the remnants of a 97 Squadron aircraft. Also Dave Stubley and Ian Blackamore of the Lincolnshire Aircraft Recovery Group, for further invaluable help in establishing the true significance of the crash site.

I would like to most sincerely thank the families of Ted Thackway, Leslie Laver, George Grundy, and Tony Lawrence, for so kindly sharing their memories and their photographs, and also Nancy Leeman and Mary Brown who knew Ted very well and who sent me the only surviving photographs of him in the RAF. In addition my thanks are due to Judith Allott, daughter of Agnes Powell, Jack's wife, and to Jack Coates, the brother of William Darby Coates who won the DFM on the night of 16th/17th December 1943.

As for information about RAF Station Bourn and 97 Squadron, my greatest thanks go to Albert East, John Arthurson, Arthur Tindall, and Arthur Spencer (who most kindly also read the entire manuscript at two stages in its development and made several invaluable points). Also Joan Beech, Geoffrey Gilbert, Maurice Hemming, Tiger Billows, Bill Ford, Bob Philips, John Jones, and Percy Smith.

Last but by no means least, Walter Bushby, a former member of the ground crew at Bourn, who also read the manuscript at a critical stage. Walter gave invaluable help in establishing Sidney Matthews' living and working conditions at Bourn, and joined happily in all the theorising as to the effect which they may have had upon his actions.

I have received the help of dozens of other people in researching this book, and this list would go on forever if I included everyone. However, I would also very much like to thank the following:

For Invaluable Local Knowledge of Bourn: Cyril Crow, Jim Hansford

Blackpool and W/Ops Training: Frank Munro

FIDO & Black Thursday: Geoffrey Williams, author of *Flying Through Fire*, a History of FIDO

The Crash of D-Donald on Ingles Farm: Colin Stocker, Don Pawley, and Clair Nutting

Texel Island: Bram van Dijk; Robert Brautigam for his translations and general help and encouragement

Ely Hospital: My uncle, Dr P M McAllen, for all his help with listing and understanding Joe's injuries, and for tracing Watson-Jones's book. Also Peter Lawler, Tom Williams, Valerie Cornford, Herbert Bailey, Les Mitchum, Leslie Morgan, Jack Reynolds, and many others.

The Leas: Above all, David Page, who worked as a remedial instructor both at Ely and The Leas and was a veritable gold-mine of information and photographs. Also Peter Ray, George Hodgson, Ken Dykes, Norman Scullard, John Gitting, Jim O'Neill, Mr and Mrs John Curwood, Mrs Shillcock, and many others.

And lastly The RAF Museum at Hendon and The Imperial War Museum at London and Duxford, in particular Christine Campbell and Mr Eddie West at the latter.

One

The Shadow of the Past

Winter, 1961

The light is off in my bedroom, but the door stands ajar. Light slants in from the hall, making a pleasant half-darkness. My bed is warm and very comfortable, the bedclothes sweet-scented with their own particular homely smell. My father sits on the edge of the bed, and his weight makes the mattress tilt, strapping down the blankets so that I can hardly move. Yet this does not bother me – in fact, I like it.

In the half-light I can just make out the features of his face. I am holding his hand, which is very smooth, very warm and rather chubby. He is telling me a bedtime story. I have heard it before – ten or twenty times at least – who knows how many? – but it never grows stale, it never fades, and each time I find it just as exciting. I often ask for it, taking great pleasure in the ritual of the telling, and he does not seem to mind how often it has to be repeated. To me, it is incomparably bewitching and atmospheric, especially as the danger is long past and Dad sits there, quite safe and warm, his living weight pinning down the bed beside me.

It is a true story, his true history, and as I hear his words I see the pictures in my mind, pictures painted in living fire on the shadows of my room. So intense is my involvement that, as he tells the tale, I find myself actually *THERE*, standing secretly in some vantage point, watching the past unroll, invisible to the actors of the drama.

One o'clock in the morning, miles from anywhere, no houses nearby, no people stirring, just winter-bitten fields with black hedgerows filing endlessly along a country lane. Night, December, cold and damp; the air hangs with a preternatural stillness, all sound and movement muffled by a dense white fog. There is a faint iron-like taste to that fog; it comes in my mouth as I breathe it. The only noise is the constant drip of moisture in the hedgerows. But I wait, and I wait, and at last I hear it – the swish of bicycle wheels approaching through the darkness.

A man is coming, hurrying back from Cambridge where he has been seeing his girlfriend. He is on his way home to a wartime base, going quickly, wasting no time – he'll be in trouble when he returns, because he has been out without permission.

And then he hears, I hear – very close – the roar of a plane's engines. Before we know it, the plane is above us, quite literally above us, looming a mere twenty or thirty feet overhead. It is a gigantic thing, massive, inconceivably huge, a jet-black cross of thunderous power. The sound of its four great engines is deafening. As it passes overhead, a gust of terrible wind sweeps over us. Something is dreadfully, dreadfully wrong – we know it but we cannot stop it – all we can do is witness it happen.

Infinitesimal moments later there comes the horrible, grinding, splintering impact of the crash as the wreck ploughs its way across a muddy field. The fog-bound night shudders and reverberates. Then once more the silence falls, a silence so unnatural that it paralyses.

Somewhere, hidden in the fog and darkness, lies the plane.

Then tiny red and gold lights begin to appear through the haze. For a moment the man on the bicycle is mesmerised, then like a mad thing he throws the bike aside, hurls himself over the field gate, and runs as fast as he can towards the wrecked aircraft.

The fire is taking hold now, beginning to creep and snake through the twisted metal, and despite the fact that it is winter the air is getting hotter and hotter, and the field is illuminated ever more brightly. Bullets begin to go off, zipping and cracking in all directions as the ammunition for the machine guns is ignited. Yet, with incredible bravery, the man enters the plane in the search for survivors.

In the middle of the plane, next to the main spar between the wings, he finds a young man, sliding in and out of dreams because of his severe injuries, loss of blood and shock. He is trapped from his waist downwards in twisted metal, and all the while the metal is getting hotter and hotter. The rescuer works, sweating and cursing, to free him. And at last, by a miracle, he succeeds; he gets his mangled and bloody legs clear and half carries, half drags him out of that wreckage. He drags him to the shelter of a hedge and gently lays him down, places him on the cold ground and wraps the folds of a parachute around him.

The young man lies there, and like a dream he sees the night, he sees the fog, he sees the flames illuminating the field, and in the centre of it all he sees the plane in which there are still six men, his crewmates.

The plane explodes into an inferno.

The wounded man on the cold grass is my father.

Spring, 1997

The farm manager, Ken Basham, drove us in his landrover down a very long straight track normally barred to public access. The spring morning was beginning to clear though it was still slightly hazy, and the landscape benefited from this milky light because to my eyes it all looked very bare, flat, dull and nondescript.

It had taken months of research to get to this place, to a farm in Cambridgeshire very close to Bourn, the RAF airfield at which my father had once been based. His aircraft had crashed in the early hours of the morning of 17th December 1943, one and a half miles from the airfield, between the two small villages of Hardwick and Caldecote. However, none of the wartime records carried a map reference, and what had brought me here were the local reports that a heavy bomber had crashed on the farm during the war.

We bumped on down the stony track, beyond which stretched the vast fields, subdivided by ditches, their crops just beginning to sprout in the hazy sunshine. And at last we came to the end of the track and the landrover stopped.

'This is the place,' said Ken Basham, 'Most of the bits of the aircraft were found roughly in the middle there. The tractor boys used to pick them up.'

We were facing the most enormous flat bare field, almost half a mile from side to side. The only thing which marked it out from the preceding prairies was a deep grass-lined ditch, straight as an arrow, which had been dug out since the war. The ditch had no trees or shrubs along its entire length, only the grass on its sides was a little more luxuriant than normal. Nor did the earth in the field in front of us have any distinguishing features. Seemingly most of the indigenous stones had been removed, and what remained, washed clean by the recent torrential rain, lay on the surface like a scattering of bone-white fragments. The soil was tan-coloured, with the faintest haze of green on it where the linseed crop was sprouting. Linseed apparently bloomed a gorgeous lavender-mauve in summer, but now it was scarcely higher than blades of lawn grass.

The farm track truncated at this field's edge, more or less in the dead centre. About 400 yards of emptiness stretched out to the left and about 400 identical yards stretched out to the right. A solitary skylark, somehow finding somewhere to live and something to eat in this inhospitable plain, hung above us in the sky, singing its fluttering and slightly melancholy song.

Ahead of us, some 300 yards away, was a hedge, the only hedge in any proximity, the hedge which marked the western boundary of the farm. Beyond it, the radio mast at the airfield, which was still in existence though no longer an RAF base, could be seen in the far distance, gleaming silver-white through the haze.

The huge block of flat land, including this field before us and the land we had just crossed, was 160 acres in all. It was known as the Hay, 'Hay' being a very old field name for enclosed land. Despite its similarity to modern prairie fields, the Hay had in fact always been this dead-straight and level. A photograph taken in 1912 proves how very little the place has changed. In the picture, Colonel S F Cody is demonstrating the abilities of a crazy-looking bi-plane, the up-and-coming weapon of war, 'the Terror that Flieth', such an amazing creation that even the King, George V, came come down to see it. The Hay made a perfect natural landing strip, and it and neighbouring fields were used throughout the First World War.

In the depression of the 1930s, the farmer who used the Hay for rough grazing let it go to seed. There were tough weeds and little stunted trees, and the indigenous plant, gorse, soon took over with its tall, yellow-flaring, iron-spiked bushes. The scrub was only cleared when the next war began and all available land was being pressed into food production. By the time the heavy bomber came to land on it, the Hay was a ploughed field, long furrows of tan-coloured mud of a peculiarly sticky and adhesive quality.

Ken Basham began to tell us what he had heard of local reports of the crash. I listened, but at the same time my attention was distracted – I just could not believe that I was here and the potential amazing significance of this place. There cannot be many less picturesque spots on earth. Over in the distance was Hardwick Wood, one or two fields away, bluish on this slightly hazy morning and probably itself full of bluebells, but it was all that attracted the eye. The immense field before us, devoid of either undulation or vegetation, was as depressing as a desert, though it must surely have gladdened the heart of a farmer, because, as Mr Basham was telling us, the soil was so good. All the same, this was apparently the least valuable land on the farm because it was so difficult to drain. It sometimes flooded and the water was very difficult to get off. Over on the far side there had once been a pond, now filled in but still getting its occasional revenge on interfering humans. The soil in the field was always heavy and damp.

This thoroughly blank canvas was potentially the scene of the greatest dramatic story of my childhood. How could this be? I could scarcely believe it.

We were just about as far away as one could possibly get from a cold foggy night in December in wartime, and yet, even allowing for that, the likelihood of this being the right place was almost impossible to grasp. I had always imagined somewhere much lusher, less barren, with mole-hummocked pastureland and thickset hedges. In my mind's eye I could still clearly see the shadow of the fire flickering on the rough grass, see the hedge beside which the wounded man lay. And of course there had to be a lane, a lane along which a man could ride his bike. I tried to reconcile my old childhood vision with what lay before me. What on earth was the rescuer, the man on the bike, doing out here in this desert in the middle of the night? Where was the lane along which he had been passing? Where was the gate over which he had flung himself? The whole thing seemed to dissolve in utter nonsense.

Yet before an hour was out, what had initially seemed so absurd and ridiculous began to make a little more sense. It was to be many months before all the pieces came together, before I knew for sure that this was really the place where my father's plane had crashed, but even as we left that afternoon it had begun to seem that the truth might indeed be there, written out in that flat uncompromising landscape.

Two

With Bomber Command

I. Joe's Early War Years

Like almost all the RAF people in this story, my father was not a professional airman. He was a civilian who, like millions of others, had his peaceful life cataclysmically disrupted when Germany broke out of her boundaries to conquer what threatened to be the whole of Europe.

At the time of the outbreak of war, on September 3rd 1939, Joe was seventeen years old. He had left school some three months earlier, and was then on a business course, prior to officially joining the family company in April 1940.

Peter Hughes Mack, always nicknamed Joe, a name he had bestowed on himself in early childhood, was the only son of Kathleen and Reginald John Mack. He was the middle child in the family, and had an older half-sister, Monica, and a younger sister, Daphne. Kathleen, who idolised her son, had been married once before, to a clergyman who had died in 1918 in the influenza pandemic. Her second marriage gave her a very pleasant life but it appears to have been one of partnership rather than passion, and her deepest affections would eventually centre on Joe.

Reginald Mack, always known simply by his initials of R.J., was a well-respected and very successful City businessman, a man of rectitude and iron will, strict but very generous to his three children. He had come from a poor background, the son of a humble schoolteacher in a small village near Liverpool, and he knew the value of hard work and self-discipline. He was also a very shrewd judge of character and must have realised quite early on that Joe would not take after him.

Joe hated being tied down to anything serious; he loved clowning about and acting the fool. He had done extremely badly at his detested public school, Sedbergh, which is why his father had taken him away early. Joe was neither academic nor gifted at sports, and his school reports had been almost uniformly appalling. His teachers, however, had acknowledged his exceptional aptitude for music, a near genius which had begun to show itself when he was only five years old.

Yet even here Joe shied away from anything serious and instead turned his talents to amusing people. He was a brilliant improviser, had an

5

excellent voice, and could be extremely funny when in high spirits, showing off at the piano or with a trumpet. A droll and endearing fellow, people loved his company and he made friends easily, though these friendships were always rather superficial.

Joe's greatest emotional support was his family. His sisters and mother indulged and petted him, and R.J. (though, like most contemporary fathers, a somewhat unapproachable figure) always carefully looked after his son's best interests. Yet though Joe loved his family, he was markedly secretive with them. He would often refuse to volunteer information, even about the most trivial things, as if he needed to keep a private world away from them. Sometimes this would result in slightly absurd situations, when he would tell funny stories about his friends at school but would completely refuse to give their names. Joe was also not above telling the occasional lie. Once again the main motivation was to preserve a private world, but he was also painfully conscious of how much his family expected of him and would sometimes fib to make himself seem more successful than he really was.

Five foot seven in height, with brown hair and hazel eyes, Joe had suffered a series of severe childhood illnesses. He had been born with spina bifida occulta, though by now he appeared to have perfectly recovered from it apart from a certain physical awkwardness and clumsiness. No one realised that the damaging effects of the spina bifida were still with him, and that there were serious long-term implications for his health. He would pass his RAF medical in 1941 with no problems, and it would not be until around 1949 that he would begin to suffer from the occasional mild epileptic fit.

The family company, Andrew Chalmers, was a large imports firm specialising in tobacco. The prospect of being a tobacco merchant had never filled Joe with any degree of enthusiasm; he had wanted to have a career in music but had lacked the will to stand up to his practical father. Yet R.J. had been right not to encourage him in his hopes – Joe would never have put in the dogged hard work necessary to succeed in such a highly competitive field.

Joe was also very fond of the status and luxuries which money brings, and Andrew Chalmers was to keep him in considerable affluence all his life. But at seventeen years old, viewing the sensible but unalluring prospects before him, he must have thought there was a lot more in him than would ever be called forth by the tobacco business. It would be the war which would give him his one great independent chance to prove himself. The RAF would be the biggest adventure of his life, and nothing which came thereafter would ever equal its emotional impact.

Andrew Chalmers' offices were in the Minories on the eastern borders of the City, situated conveniently close to the London Docks. However, on the outbreak of war, with habitual caution R.J. moved the company's main operations out to Hertfordshire, to the family home, long the unofficial centre of the business. Little Kendals, though neither large nor grand, was set in its own extensive fields and woods, some way outside the large village of Radlett. Its best feature was the very long and beautiful entrance avenue, which gave what was otherwise a fairly simple Victorian farmstead the air of something grand.

Delighted to be away from the hated constraints of boarding school, Joe settled down quickly to his new routine. It was the period of the Phoney War, months of uneasy quiet in which nothing seemed to be happening. With the ebullience of youth, Joe made the best of it, and seems to have rather enjoyed living and working at home – it had a multitude of small benefits, such as playing bowls on the lawn during the lunch break in fine weather.

By the summer of 1940, however, the fine weather no longer seemed so halcyon. Denmark, Norway, Holland, Belgium, and France had been occupied. It was the height of the Battle of Britain, when Fighter Command fought against massive odds to keep their airfields operational and their planes in the air. Devastating German attacks were mounted on Britain's fighter airfields in an attempt to pulverise the air defences prior to an all-out invasion. Perhaps when Joe stood outside in the garden, playing bowls, he may occasionally have seen one of the dog fights which so enthralled and horrified those who watched from the ground that summer. It was a desperate struggle, and the Luftwaffe came very near to winning it. British losses were terrible, though the figures were exaggerated by poor intelligence and the Germans believed them to be worse than they really were. The Germans' sudden switch of tactics to bombing British cities was made as much in the hope of drawing out the remaining fighters and destroying them as in the expectation of crushing civilian morale.

So began the Blitz. The abrupt change of tactics, together with the overwhelming force of the opening raid on London, took the defenders by surprise. The Germans attacked the capital without warning during the afternoon of 7th September and then again that evening, the prelude to two months of ferocious attacks, 2nd November being the only raid-free night of the whole period.

On only the third night of the raids, the premises of Andrew Chalmers were hit. Number 22 Minories, a dark rambling old-fashioned building on four floors, which had been the firm's London home since 1919, was totally gutted by incendiary bombs. Defensive precautions against the raids were shambolic, and Number 22 Minories, just as thousands of buildings like it, was lost because there were no fire-watchers.

Over the remainder of 1940 and throughout 1941, the Germans mounted horrendous bombings of London, Liverpool, Southampton, Portsmouth, Plymouth, Birmingham, Coventry, Bristol, and many other British cities. Casualties were huge. In the first four months of the Blitz 22,000 civilians were killed, nearly 13,500 in London alone. Many thousands more were injured. During 1941, a further 20,000 died.

Both Joe and R.J. had by now joined the Local Defence Volunteers (later the Home Guard), and were also on Air Raid Precautions duty in the evenings after work. In old age my father would write a memoir about his life, a short and sketchy account which he never finished, and this contained several anecdotes about his war years, beginning with his service in the ARP:

> At the bottom of Gills Hill there was a Bomb Shelter, half-buried on purpose . . . Six of us used to sit around this shelter at desks with telephones waiting for a signal to be alerted and at right angles to these desks was another desk looking a bit more important where the man in charge used to sit. Dad used to do that quite regularly. We used to be on shift work, and I remember the earliest time I had to report for duty was 5.30 a.m. and all this was on top of whatever work we were doing during normal business hours . . . What I was supposed to do in the event of a real raid was to ride my bicycle to King Street, Watford, and alert Headquarters; why I could not have done that on the telephone defeats me. There was only one occasion on which I had to do this and it turned out to be a false alarm.

Watford was six miles away, a distance which even as an eighteen year old my father would have considered most strenuous for a bike ride.

Joe's life changed forever when, shortly after his nineteenth birthday, he joined the RAF Volunteer Reserves on 24th April 1941. Conscription would have been coming to him anyway, and volunteering gave him some element of choice over what happened to him. However, there was also a very large element of patriotism, pride and excitement about taking this dramatic action, stepping aside from the path which had been so carefully planned out for him by his father, and going off into the unknown to make something of himself. It must have been an anxious time before he knew that he had passed the tests of the Euston Air Candidate Selection Board, which was based at Euston House, Eversholt Street, in north-west London. When he was told he had been accepted for aircrew training – this young man who had failed to make the grade in just about every subject at school – it must have been one of the most gratifying moments of his life, for he had won his place despite a fair degree of competition.

All RAF aircrew were volunteers, and the service had their pick from a large number of applicants. Since the Battle of Britain, the RAF had become the most glamorous and exciting of the services, and everyone wanted to be a fighter pilot, one of those legendary awe-inspiring figures who had won the adulation of the entire nation.

Fighter boys looked the part, being allowed a degree of latitude in dress and behaviour which would have been unthinkable in the Army or the Navy. Far less publicity was given to the crews of Bomber Command, who had stoically gone through the most awesome feats of endurance to fight their relatively unknown battles. Guy Gibson, in his classic book *Enemy Coast Ahead*, wrote amusingly of the clashes between the 'two age-old rivals – the Bomber Barons and the Fighter Glamour Boys', contrasting the flattery and adulation so lavishly bestowed on 'the flying-booted, scarf-flapping' fighter pilots with the more spartan and anonymous lot which was that of the bomber crews. This rivalry eventually led to the wartime Battle of the Snake-Pit, an affair of purloined squadron crests and kidnapped Wing Commanders, which is detailed in all its trivial but hilarious detail in Gibson's book.

I do not know if my father ever aspired to be with Fighter Command, but one thing is for sure – no one ever thought of him as pilot material. He was uncoordinated, a little clumsy, maladroit (and was later to be a terrible car driver); no one in their right mind would have put him in charge of an aircraft. Instead, No 11 Air Crew Selection Board commented on his papers as they accepted him: 'Recommended for training as OBSERVER and for commissioned rank'. He was destined to become an officer, with an officer's job. There can be no doubt that Joe's prosperous middle-class background, together with the accent and manners acquired from his public school education, had won him this favourable verdict. His poor academic and athletic achievements appeared unimportant to the selectors because in other ways he was their ideal type of recruit.

Joe, like the thousands of others who joined the RAF in 1941, could never have foreseen his eventual involvement in Bomber Command's campaign of area bombing, when Germany would be plastered with thousands of tons of explosives, and thousands of young men would die in delivering them. When RAF recruits enlisted, they placed their fate in the hands of their masters – they had very little control over what use their masters chose to make of them.

There were still some months to go before that extraordinarily controversial historical figure, Arthur Travers Harris, took over as Air Officer Commanding in Chief, but already Bomber Command was expanding dramatically. From being a minuscule Command in September 1939, numbering approximately 14,280 men, the Command was to grow into a mighty war-machine with the most voracious appetite for personnel. The number of men being transferred into the Command as the war progressed was nothing short of amazing. By July 1943, at the time my father began training on heavy bombers, the personnel in the Command had risen to 192,494. One year later, the peak figure of 226,294 was achieved.

So important was Bomber Command's contribution to the war effort deemed that eventually it had an industrial capacity equal to that devoted to the entire British army. Alongside the colossal expansion in manpower ran an equally staggering investment in planes and airfields. At one stage in 1942, at the height of the construction program, a new airfield was being opened every week after an average of eighteen months spent on its development. John Maynard, in *Bennett and the Pathfinders*, has compared this feat, with its roving bands of navvies, to the early days of railway building. Like the increase in the number of airmen, this program represented the expansion of Bomber Command on the most stupendous scale.

Joe had no foreknowledge when he joined the RAF of what contribution he would eventually make as a minute cog in this immense war-machine, but he knew that he had been selected for the prestigious ranks of the aircrew and the glamour of it must have thrilled his heart.

Though he had passed the RAF selection procedure in April, Joe did not begin his training until June of that same year. He waited some three months to be called back, though during this time he could proudly wear the RAF Volunteer Reserve badge which had been issued to him on enlistment. Eventually, however, the small buff piece of paper came, 'Notice to Recruit to Rejoin for Service', with a railway warrant attached for the journey to his training station. He was told to bring with him the RAFVR badge, his National Registration Identity card and Civilian Ration Book, his Unemployment Book and Health and Pensions Insurance Card, his gas-mask, and an absolute minimum of personal requirements – a uniform would be issued as soon as he arrived. This journey into the unknown with so little baggage from his former life would be a stripping away of both emotional ties and his former civilian identity. He would be leaving his family, his protective parents, and his pleasant middle-class home, to join instead the community of airmen, to experience the comradeship and friendship only to be found in service life and to experience its draconian discipline, its spartan living conditions, and – for the time being at least – an almost complete loss of personal autonomy.

And so Joe left his comfortable life, thereafter to enter, so far as his traceable history is concerned, a sort of featureless blank or Dark Ages. Only a skeletal outline of the next two years can be drawn, based upon the bare facts in his MOD service record. These tell of what mustering or trade he was listed under, and at which training camps he was based. The other thing they show, just perceivable behind the terse hieroglyphics and cabalistic squiggles, is that his progress in the RAF was initially rather faltering.

His initial mustering was ACH/OBSERVER, the ACH standing for Aircrafthand. 'Observer' was an already antiquated title, referring back to the days of two-man planes, when one man would be the pilot and the other would be lookout, gunner and navigator. In 1942, as roles in the RAF became increasingly specialised, the title of 'observer' would be replaced by that of 'navigator'. Nonetheless, the badge they wore would for some time continue to be an 'O'.

Navigators were highly esteemed. Together with pilots and bomb aimers, they were classified as the PNB group; these were the core members of any Lancaster bomber crew and thus likely to soon be promoted to be officers.

The other three roles on Lancasters by the time my father joined his crew were wireless operator, air gunner, and flight engineer. These men were not so highly skilled and this was reflected in the fact that they generally held a lower rank and often remained Non-Commissioned Officers, NCOs. By the time Joe had become, in fact, not a navigator but a wireless operator, ALL bomber crews were of the NCO class or above, for it had been decreed, in recognition of the appalling risks they ran, that none should be below the rank of Sergeant.

It must be said, however, that the RAF was by far the most egalitarian branch of the three services, and rank for its own sake was not greatly respected. The command structures of the bomber crews were of necessity very fluid, for every member was critically important to the plane's survival. A pilot who was a squadron leader would react instantaneously to the commands given to him by the lowly sergeant acting as his rear gunner, because hesitation all too often meant that the whole crew died. With such an intense need to trust and depend on one another, officers and NCOs did not bother overmuch with the niceties of who was supposedly more important than whom.

As Aircraftman 2nd Class (AC2), the very lowest rank in the RAF, Joe commenced his training at 'Stratford/Avon', the home of both No 9 Receiving Wing and No 9 Initial Training Wing, which would have handled the earliest induction procedures.

There is a photograph taken at this time which shows him with a group of fellow RAF trainees. The white flashes on their caps, just behind the front brim, indicate that all of them have been selected for aircrew. All wear immaculate but basic uniforms, with no insignia or special emblems. They are grinning like a group of Cheshire cats, and all look most happy and cheerful. Annoyingly (though probably it was intentional, given strict security in wartime), the sign on the building behind them is obscured.

By August, Joe had risen two ranks, from Aircraftman 2nd Class, through Aircraftman 1st Class (AC1), to Leading Aircraftman (LAC). At this point his service papers show he is still mustered as an observer, that is to say a navigator, and indeed it is probably at this point that he begins his navigator's course, having completed basic training.

By March of 1942, however, he has lost his promotion and reverted back to AC1, a rank he keeps for the following fourteen months. His mustering is also reclassified, and from thenceforth he is set down as WO/AG, wireless operator/air gunner. The inference is obvious – he has failed to make the grade as navigator. Throughout his training period his character has been noted as 'vg', 'very good', so his demotion has not been caused by bad behaviour – he just hasn't been strong enough in the technical sense.

His failure was not really that surprising. A navigator's was a job which above all demanded the uttermost meticulousness and precision. A navigator had to work in a very cramped poorly lit space, plotting his charts, working his sums, measuring angles and distances precisely, never losing his concentration for one moment. Joe simply did not have that kind of mental ability. He was a slow learner, a dawdler and a daydreamer, something which had been frequently noted at his schools, where his inattention and lack of focus had infuriated his teachers.

Equally clear was the reason for his new speciality. The primary requirement for a wireless operator was Morse code at a minimum of 18 words per minute. If one considers that each word meant 3 or 4 beats *per letter*, in the characteristic Morse pattern of dashes or dots, one can easily see the level of skill in this. Being an exceptionally good piano player, with nimble fingers and an instinctive feel for sound patterns, must have given Joe a head start. But all the same, losing his role as navigator was a very considerable step-down for him; it was a humiliating failure and he knew it. It also meant that in the long run he was unlikely to win his commission, or ever rise above the rank of Warrant Officer.

Prior to Joe's remustering, he had moved to the Reception and Despatch Unit in Blackpool. The R&D unit had its headquarters at the Winter Gardens (later 82-84 Topping Street). From the outbreak of the war, the RAF had moved into Blackpool in a very big way. Requisitioning had been carried out on an enormous scale and every possible building was used; church halls, cafes, garages, even the town football pitch had been taken over, together with almost all the seaside lodging houses and all the hotels. There was sleeping, working, medical and teaching accommodation for many thousands of RAF men and WAAFs, almost all being trained as wireless operators or 'w/ops'. At peak periods, there might be as many as 40,000 extra people to be catered for. It was only in 1943 that the huge numbers began to drop a little. Frank Munro, an ex-airman who commenced his w/op training in Blackpool in January 1943, remembers that 'locals used to mention that it was better now "because some of you lot have left"'.

In his massive three volume tome, *The RAF Medical Services*, S C Rexford-Welch mentions some of the problems of this mass feeding and housing. Many of the apartment houses 'fell far below either normal civilian or Service standards of habitability, and often the dirt and decay of years was all too evident; washing and lavatory facilities were ill-kept, and many of the basement kitchens were infested by pests'. The problems were compounded by the unsympathetic attitude of many landladies who did not respond well to 'this call to patriotism and the opportunity to assist the war effort'. Rexford-Welch records how 'certain landladies with an eye to pecuniary advantage' created numerous difficulties as they tried to gain exemption from billeting, either by claiming personal ill health or by accusing their billetees of such heinous crimes as bed-wetting, 'the whole matter causing considerable embarrassment to all concerned'.

Joe was to spend the first eight months of 1942 in this region of harridan landladies. I have no information about his time there other than what he once told my brother, Rick. He said that he had had a great time in Blackpool, and that his landlady (whom Rick laughingly dubbed Mrs

Miggins) had been very good. He had also met a very nice girl there. And that minute scrap of information is all there is.

Others remember Blackpool rather more vividly and rather less flatteringly. Frank Munro recalls that he and his fellow billetees were immediately allocated duties at their boarding house by 'Him and Her' – peeling potatoes, washing up, and so forth – and were also told in no uncertain terms that they were forbidden to use the bath. 'Once a week we marched to the Derby Baths in North Blackpool and everybody had to remove all their clothing and swim in the large pool. No soap was allowed, so you get the idea . . .'

Blackpool was parlous cold in winter, miserable and bitterly depressing, with incessant rain and wind. However, in compensation there was plenty of good, cheap entertainment. There was the Ice Rink, together with numerous dance halls, cinemas, music halls, and theatres. A popular attraction was the evening singsongs at the Tower with Reginald Dixon on the Mighty Wurlitzer organ, later to be parodied by a thousand rear-gunners when they called their revolving gunturrets their Mighty Wurlitzers. The sing-songs attracted huge crowds. Pip Beck wrote, in *A WAAF in Bomber Command*, of 'becoming part of a vast assorted choir, singing old songs, popular songs, creating with our massed voices a great wave of sound . . . crashing against the walls like the sea-waves outside . . . Coming away at the end of it we felt light-headed and wonderfully free – and it was cheaper than alcohol.'

In the daytime, the training was intensive. By April, Joe had begun at No 10 (Signals) Recruiting Centre – it was as a Signaller that he was eventually to qualify, and the 'S' insignia can be clearly seen in the last photograph of him in the RAF, taken the following year when he became a Pathfinder.

As so many others did, Joe would have known the Olympia Hall in the Winter Garden all too well. The Hall was a massive place, inhospitable, echoing, and bitterly cold. In it were dozens of long tables, on each side of which sat numerous airmen with earphones clamped on their heads. Frank Munro paints a slightly lurid picture of the place, but it is quite obvious that the incessant, unrelenting buzzing and humming of the Morse in the earphones could drive sensitive people into fits:

> The Corporal at the end of each table sat there and instructed us in the Morse Code . . . we were to remove the earphones if the Morse became too much for one to put up with. Many did not make the grade. It sent them a bit round the bend and always there were SPs [Service Police] at the end of the Hall. They moved sharply towards the table where the Airman was shouting or kicking the seat. He would be removed and we never saw him again. I think they were removed and spent a couple of days in hospital and were then posted on somewhere else in some other trade.

The trainees were also allocated other duties, including fire-watching on some nights. Every so often there would be an Active Defence Exercise, which typically would involve a forced march of five or six miles, followed by firing from 200 and 100 yards, and finally 'charging the target'. There was also the much loathed square-bashing and marching in formation through the streets of Blackpool. Mass PT was held in the Tower Ballroom, or even on the beach, blasted by wind and salt spray. Bayonet Fighting and Grenade Training also took place in full public view at the Concourse Field.

Frank Munro remembers the compulsory attendance at the rifle ranges:

> Much shouting from the NCOs – 'Keep the bloody gun pointed towards the target, don't swing around and point it at your mates', and so on and so on.
>
> Another thing we had to put up with was 'Get your hair cut'. For the service personnel one could obtain a haircut for 4d.
>
> On Sundays if there were no Church parades we would walk or travel by tram to South Beach. This was a huge funfair . . .
>
> This went on for sixteen weeks with the square-bashing mixed in with it and the once a week bath.

At the end of August 1942, his Morse up to speed, Joe left Blackpool for No 3 Signals School, situated at Compton Bassett, near Calne in Wiltshire. Compton Bassett took many airmen from the Blackpool training centre as did its nearby sister station, No 2 Radio School at Yatesbury, the eventual destination of Frank Munro.

The standard course at Compton Bassett was thirteen weeks, and in this period you were trained as a Ground Wireless Operator. You needed a further period of training, of approximately the same duration, if you were destined to become an Air Wireless Operator. And even then your training was not complete, for there was a further fortnight to be spent on air gunnery – at this stage in the war wireless operators were still being trained to double as air gunners.

The Ground Wireless Operator course at Compton Bassett ran strictly to timetable. Summer Reveille was at six o'clock in the morning, breakfast at seven and first parade at eight. Study periods began at 8.15 and continued throughout the day until quarter to six at night, though there was a twenty minute break in the morning, one hour for lunch, and half an hour of mass PT in the afternoon. There were no classes on a Sunday, though one would not be allowed off the camp without permission. Only one weekend of leave was allowed during the entire course, between the fifth and eighth week after commencing training.

As before, one or more evenings per week had to be devoted to defence exercises, and there were other duties such as cleaning the school building. The trainees' lives were as regimented as ever and much attention was paid to military discipline. The syllabus of instruction notes, 'It is essential that strict march discipline be maintained when trainees are being marched to and from instructional centres, etc, and that particular attention be paid to their discipline, bearing and dress at all times'.

Either Joe had to take some aspect of this course again, or it overran, perhaps due to one of the frequent log-jams which were occurring when the system just could not cope with the huge numbers it was processing. In the end, Joe only just scraped through with a poor grade of 45%. He did not move to his next posting until 30th December, when he went for a very short while to the Heavy Glider Conversion Unit at Brize Norton west of Oxford, another training outfit. Then it was on to Number 4 Radio School, at Madley, about ten miles west of Hereford. It was only now that he began training as an Air Wireless Operator, the role he eventually performed in Bomber Command.

Joe completed the course at Madley in May 1943, and on 12th May, once again promoted to the rank of Leading Aircraftman, moved onto No 7 Air Gunnery School, at Stormy Down, near Porthcawl, Glamorgan, South Wales. It is here that he took a short course in how to fire a bomber's defensive guns. No 11 W.Op/AG Short Gunnery Course ended on 26th May, and Joe was awarded 78%, a very respectable result. He was also given a step up in rank to mark the successful completion of his course of studies. Normally this would have taken him to Corporal but instead he became a Sergeant since all Bomber Command aircrew had to be of Sergeant's rank and upwards, even if this meant giving them a temporary rise in rank.

There were four weeks to use up before he could commence the next phase of his training. After a brief detour to No 9 (Observers) Air Flying Unit located at Penrhos, Pwllheli, North Wales, he finally arrived at No 17 Operational Training Unit, based at Silverstone between Banbury and Milton Keynes, now the site of the racing track. This was where his real training for flying in heavy bombers would begin and where at last he would join his crew.

Joe's first two years in the RAF had been a succession of moves from training camp to training camp, in a criss-cross pattern across a country which – for the first time since the Civil War, three hundred years earlier – had been mobilised and militarised from Scotland to Cornwall.

II. The Crew
Joe's relationship with the six men on his crew commenced in the most casual way and yet, as was the case with almost all Lancaster crews, the seemingly haphazard method proved remarkably effective.

The initial grouping was, as was usual, only five men – Ted Thackway, Jack Powell, Sandy Grant, Joe Mack, and Leslie Laver, respectively pilot, navigator, bomb aimer, wireless operator, and rear gunner. It would only be in late September, at the Heavy Conversion Unit (abbreviated to HCU or CU), when the crew began to train on Lancasters, that the last two vital members of the team would be added – George Grundy, the flight engineer, and Tony Lawrence, the mid-upper gunner.

Joe arrived for No 65 Course on 29th June. He and his group of fellow wireless operators were evidently the first trade to arrive at Silverstone. Sandy, Ted and Jack came on 13th July; Leslie came even later, on 27th July, after a hastily condensed gunners' course.

Once all the trades had arrived, the men were assembled in a large drill-hangar on the airfield. The Chief Ground Instructor wished them good morning, told them they were there for crewing-up, uttered some equivalent of the time-honoured words, 'Right, chaps, sort yourselves out', and then disappeared and left them to get on with it. Amazingly, within a couple of days chaos had become order, and instead of an inchoate mass there were now several five man crews.

Small nuclei or allegiances had been very quickly formed – men who had come across one another during their training, or who were drawn to one another because they shared a common background. In the case of my father's crew, the initial grouping was almost certainly pilot and bomb aimer, for Sandy was a Canadian and Ted had completed his flying training in Canada – it is highly possible that they had met there. There was also a connection between Ted and Jack, for both were Yorkshiremen who had grown up respectively in Harrogate and Wakefield, towns only twenty miles apart. There were even certain similarities in the background of Ted and Leslie, which I will describe in a moment. However, there *was* an odd man out and that was my father, and why he was chosen by the others I do not know.

Ted, Leslie, and Jack (and probably Sandy also) all came from poor, working-class families, and all had had a hard beginning in life. Joe was the only one who approximated to the stereotype of the wartime RAF, coming as he did from a prosperous middle-class background with an expensive education at a minor public school. Yet, despite his advantages, he had so far not exactly excelled in anything the RAF had offered him. In his favour was the fact that he was a likeable sort of fellow, amusing, entertaining, fun to be around, and perfectly cut out to play the role of crew clown. Perhaps the other four were happy to 'adopt' him, to be protective and elder-brotherly towards him, for throughout his life Joe had a highly pronounced tendency to lean on other people. For his own part, he probably felt happier with those who were his supposed social inferiors; their abilities put him at less of a disadvantage than would those of similarly talented men of his own background and class.

The skipper, Ted, is the only one of his crewmates my father ever described; in words so spare they can hardly be called description, in his memoir he calls Ted 'a tall Yorkshireman from Ripon'. Six foot one, Ted had in fact grown up in Bilton, a northern suburb of Harrogate on the road to Ripon.

Ted's background had been a difficult one. His father, George, was fourteen years older than his mother, Elsie, and they had married when she was already pregnant – the baby Ted would be born only three months after the wedding, on January 10th 1920. In December of the following year, a second son, James, always known as Jim, was born, but George – a tailor by trade – was something of a wanderer and soon disappeared from the family home, off on twenty odd years of peregrinations. Elsie was to bring up her two boys almost entirely on her own, working as a seamstress at Marshall and Snelgrove in Harrogate.

Ted was dark-haired whilst Jim was ginger-haired. Jim looked up to and adored his gifted brother, who had taken on responsibility early. Ted's was a very strong, loyal and affectionate character, and as a boy he was very much his mother's mainstay. Even whilst at Christ Church, the Harrogate grammar school, he was earning extra money for the household, working as a milkman's delivery boy to supplement the meagre family income, and his customers liked him very much, coming up the garden path every morning always cheerful, always whistling – he was proverbial for his good nature, and people remember him for it even now.

In the early 1930s, George came home long enough to give Elsie another son, John, before vanishing for another few years. At about this same time, Ted left Christ Church and for two years attended Harrogate Technical School, leaving at the age of fifteen. For someone of his background, the employment prospects were dismal, and so Ted became a dairy man at Bilton Dene Farm and later a van driver for Bilton Grange Stores.

In June 1939, at the age of nineteen, he signed up with the RAF for six years, and from then on things began to go very well for him. He began as an Aircrafthand/Flight Mechanic, but such was his natural ability that by September 1941 he had been recommended for training as aircrew either as a pilot or navigator. Like nearly everyone, his first choice was to be a pilot. His pilot training began in January 1942, and he soon proved to be an exceptional student. By the end of the year, he had done so well that he had won his temporary wartime commission, jumping from humble LAC to Pilot Officer in one single giant step.

Ted had a lovely friendly open face, fine dark eyes, and an endearing smile. He was quiet, unassuming, and unaffected. Amongst his attributes was the strength of character to foster a team spirit in the crew. His was the final responsibility for the aircraft and the safety of everyone on board; his decisions had to be accepted without question and obeyed instantly, and pilots had to earn this respect – it was not automatically bestowed.

Ted was amazingly even-tempered, slow to anger, and very self-controlled. At the same time he was always ready to laugh, he always saw the funny side of things. Serious and ambitious enough to have qualified as a pilot and to have become an officer, no easy thing for someone of his background, at the same time he was equable, likeable, and easy-going.

Like Ted, Jack Powell, the navigator, came from Yorkshire; he was 31 at the time of his death, old for the wartime RAF and the oldest man in the crew. Five foot nine inches, with brown hair, blue eyes, and a thoughtful, serious and determined face, Jack had spent most of his life in the large manufacturing town of Wakefield. His mother had been a fishmonger's assistant, his father a stable-man, who had miraculously survived the carnage of the First World War to return and complete the family of two sons with a single daughter, Barbara.

At some stage – from what source is unknown – a reasonable amount of money apparently came into this otherwise lowly family. It must have been this new-found wealth which permitted Jack to escape the usual fate of gifted working class boys, for instead of having to leave school early he was able to continue his education. In his late teens he was articled to a Mr Donald Milner at City Chambers in Wakefield, and by the age of twenty-three had qualified as a chartered accountant, passing his examinations first time. Thereafter he would work for the audit departments of West Riding and Wiltshire County Councils. That he was very well thought of is obvious from the tributes paid to him both before and after his death. The Treasurer of West Riding described him on his transfer to Wiltshire as 'a man of excellent personality', and said he had 'every confidence in his integrity and honesty . . . he has proved a loyal, conscientious and capable officer'.

In local government circles Jack would definitely have been regarded as a high flyer and would probably have ended up as a County Council Treasurer. With his independence assured, he was able to go ahead and marry his long-time sweetheart Agnes. It was a match made against the wishes of his family, who despite their own poor origins now apparently considered that Agnes was beneath him – she was only a mill girl, after all. Agnes, however, was also extremely pretty, and a very positive, determined and strong-minded young woman who passionately wanted to better herself. She had superb dress sense and always looked elegant; if she could not afford something, she would save until she could get the best. Jack too had a natural elegance about him, and they made a most handsome couple. In the wedding photographs – they married on Christmas Eve 1937 when both were twenty-five – the pair of them look most beautifully turned out. The marriage appears to have led to a permanent rupture with his family; only his sister Barbara stuck by him and acted as witness on the marriage certificate.

For some while afterwards Agnes and Jack continued to live in Wakefield, in a very pleasant semi-detached house with a large bay window. Later there came the move to Wiltshire in that same year that the war which had so long threatened broke out. They settled in Trowbridge, a small town between Bath and Salisbury Plain, in another very nice house – number 48, The Down. This was the height of Agnes's prosperity, but she was only able to enjoy it for two years against a backdrop of Jack's growing unease with his situation. He was in a reserved occupation, quite safe from danger, but after a long struggle with his conscience he told Agnes he was going to volunteer, he did not want other people to fight his battles on his behalf. Poor Agnes found it very hard to accept his decision.

Jack joined the RAF in the same year as my father, 1941, but unlike him would become a first-class navigator. Commencing on 24th September, his training was long and arduous, and eventually took him overseas for many months. The Trowbridge house had to be given up and Agnes moved back to her family in Wakefield, taking work in a munitions factory to help the war effort. She treasured all the letters from her adored husband, which often arrived with photographs of himself and service pals in various exotic locations. Though the strain of missing Agnes and his homeland was always great, like many servicemen Jack was seeing a far wider life than he would ever have done otherwise and he always looks happy in these snapshots, albeit with the same thoughtful and even rather grave expression. He aged rapidly and soon appeared quite considerably older than his youthful companions. However, with his pleasant easy-going nature he would have fitted in well despite the age gap – as his brother-in-law Bill, a miner, said of him, 'Jack would thee and thou it with anyone', and coming from Bill this was the greatest compliment.

One of the best overseas snapshots of Jack was taken in October 1942, as a Christmas greeting to Bill and Mary, Agnes's sister, and their family. It shows Jack and five young airman from No 41 Air School, East London, South Africa. All have just been swimming, and stand grinning in various states of undress in front of a handsome shiny car. In the accompanying note, Jack wrote in his tiny, meticulous handwriting, 'This is a bit early for Xmas Greetings but unless I get it off this weekend you won't have it in time . . . I am more than sorry, as you might imagine, that I shan't be able to see you as usual this year. However – perhaps soon, you never know.'

He would eventually arrive back in England on 6th January the following year.

Sandy Grant, the bomb aimer, must like Jack have been extremely proficient, being the third vital member of the PNB group which was the core of all the Lancaster crews. Sandy held the same senior rank as Ted, being a temporary Flying Officer at the end of 1943; he and Ted were the only officers on the crew.

Sandy's full name was Leslie Kenneth Alexander Grant, but the crew always called him Sandy, an abbreviation of his third name which both reflected his hair colour and usefully distinguished him from the other Leslie on the crew. He was a small man, slight and short, with a reddish Celtic colouring and a little moustache. Born in 1920 and thus the same age as his skipper, his father was Canadian, his mother Scottish. His early childhood had been spent in Princeton, British Columbia, but at some stage the family had moved to Vancouver – the family home was at 955 Thurlow Street.

At the age of 18 Sandy had joined the Royal Canadian Signal Corps, but only remained with them for six months. The rather odd occupation he took up thereafter was that of painter and interior decorator at the Ritz

Apartment Hotel. He joined the Royal Canadian Air Force in June 1940, and thereafter prospered. His initial training was in navigation, always a useful skill for a bomb aimer, a large part of whose work was in assisting the navigator to plot an accurate course. He finally won his Observer Badge on 19th March 1943, and only one month later, on 29th April, embarked for England – he would never see his homeland again.

The fifth member of the crew, the rear gunner, was Leslie Norman John Laver.

Leslie is of enormous significance in this story. Contrary to what my father told me as a child, he in fact survived the aircrash. Not only did he survive but he was completely uninjured, and would help 'the man on the bike' to rescue my father from the burning plane. The complicated reasons why Leslie was never mentioned during the bedtime story (though my father would many years later give some scant details of him in his memoir) will become clearer later in this book.

At the time of the crash Leslie was just 20 years old – his birthday had been on 30th September. His mother's name was Jenny. Before her marriage in 1911 at the age of 22, she had trimmed hats and other such luxury items – her profession on the marriage certificate is given as 'Ostrich Feather Mounter'. She and her husband, Edward Cyril Laver, were Catholics and both came from struggling working-class families, his father being a newsagent/carman and hers a journeyman baker. However, it is not Edward Cyril Laver on Leslie's birth certificate but William Laver, a 'Draper's Carman' or delivery man. Leslie was born at home, at 6 Calmington Road, in the poor densely built streets of south London, between Elephant and Castle and Peckham. The address was about half a mile from the original matrimonial home of 50 Carter Street – for whatever reason, Jenny had changed partners, perhaps to a brother or cousin of her husband's.

Later Jenny remarried and became a Mrs Crockett, but her last husband died prematurely.

The family now consisted of eight members, the mother Jenny, the three boys, Cyril, Walter (or Wally), and Leslie, and the four sisters, Marjorie, Irene, Jessie and Dorothy. The only work Jenny could get now was as a cleaner at the London theatres, and the family was extremely poor, yet they were all quite happy together. The children helped out by running errands or earning little sums of money. Brought up as Catholics, they all took turns to be the one who stayed behind on Sundays and cooked the breakfast for those returning from Communion. All the boys had been taught to cook by Jenny, 'because you might have to do it when you're married'.

Leslie grew up to be a good-looking lad, with fine features, dark brown hair, and strikingly beautiful grey-green eyes. He was very slight, just under five foot six in height, but his slimness of build would prove a great advantage when he became a rear gunner because of the appallingly cramped nature of the gun turret. Like his skipper who had also been brought up by a mother on her own, Leslie left school early, between fourteen and fifteen years of age, and began work as a milkman. Again as with Ted, the war would offer him chances otherwise not provided by his background.

Leslie joined the RAF just before his nineteenth birthday, on 8th August 1942, but was not called to the Volunteer Reserve until 22nd March, 1943 – he would only be in the RAF for 10 months. His first ambition had been to train as a pilot and his initial mustering is shown on his papers as Aircrafthand/Pilot. However, at his own request he was regraded to Air Gunner after almost seven months of waiting to be called up. He had been told it would take even longer before he could commence training as a pilot and Leslie did not want to wait. His brother Wally told him he was mad, but Leslie said it would all take too long – he wanted to get into action as quickly as possible. Just over three weeks later, he commenced his training.

The gunners' courses were very short and by this stage of the war extremely concentrated and very hard work. In a letter to his sister Jessie, written from Bridlington in Yorkshire on a Sunday evening around the middle of June, Leslie wrote:

> Have at last found some spare time in which to write to you, and even this has to be while I am on Fire Picquet. I haven't had any spare time at all until today, and that is only because we are on duty all night. We have had our course cut down from twelve weeks to five weeks now, and that only came through officially on Thursday, so you can guess that we have quite a busy time in front of us. If I pass right through this next four weeks, I shall come home on leave, but unfortunately not as an Air Gunner, that will come about three weeks after my leave I hope.

The coveted moment when he could at last sew the 'AG' of the Air Gunner's badge on his uniform came shortly before he arrived at Silverstone. He had passed his course with a mark of 73.7%.

This then was the nucleus of the crew. At the OTU and later at the CU, they were to spend some four and half months learning new skills, and how to cooperate with one another and function as a team. Along with daily training flights, there was a multitude of other things to learn – about the stars and the moon, how to understand weather conditions, cloud base and safety height, what types of clouds there were and what they meant, dewpoint (the temperature at which condensation sets in and the atmosphere becomes saturated with moisture), how to deal with fog and electrical storms, or conditions where the plane suddenly became encrusted with ice. Then there were the unnatural hazards – flak, fighters, how to recognise an enemy or a friendly aircraft, where the potentially fatal British balloon barrages were, and what to do if one accidentally strayed into them.

Aircraft recognition – a most vital matter – was taught in a room resembling a macabre child's bedroom. The ceiling was painted blue with white puffy clouds, and model aeroplanes hung down from it. The main piece of equipment was an Epidiascope, a gadget that projected an image onto a large screen; this was ideal for demonstrating the silhouettes of the different aircraft. Soon you would put this into effect when you took part in fighter affiliation exercises. In this simulated aerial combat, a fighter would suddenly come hurtling down on your aircraft with his camera-guns blazing – your skipper would try to escape him by turning, twisting and diving, sometimes so violently that it seemed that the wings of the aircraft would break off.

For a crew who loved their work and were good at it, life at Silverstone was often ideal. Particularly on fine days when they were up in the aircraft away from all the petty rules and restrictions on the ground, nothing could be more thrilling and exciting. Ted banked the Wellington in a sideways turn as it climbed, and they all looked down upon the rich landscape of England, the ripening cornfields, the oaks and the elms, the hedges and the copses, the clustered dollshouses with their bright scraps of garden. It was so hot up there in the bright blue sky, the sun beating on the perspex windows, that they flew in shirtsleeves. They were as happy then as it is possible to be. They were a great team, one of the best on the course, and probably they couldn't help thinking that when the time came for them to go into action, they would really do something special for the war effort.

That time was still two or three months off. Meanwhile, the nearest they could get to it was vicariously through their instructors, tour-expired men who had already finished a tour, or even two, somehow emerging from that mortally dangerous run of ops unscathed. Other instructors were drawn from the ranks of those who had been severely injured and, once recovered, did not have sufficient mobility to continue operational flying. George Hodgson was one such, lecturing in aircraft recognition at Silverstone in the summer of 1943. He had moved there from a convalescent centre called The Leas after recovering from a very serious back injury. Less than 10 months later, my father, the sole survivor of his crew, would himself arrive on crutches at The Leas.

The crew was training on the twin-engined Wellington, an aircraft now well past its prime having been outmoded by the Lancaster. Wellingtons were no longer used in major raids from August 1943 onwards, and though some squadrons remained in Bomber Command until well into 1944, they were only flying limited operations, mainly minelaying. Nonetheless, as was customary towards the end of OTU training, Ted's crew were sent in their Wellington, LN444, on a short and comparatively easy sortie to the north coast of France. It was on the 8th September and it was the first time that the crew had committed a violent act of war. They took off at ten to ten that night and returned at half past twelve, having been part of a large force attacking a German long-range gun battery in the Boulogne area. Neither the target marking nor the bombing were accurate, and the gun battery was apparently not damaged. All the attacking aircraft returned safely.

In his memoir my father gives what must be an account of this trip though he does not specify the date or the fact that he was still in training. The account begins: 'Whilst flying in Wellingtons we were given the opportunity to participate in a raid on Occupied France. This was relatively easy and undramatic, in that we did not have a very long journey.' Note the use of the phrase 'we were given the opportunity to participate' – this is obviously not the wording one would use if one was actually flying on operations – there would be no such footling, elegant delicacy about it.

What he remembers as most notable about this trip was the fact that the photoflash which fell with the bombs got stuck in its tube and he managed to re-fuse it, so saving 'the aeroplane and crew [from] being blown up in a fatal explosion'. The other thing which he recounts was that there was a fault in his oxygen supply. He went for the emergency oxygen cylinder, but 'the effort must have been too much as I became unconscious and lay on the floor of the aeroplane. Another crew member, seeing what had happened, revived me with the emergency supply . . .'

What I find so odd about these extremely sketchy anecdotes is that my father does not name the men he was flying with, or say that they were the same men who were in the fatal crash of December. Surely he cannot have forgotten. He refers to just 'another crew member'. By now he had been in training with Ted, Sandy, Jack and Leslie for several very momentous weeks. These men, who were of such dramatic significance in his life, are completely erased from the picture which he paints of the Boulogne operation.

One of the four other No 65 Course crews who flew from Silverstone to Boulogne that night was captained by William Darby Coates, a young Yorkshireman only just twenty years old and still a sergeant. There must have been considerable friendly rivalry between the Coates and Thackway crews, both the pilots being working-class Yorkshiremen who had trained in Canada, and both the bomb aimers – Sandy and the splendidly named John Moody Baldwin – being Canadian officers. The two crews would go through all their OTU and CU training together, first at Silverstone and then at Wigsley, and finally both would have the honour of being selected for the Pathfinders. Both would be posted to the same squadron, and Bill Coates would win the Distinguished Flying Medal on the night that Ted died.

III. Wigsley

Two weeks after the flight to Boulogne, No 65 Course ended. The crew were granted seven days leave, and went their separate ways home.

Ted travelled back to Harrogate. The family house was at 97 St John's Grove, Bilton, on an estate of small, plain, semi-detached council houses. When this tall, dark, impressive-looking young man, now an officer and a pilot, came walking up the curving road, it must have been a source of the

most enormous joy and pride to his mother, Elsie. Though she had already
seen him since his return from Canada (and had even met one of his Royal
Canadian Air Force friends, an older man called Tom Acton, who was
eventually to be her second husband), the transformation which four years
in the RAF had wrought in Ted was still something of a marvel. Hard to
recognise in this handsome Flying Officer the young lad who could only
get a job as a dairyman on leaving school. Ted had gained poise and
maturity, and a quiet but immensely strong self-confidence.

All his Harrogate friends noticed the change in him. Ted had been so
enthralled and excited by his flying training in Canada that he had always
been writing home about it to his close friend, Mary Brown, who said,
laughing, 'he put so much of it down in his letters that I could nearly learn
how to be a pilot'. Now, however, he seldom mentioned service life. He
never talked much about it to Nancy, another friend he was close to in the
last months of his life, who nonetheless knew that the RAF was a special
part of his life, a part of which he was enormously proud. He adored his
work as a pilot – 'it was his dream come true when he got his wings'.
Nancy said you could see the glow of happiness in his face; he had come a
long way under not very propitious circumstances, and 'you couldn't help
but be proud of him', for he had really made something of himself.

Nancy worked as a seamstress at Marshall and Snelgrove with Elsie. She
and Ted had known each other a long time, and before he came home on
leave he always used to send her a postcard with the dates and the message,
'Nan – get your dancing pumps out!' Ted was a super dancer, he had a fine
figure and his bearing was very good. As Nancy was also very tall, they
made a good team, and both delighted in spending his leave dancing.

On this last leave, it seemed that the long-time friendship between them
might be turning into something different – 'I had always known him,
always seemed to know him, then suddenly we were that little bit closer'.
But the days went by so quickly and, before she or Elsie could believe it, it
was time for him to go again.

On the very last day of September, Ted travelled by train to Lincoln,
where transports were waiting for him and the other airmen now arriving
for their Lancaster course at 1654 Conversion Unit, based at Wigsley.

On the same day that he arrived at Wigsley, Ted met Edna Shaw, always
nicknamed Jill. Jill was an extremely pretty Liverpudlian, a bottle-blonde
with fine blue eyes who worked as a WAAF in the Officers' Mess. She
would always remember her first sight of Ted, sitting on his own, waiting
for his crew to arrive. 'He was having a coffee in the ante-room and looking
very forlorn, so like a good Samaritan I took him under my wing. He was
in the battle dress of the time, and on one side of his chest he had his wings
and on the other, on a strip of brown leather, his name E. Thackway. I
thought to myself what a funny name. I didn't realise then it would become
my name.'

Not long afterwards, they began going out together. Ted rapidly fell madly in love. As Jill wrote, 'There was many a time I very nearly lost my Honour with Ted, he was a very loving man'.

They almost always went into Lincoln for their dates. However, after one dance on the camp on a very cold night, they slipped off afterwards to an empty workman's hut, and were sitting there quietly, cuddling and kissing and saying a prolonged goodnight, when suddenly a bright torch light was shone in on them – it was the Service Police snooping round, checking up. Ted and Jill were marched off separately in disgrace.

It was very much frowned upon for NCO WAAFs to associate with officers. Ted, despite his protestations, saying that it was all his fault, was only given a ticking off, but Jill was posted away to Scampton, eight miles to the north. The pair continued to meet in Lincoln. Things became so serious that he asked her to marry him. She was only 20 and felt she was too young, not ready for such a commitment, and so it was agreed that they would marry on Ted's next leave, after he had finished his training and flown a few ops.

Jill would always remember Ted and Sandy's frequent appearances together, for they were something of an odd couple due to the great disparity in their sizes, Ted being very tall and dark, and Sandy very small and ginger. It was obvious, however, that the two were extremely good friends, who were always together except on the times when Ted and Jill wanted to be alone. Sandy seemed to follow Ted like a shadow; being rather shy, he looked up to Ted and used to rely on him like a big brother. As Jill said 'Sandy was so small that I think Ted felt responsible for him. Ted was very friendly to him. But then Ted was friendly to everyone.'

Unfortunately Jill has no recollection of the five other members of the crew, all of whom were NCOs, including the last two who now joined it on the same haphazard basis as at Silverstone.

George Grundy, the flight engineer, was, like his pilot and navigator, a Yorkshireman, and like them came from a poor working-class family. 21 years old at the time of his death, he hailed from Eccleshill, a suburb of Bradford, about twelve miles west of Harrogate. His father, Frank, seems to have been something of a rolling stone, for his occupation changed from general labourer to fruit salesman to carter with the birth of his children, George, Joyce, and the much younger Alan and Maureen. By the slump of the 1930s, Frank was permanently unemployed, and money was exceedingly short in the house.

George was a very clever lad, always top of his class at school, but, as was so common in that era, economic necessity forced him to leave school at an early age. Just fourteen, he obtained an apprenticeship as a joiner and shop fitter, and with the scant wages he earned as an apprentice did the best he could for his family. As there was only a two year gap between them and they shared the same friends, he and his sister Joyce were particularly close. His brother, Alan, would always remember George buying Joyce a party dress that she needed and paying for her to go on school trips despite the fact that it left him with hardly any money for himself.

George volunteered for the RAF as soon as he could, joining in August 1941, at nineteen years of age, as a flight mechanic specialising in air frames. Twenty-two months later, when the RAF asked for volunteers to become flight engineers, he began to train as aircrew. The position of flight engineer had been set up after the RAF had decided it could no longer afford the loss of so many second pilots. The flight engineer sat together with the pilot in the cockpit, constantly watching the complex series of instruments in the Lancaster, monitoring the four engines and the electrical system, checking and logging the fuel supply. He also checked the course, height and airspeed, and generally acted as the pilot's right-hand man. Lastly, he was trained in basic flying techniques 'just in case', and would occasionally take over the Lancaster's controls on cross-country practice flights.

Flight engineers had a much shorter training period than the highly skilled pilots, in George's case a mere three months. This he spent at No. 4 School of Technical Training at St Athan in South Wales, the same station at which Ted himself had trained some three years earlier. George completed his course on 20th September with a mark of 65.6%, and was at once promoted from AC1 to Temporary Sergeant. On the 25th, he arrived at Wigsley, where he had five days to wait before the five-man core crews started to arrive.

Dark-haired with grey eyes and a cheerful smiling face, George was a good-looking fellow. At five foot five, though, he was no taller than Leslie, and even slimmer in build. Perhaps the reason why my father bestowed on Ted the single adjective, 'tall', which described his crewmates was because Ted's height was so striking in contrast to what was in the main a very short crew.

The seventh and last member of the crew was Tony Lawrence, the mid-upper gunner, just 20 years old at the time of his death. That he was of great personal significance to my father cannot be doubted; in his memoir, my father described him as 'a close friend of mine' and 'my closest friend', and on one solitary occasion (not naming him but later it became obvious whom he was referring to) he mentioned him to me and my brother as 'my best friend'. Other than this, however, not a syllable ever left his lips about Tony Lawrence; his memory was forever enshrouded in the same deliberate obscurity as the rest of the crew.

Why was Tony so significant to Joe? Because in Tony he had for the first time a crewmate with a similar background, preoccupations and aspirations. Joe was very musical, Tony very artistic, neither was in the least bit academically inclined, and both came from prosperous middle-class families in business.

Where Tony differed from Joe was in the circumstances of his birth. There was a very old scandal attached to this, though it was all kept so quiet that it is possible even Tony himself did not know about it. In a strange parallel of the upbringing of Ted and Leslie, Tony had also been brought up by a mother on her own, albeit one in a far more comfortable way of life.

Tony's mother, Peggy, was the only daughter of Mabel and Lawrence Burroughes, the latter always known affectionately in the family as 'Pang'. Peggy was very close to her brothers, Tom and Guy; the fourth child George was something of a loner, and did not share the others' passion for parties, boating, horse racing and country sports. Peggy in particular was mad on horses, dogs, and hunting. The family wealth had come from the firm of Burroughes and Watts, which in the Victorian era had made a fortune out of the manufacture of billiard tables. Already, however, a generation down, much of the money had melted away and as a young woman Peggy would work for a pittance as a groom, a job which would prepare her for work in the Land Army during the war, and eventually, when she remarried in her sixties, the rugged life of an Exmoor farmer.

At nineteen years of age, Peggy was attractive, impetuous, and headstrong. Her family lived at Heath Lodge in Shurlock Row, a village in Berkshire between Windsor and Reading. Heath Lodge (of which a pen and ink drawing by Tony still exists) was mellow and sprawling, and attached to it was a large stableblock consisting of looseboxes with small rooms over them, the sort which in those days would have been occupied by a groom or chauffeur. In January of 1923, however, one of these rooms was lent to William Frederick Lawrence, a builder and decorator from Sidcup in Kent. The likeliest surmise is that William had been employed by Peggy's father to work on Heath Lodge. However, in his leisure time the handsome twenty-eight year old charmed the daughter of the house so effectively that she soon became pregnant with Tony, her only child.

When Pang and Mabel found out, they must have been utterly horrified. William came from a poor family, living in a cramped tenement and following without notable success their traditional calling as painters, plumbers, and labourers. It is thought that William was bought off by Pang for £200, a huge sum of money in those days, the agreement being that he should marry Peggy and then leave her life for good.

On 4th July, 1923, when she was five months pregnant, Peggy and William were married in a registry office in London, her father and mother being the only witnesses. Peggy's residence at the time of her marriage was given as Hotel Great Central in Marylebone, London. Opened in 1899, this was the last of the grand Victorian railway hotels constructed during the golden age of steam. Adjoining Marylebone Station, it was massive, with 700 bedrooms, and the ideal place to preserve secrecy.

By the time Tony was born on 3rd November, his parents were permanently estranged, Peggy living at number 59b Warrington Crescent within walking distance of Hotel Great Central, he back at Sidcup in Kent.

It must have been a great relief to Peggy when she could finally leave London and get back to her beloved countryside. Due to her various jobs with horses and dogs, Tony would be mainly brought up by his grandparents, Pang and Mabel, and would live with them at Heath Lodge.

Pang would be his grandson's chief mentor and protector. Like all the family, he was addicted to country sports, a kindly man with a sense of humour whose will (he died two years after Tony, in 1945) characteristically ends, 'I desire that my body shall be cremated and the ashes scattered to the winds and that there shall be no flowers or mourning, no long faces but a smile'. Mabel was a far more daunting prospect, a strong-minded and at times autocratic lady who was fond of writing down little quotations and sayings, and who was probably the one who eventually selected the epitaph for Tony's tombstone.

Pang had a highly prized collection of valuable shotguns with which he taught his grandson to shoot. Tony soon became an absolutely lethal shot, and won competitions and certificates for his accuracy. The keenness of his eye was obvious in other matters too, for he was a very capable draughtsman and altogether artistic. Pang, as director of the family firm, often took him to the billiard table factory. The billiard balls were made out of ivory, and Tony used to take the offcuts and carve minute netsukes out of them, the subjects reflecting the family's love of horses and the countryside, being such things as tiny boots, spurs, stirrups and whips. A little display case of these charming artefacts still exists.

By the time my father met him, Tony was a slim, tall and dramatically good-looking young man, just under five foot eleven in height, with auburn hair and blue-grey eyes. Like Joe, he may well have been destined for the family firm, but the war disrupted these plans just as they disrupted those of Joe's father. Like many young men, Tony was keen to get into action as soon as possible. Aged eighteen, he first enlisted in the Royal Navy in September 1942 as Naval Airman 2nd Class. He trained at Skegness and Portsmouth before moving on to the Fleet Air Arm Station at Lee-on-Solent, thereafter serving briefly on HMS *St Vincent* and HMS *Daedalus*. Whether it had always been understood that he would eventually join the RAF is not known, but he was discharged from the service in mid-April 1943.

Only one month later, on May 17th, Tony joined the RAF as an Aircrafthand/Air Gunner. Seven months later to the day, he would be killed in the aircrash. My father only knew him for eleven weeks, but his memory would always be fraught with pain.

And so, in October 1943, the crew was complete, the full Lancaster compliment of seven men. After a couple of familiarisation flights in a four-engined Halifax, they finally took to the air in a Lancaster, the absolute cream of Bomber Command's aircraft.

The handful of Lancasters still in existence are most jealously tended and guarded. Of the 7,377 built, in Britain there remain only four complete planes, one at Hendon, one at Duxford, one at East Kirkby, and one still owned by the RAF and stationed at Coningsby, the Battle of Britain Memorial Flight Lancaster which is called the 'City of Lincoln'. 'City of

Lincoln' is the only one which still flies. You can see it at summer airshows, making its graceful, slow, almost stately progress through a blue sky decked with huge white clouds. In silhouette it has almost a glider's shape, so abnormally long are its wings, and it looks rather slender and fragile despite its four massive engines. In profile, it is entirely different, blunt-nosed and dominating, with a generally pugnacious look about it. Though it seems incredibly slow compared to modern planes and even contemporary Second World War fighter planes, it possesses stunning charisma and majesty, both in the air and on the ground.

The Lancaster was the supreme heavy night bomber of the Second World War – all books on the bombing campaign will repeat some variant of this phrase. Though the frame was staggeringly huge – almost 70 feet long with a wingspan of 102 feet – the aircraft was highly manoeuvrable. After the lumbering heaviness of other aircraft, Lancasters seemed to fly with the lightness of a bird, and pilots transferring onto them were generally ecstatic. Though their maximum speed was only 287 mph, a tail wind could make the true speed over 400 mph. They handled easily, even when carrying several tons of fuel and explosives. Unloaded, they flew with an easy grace and never liked to stall – pilots had to learn not to overshoot the runways because the aircraft would float forever if the approach speed was too high.

These beauties, however, were not without their personal flaws. The wartime operational Lancasters would not have remotely looked like the immaculate gleaming specimens in modern-day museums. They were battered, beaten up and tatty, with massive dents and scratches on their fuselage, their skin rippling where undue strain had been put on some part of the framework. The topmost parts were painted a dull green and brown, but their main colour was a peculiarly soft, dense, absorbent sooty black, designed to give the least possible reflection to searchlights and flares, and to make the massive shape blend better into the night sky.

The interior was painted in a particularly insalubrious bile-green. In several places the ceiling was so low that one could only get about by slithering and contortions, thereby getting covered in whatever dirt or oil had been left by the rigger. The fuselage was unpressurised, so above 8,000 feet oxygen masks had to be worn, and when moving from crew position to position portable oxygen cylinders had to be carried. The meal eaten before an operation had to be easily digestible, as the build-up of gas in the stomach when flying at great height in an unpressurised plane could be acutely painful. It made some people want to fart continually. Nor was the aircraft heated effectively, and the temperature could fall so low that frostbite of the hands and feet could result.

The flying controls were not power-assisted, and it was extremely physically demanding for the pilot to throw his heavy aircraft around the sky when taking evasive action. If the plane was hit, the odds of getting out of it were very poor – the G-force could virtually paralyse you, and the escape hatches were not easy to use. Though in combat the Lancaster looked after its crews better than any other bomber, when mortally wounded it could be a death-trap.

In flight, they shook with massive vibrations, the noise was absolutely terrific, they stunk of petrol and oil mingled with the sloshing stink of the disinfectant in the Elsan toilet. To those sensitive to airsickness, they had a peculiar sliding yawing motion, like a boat on an ocean swell, and some crew members were routinely sick on every journey. When the pilot made a violent evasive movement, diving hundreds of feet in seconds, even the toughest were inclined to puke.

However, there is not the slightest doubt that the Lancasters inspired great loyalty, and that they deserved all the care and superstitious reverence which were lavished upon them. They were highly manoeuvrable and very robust, able to fly well after considerable battle damage, and there was an undeniable magnificence about them. It is hardly surprising that they were loved.

The Lancasters at Wigsley were like old warhorses put out to grass, having reached the end of their fighting life. New Lancasters seldom ended up at the Heavy Conversion Units, unless they were those which had been knocked about so badly that they were no longer considered safe for the extreme strains and stresses of operational flying. However, all the crew were delighted to be flying in these great black monsters at last, no matter if they were rather arthritic specimens.

By the end of October, it had become obvious to the Wigsley instructors that Ted's was a first-class crew. At some point someone evidently told them that they stood an extremely good chance of being accepted for the Pathfinder Force.

By the autumn of 1943, Arthur Travers Harris had been supreme commander of Bomber Command for some eighteen months. During this period he had transformed a demoralised and largely ineffectual Command into the awesome striking force which was now targeting all the major industrial cities of Germany.

The bomber squadrons under Harris's command were organised into two main roles – there was Main Force, as the ordinary bomber squadrons were collectively known, and there was the Pathfinder Force, set up in August 1942. The commander of the latter was Donald Bennett, an outstandingly gifted Australian in his early thirties, twenty years younger than his fellow Group Commanders. Despite an inauspicious start when Harris had told Bennett face to face that he was opposed to the whole idea of the Pathfinders, Harris soon came to have the greatest faith in Bennett, and when the Pathfinder Force became a separate Group, 8 Group, in January 1943, Bennett wrote that Harris 'fought the bureaucrats who wanted some senior and senile stooge to command it. He won the day for me, and I was promoted to Air Commodore.'

8 Group's motto was 'We Guide to Strike'. Pathfinders were the leaders of Main Force, the Mosquitos and Lancasters flying at their head as the massive bombing stream swarmed out from Britain on a raid, a truly awesome snake-like entity perhaps seventy miles long and 3,000 feet deep, the width of the stream depending on the accuracy of navigation. Within this mass might be flying 400 to 700 aircraft, each moving at its preallocated speed and height along the route carefully designated by Command. At this stage of the war, such raids always took place at night because it was suicidal to fly them in the day. In the darkness the huge force swamped the defences; safety lay in numbers and the bomber stream was meant to keep together as compactly as possible, but the extreme difficulties of navigation with comparatively primitive aids meant that mistakes of judgement were all too easily made.

The Pathfinders were the guides to Main Force, not only as route-markers on the long hazardous trip to the target but also over the target itself, where, with their better navigational techniques and technology, they had the task of pinpointing the areas where the bombs should be released. An advance party of 'illuminators' lit the general target area, and a second group, the 'visual markers', identified the actual aiming point and marked it by coloured flares. A third wave, the 'backers-up', dropped target indicators, usually of a different colour to the primary markers. Junior PFF crews would also fly, dropping only bombs until they had gained sufficient experience. At least part of the PFF would be over the target for the entire duration of the raid, so that they could top up the markers and re-centre the attacks as it became necessary.

The Pathfinders were critical to the success of the bombing raids, which were planned to the most minutely exact timetable. They had to reach the target despite all the difficulties of navigation – changing weather conditions, variable winds, German nightfighters and flak defences – within a tolerance of only one minute. They had to drop their target indicators on exactly the right spot even though the whole scene might be enveloped in dense cloud and high winds might shift the flares miles off target. When they failed, which they not infrequently did, the resulting confusion had a disastrous knock-on effect on Main Force.

Despite the critical nature of their role, Pathfinder crews were not a hand-picked elite. Crews reached 8 Group by different routes, about two-thirds coming with considerable experience from Main Force squadrons, the rest from Coastal Command, the Middle East, or any other place where good crews could be found, including directly from the training units with no operational experience. The Pathfinders' general level of experience and competence seems to have been much lower than Bennett would have liked, and this trend became particularly marked during the Battle of Berlin when the appalling loss rate drained the Group. In one horrendous six week period between 16th December 1943 and the end of January 1944, 87 Pathfinder crews, including my father's, became casualties in missing or crashed aircraft.

The loss rate was compounded by the fact that many of these PFF crews were very inexperienced – my father's crew was representative. Throughout the campaign, novice crews were known to be at very high risk during their first five operations – once they had become a little battle-hardened, their chances improved.

Nonetheless, the odds stacked against all bomber crews, Pathfinder or Main Force, were appalling. Heavier armaments had been sacrificed for a heavier bombload, and the Lancasters simply did not have the firepower to outgun their enemies. The situation for any crew hunted by a German nightfighter was dire. Their best option was to stay out of trouble – if they saw a fighter they did not engage in combat but tried to get out of the area before he spotted them. If it became obvious they were the target, escape might just be possible via violent evasive manoeuvres, the Lancaster plunging madly through the darkness at hundreds of feet in seconds.

Flak, too, was an awesome menace, both over land and an apparently empty sea where ships targeted their high-flying prey by radar. But it was flak over the targets which provided the most horrific scenes. Many crews saw the last moments of a stricken plane, coned in the blazing silver of the searchlights whilst shells climbed unhurriedly towards her, bursting orange and black, until at last they found her height. Only if the flames took hold gradually might the men on board have time to bail out, into the boiling maelstrom of bombs, flares, shells, and hundreds of other aircraft, whilst 18-20,000 feet below, the very earth seemed on fire.

Even the Germans could be moved by the sight of the pathetic corpses, hurled as if from another planet, which came down in their midst. The bodies of those who fell without parachutes were so comprehensively fractured that the limbs had become doughlike; as one German boy said, 'they appeared to have no bones'.

Being in Bomber Command was an extremely dangerous way of life. Of the 125,000 aircrew who served in Bomber Command during the Second World War, 56,000 would be killed.

When they volunteered for the PFF, my father's crew would have been aware that, if accepted, they would be signing on for a tour of 45 operations without a break (Main Force flew a first tour of 30 and a second tour of 20). The compensation for this dangerously extended tour was being one step higher in rank than in Main Force, with attendant increase in pay, but a much more compelling motive was the exclusivity, honour and glamour of belonging to the Pathfinders. This privilege was symbolised by the Pathfinder badge. Though valueless in itself, the small hovering gold eagle was an emblem of very special status, and what it represented so secret that it was never worn on operations.

Once they had volunteered, my father's crew were checked out by their departmental instructors, completing at least one simulated bombing test to prove the accuracy of their critical night-flying and navigational skills.

After a seemingly interminable period of waiting for the results, they learned to their delight that they had been accepted. This meant that they would soon be posted to one of the PFF stations clustered around Huntingdon. Though Ted's girlfriend, Jill, had hoped that the crew would get a posting to Main Force at one of the many RAF stations close to Lincoln, she was pleased for Ted's sake that things had worked out so well. 'Ted was very thrilled to have been chosen to be a Pathfinder – as you know, they only chose the best.'

On his last day at Wigsley, Ted and Jill took a last walk along the road together so that they could get away from the crowded camp and be alone for a while. The knowledge that they would soon be parted was very painful, but they comforted each other with the hope that it would not be for long, that around Christmas they would be married. As they walked slowly along, his arm entwined around her waist, her head resting on his shoulder, a black cat emerged seemingly from nowhere. It would not leave them alone, but kept following them, twining sinuously between their legs. 'It's lucky,' Ted told Jill with a smile to cheer her up, and though the good omen, they knew, was an absurd small thing, it gave them faith that things would come right for them and that they would soon be together again.

On 19th November, Ted, George, Sandy, Jack, Joe, Tony and Leslie left Wigsley for Wyton. Wyton was the main PFF airfield, because it was so close to Huntingdon where Bennett's headquarters were situated and Bennett's marital home was actually on the station.

At this period of the war, the Pathfinder Force consisted of 10 squadrons: four Mosquito, one Halifax, and five Lancaster. The latter were all in a relatively small geographical area. Wyton to the east of Huntingdon was the home of 83 Squadron; Upwood and Warboys to the north were respectively the PFF training centre and the home of 156 Squadron (they were to swop these roles in early 1944). To the south-east lay Oakington with 7 Squadron, whilst to the south, very close together, were Graveley (35 Squadron still flying Halifaxes), Gransden Lodge (405 Squadron), and Bourn (97 Squadron). These last three were to be the Pathfinder stations most seriously affected by the disastrous events of 16th/17th December 1943.

Ted's crew were first entered in the Operations Record Book (commonly abbreviated to ORB) of 83 Squadron. However, for whatever reason, they were immediately transferred that same day to the strength of 97 Squadron, and the appropriate entry appears in 97 Squadron's records.

They had one last fortnight of training to complete, the PFF's specialised course in advanced navigational and target-finding procedures which took place at Upwood. Only three crews at a time attended the Upwood course, and as Bennett made a point of addressing each new intake personally, Ted's crew must have met their impatient, austere, perfectionist commander before the month of November was out.

Bennett was one of the most brilliant technical airmen of his generation. A superb pilot, he also had a First Class Navigator's Licence and a Wireless Operator's Licence, being probably the only pilot in the world to possess both. He was perfectly capable of engineering jobs like stripping a wireless set or overhauling an engine. He had seen action in the most dramatic way – whilst commanding a Halifax squadron, he had been shot down close to a Norwegian fjord when attacking the *Tirpitz*, the pride of the German fleet, and had made a successful escape home through Norway and Sweden.

Bennett was very much a hands-on commander who kept in close touch with the men and stations under his command. At HQ, there was a signed notice from him in the foyer which read, 'Every officer in this Group has direct access to me'. He never allowed himself to become removed from the actualities his crews were facing, and even went to the extreme of flying surreptitiously on operations, something which had been categorically forbidden by Harris.

Hawk-faced, austerely handsome, intolerant, intense, severe, and always immaculately dressed in an impossibly perfect uniform, Bennett could be coldly ruthless towards those who did not achieve the high standards he demanded. Yet he was not a hard man, and his involvement was such that he was emotionally affected by the loss of his crews. As the pressures of the bombing campaign mounted, he lost many people whom he regarded as good friends. He got to know most of the senior pilots fairly well, and when they went missing it was a personal blow. Occasionally, when driving home from a squadron base in the early hours of the morning after learning of yet another tragic loss, he found it hard to avoid breaking down and shedding a few tears.

That sensitivity would not, of course, have been obvious to my father's crew when they saw Bennett at Upwood. His exalted rank and awesome competence put him so far above them that it would have been like meeting a living legend. Bennett's manner would have been stern, even threatening, as he impressed upon them with the greatest force the singular importance of their destiny and the supreme standards of excellence which he expected from them.

IV. RAF Station Bourn

On 2nd December, having completed their PFF course, my father and his crew left the training centre at Upwood and made the fifteen mile journey through flat wintery countryside to their first operational posting. At Bourn, it had been raining all morning, but by afternoon the rain had turned to mist. When the crew arrived, last minute preparations were taking place for the departure to Berlin of 16 Lancasters, a low number for 97 Squadron. The Lancasters took off with an almighty roar not long after darkness fell.

By that time, the crew had been allocated their beds – Ted and Sandy in the officers' more spacious sleeping quarters, the other five in the NCO sleeping quarters, which had two or three beds to each small room, the rooms opening off a main corridor.

Once they had dumped their kit bags, they went out to take a look at the camp. In the rainy twilight of a winter's afternoon, it could not have looked a very attractive sight. The only solidly constructed building was the Control Tower, the central nucleus around which the station revolved. Austere and utilitarian in style, a grey-hued block pierced by many large windows, it dominated the skyline on the edge of the airfield in the perfect position to oversee the three runways. Numerous one-storey prefab huts clustered behind it, some with pitched roofs, some with rounded. Similar clusters of buildings could be seen behind the bare hedges and trees edging the road which intersected the camp, whilst down at the bottom of the airfield the tall narrow shape of Bourn Grange heralded yet another extensive huddle of Nissen huts, those of Station Sick Quarters with its hospital, ambulance garage, and mortuary.

Approached via an avenue edged by fine trees, The Grange was a handsome, greyish-yellow Victorian building with a slate roof, one of the very few permanent buildings on the station. The temporary nature of the encampment was everywhere apparent. Some 2,500 people were living and working in this makeshift town pieced together from concrete and corrugated iron, sometimes wood but rarely brick. Many of the arrangements were suitably make-do-and-mend. Though a fifty-foot-wide concrete track ran round the perimeter, the huts themselves were linked by blackened cinder paths, by-products of the camp's many coke-burning stoves. Strong-smelling and dismal in colouring, their pitted surface full of puddles, at night these highways would be impudently used by the local rats who had left their farmsteads for the rich pickings to be had at the camp.

The airfield stretched away far into the distance, a vast flat acreage intersected only by the concrete runways. The fading light glinted in the multitudes of wheel ruts, brimful of water, where vehicles had driven off the perimeter track onto the muddy grass. Out at the dispersals, obscured by a faint mist, could be seen the Lancasters which had not departed for Berlin. Of huge size and dull black in colouring, they stood like gigantic totemic beasts, heavy tarpaulins muffling their shape. Beyond them, in the gathering darkness, was an empty dripping melancholy landscape, ploughed fields, bare hedges, the occasional cottage or farmhouse, dark woods bare of any leaves.

Though it was twilight, no lights were coming on, for the whole station was under a strict blackout. The air was heavy with the smell of coal tar from the numerous stoves burning in the huts. The grey-blue of the RAF uniform harmonised all too well with the dismal, saturated tones of both sky and camp, as a few lone figures hurried squelching from one damp coke-heated prefab to another.

The crew took all this in fairly quickly, before making for the comparative warmth, light and cheer of the Sergeants' or Officers' Mess. Like most crews, fed up with months of living in the cold, damp, drafty

Nissen huts of the training units, they had probably hoped for a posting to a pre-war airfield like Wyton, well-planned, brick-built, and centrally heated (though in reality massively overcrowded). Looking at the makeshift squatters' camp they had drawn instead, they grumbled a little, good-naturedly, until Joe, playing the fool as usual, cracked a series of jokes which made them all laugh.

Later that night, they would hear the Lancasters returning from Berlin, and like everyone else on the station, they would begin to count them. One Lancaster had already been back for hours, returning 90 minutes after take-off because the captain, Pilot Officer Billing, had fainted at 13,000 feet. Fifteen other planes were due back from eleven o'clock onwards, but only fourteen would return. Pilot Officer Coleman's limped back with flak damage and an injured flight engineer. The aircraft which did not return was captained by Squadron Leader Garlick, the Commander of B Flight and one of the squadron's most highly valued pilots. Though it would not be known at Bourn for weeks, Garlick and one other crew member had been killed – the rest of the crew would eke out the war as PoWs.

RAF Station Bourn had only been in existence for two years. Sited on the extensive lands of Bourn Grange, between the Grange itself and what little remained of the buildings of the home farm, Grange Farm, the station was in fact much closer to Caldecote and Highfields than Bourn, but it was from the Grange that it had taken its name.

Prior to being commandeered in 1940, the land had been in the ownership of a man called Wells. The Wells family lived at the Grange and had to vacate the fine house when the RAF took over, though they were well compensated when the whole estate was bought outright. Grange Farm had been a mixed farm – dairy, sheep, and poultry, together with wheat, barley, beans and oats, mostly grown for cattlefood. All this was obliterated once the engineers and navvies moved in. The fields disappeared beneath tons of concrete and a huge number of temporary buildings. Most of these were to the west and south of the airfield, but in the north-east, close to Grange Farm, a large hangar for aircraft repairs was built, together with facilities for petrol and oil storage.

On the north side, the airfield was bordered by the St Neots to Cambridge road, and on the east by the small settlement of Highfields, beyond which lay the village of Hardwick. A thick tree belt ran along the southern side, whilst along the west side ran the public highway, Broad Way. A security checkpoint with a pole stood by Great Common Farm, at the junction where all the heavy duty and supply vehicles came into the camp. Civilians travelling along Broad Way were required to have passes to go through the checkpoint, and those who did not, to their singular annoyance, had to go the extremely long way round the outskirts of the camp.

The barbed wire perimeter fence was patrolled daily by Service Police, but in many ways security was rather lax. Folk memory has it that there were various half-concealed gaps in the barbed wire, holes deliberately created by the station's ground crew to link up with the extensive local network of footpaths. These not only gave quick access to favoured pubs such as The Chequers at Hardwick, but also meant that ground crew could occasionally bend the rules a little. An erk might thereby sneak out of the camp without permission, knowing he could get back unseen by the watchful SPs on the main gate, who otherwise would have put him on a charge immediately.

When completed in 1941, the airfield had mainly been grass surface, but as the bombing campaign accelerated so the facilities had been significantly upgraded. The three runways were hard-surfaced and in the latter part of 1942 extended to 2,000 yards, 1,650 yards and 1,000 yards. When the Pathfinders came in the spring of 1943, the 1,000 yard runway was extended to 1,450, and a homing system called SBA was installed. The airfield's beacons were placed at either end of the main NE.-SW. runway, with the main beacon near the camp's domestic sites, including the Waafery, and the inner marker on the far side of the St Neots-Cambridge road, the closest building to it being Two Pots Farmhouse.

The three massive runways crossed over one another, making a very powerful and striking geometric shape when seen from the air. The prevailing winds were south-westerly. It was therefore seldom that the Lancasters of 97 Squadron would take off using the shortest runway of all, NW.-SE., which meant that just after becoming airborne they would pass over Highfields and Hardwick, close to St Mary's Church. When they did so, it was an awesome experience for the village folk. A local man, Bob Plane, who was 14 in 1943, well remembered the war years and their excitement, and particularly the repercussions of living so close to the airfield. There were several crashes in the area, and he said with a laugh, 'we were more afraid of planes crashing than the Germans bombing'. He recalled the Lancasters straining and labouring to gain height as they came directly over Hardwick:

> They used to come over the tops of the houses, laden with bombs, and one would think 'Please God, let them get over'. You would be sitting there with a cup of tea, and when they had gone over the saucer was full of tea and the cup was only half full because of the vibrations.

The bombers would all conglomerate overhead, gathering together before they headed off for Germany, 'it was a hell of a noise'. Together with the roar of Bourn's aircraft taking off, there would be the distant growl of others taking off from neighbouring airfields, and then the huge pack would set out into the gathering darkness, the roar of their great engines gradually receding.

Though ground crew came to drink at Hardwick (as they also went to

Bourn village, a similar distance from the airfield), there was little direct contact between aircrew and village folk. Aircrew had little time for socialising, and in any case most preferred to go to Cambridge, or to the Messes and cinema on the camp itself. There were frequent station dances, with plenty of girls in uniform, mostly WAAFs and local ATS girls. Aircrew, who had it constantly drummed into them that careless talk cost lives, were very careful what they said to any civilians they met, and to a large degree kept to their own social circles.

In response, the attitude of the locals was mixed. Some displayed an element of resentment towards the huge encampment which had been plonked down unceremoniously in the midst of a quiet, old-fashioned, farming community. It was not just the airfield, for there were also soldiers based at the nearby village of Caxton, Land Army girls working on the local farms, and, towards the village of Toft, a prisoner of war camp, with mostly Italians but some Germans as well. Geoffrey Gilbert, of 61 Squadron, also in Bomber Command, whose family home was near Bourn, used to come home on leave to find what seemed a hive of service activity – 'I'd come home and be surrounded by three airfields, Gransden, Graveley, and Bourn, so it was not like getting away'. Though the Lancasters only flew ops at night-time, they would be out in the day on tests or training exercises (the latter including the somewhat ominously named 'circuits and bumps'), and the huge black planes were a highly visible and aural presence. Some of the locals used to grumble about the noise the planes made. As Arthur Spencer, a 97 Squadron navigator, said, 'I don't think they were very pleased to have us there, the Lancs were so noisy – the Stirlings that had been there before were much quieter'.

But local people were not immune to the drama and magic of the Lancasters. A particularly striking demonstration of this could be seen on operational nights, by the disputatious checkpoint. Here the perimeter track which linked the westerly dispersal points to the airfield actually crossed Broad Way in two places. Bill Ford, one of the old ground crew, remembered that on summer evenings there would be quite a crowd of village people on the road, waiting to see the Lancasters go across. The heavily laden aircraft would taxi slowly past, all four props spinning, before lift-off towards enemy territory. The onlookers would stroll up, maybe two or three dozen of them, and he always wondered if that was because security at the station was a bit lax or just because the locals could hear the engines being run up.

In winter, when the planes were taking off either at twilight or in the dark, the divorce of station from local community was far more complete. To those who lived on the camp, RAF Station Bourn at times felt very cut off, damp, dreary, dark, cold, isolated, and melancholy. When the rain, mists and fogs closed in, it became a little world on its own. Such dismal weather was to prevail for the first seventeen days of December 1943, and when the worst night in the squadron's fortunes came it was comparatively easy to keep matters a close secret. Cyril Crow, who during the war farmed at Gills Hill Farm, near Bourn village, told me how little was known about the disastrous events of that December night when RAF Station Bourn lost so many planes and crew. 'We could hear there was a lot of trouble going on and we could see the fires, but we did not really know what was going on. We never got to hear much about it afterwards – Air Force people did not talk about what was going on – it was all very hush-hush in those days.' The official wartime stranglehold on information meant that the squadron suffered its disastrous losses in silence, and the local community was never involved.

The crashed planes had gone down on local farms, but all the wrecks were closely guarded and all civilians were kept away. Later, local gossips would pool information about the lost planes and thus compile a sort of picture, one which as the years went by became progressively more exaggerated and distorted. 'They lost half the squadron that night', that was what I was first told when I tried to find out what local memory said. On another occasion, it was 7 planes out of 14; the last, even wilder, version was 15 out of 30. In fact, they lost five crashed in England and one over Berlin, six out of the 21 sent to Berlin, unless you also count the two abandoned aircraft in which no lives were lost. Yet when I pointed this out, my informant became sniffy, as if I was minimising the significance of what had happened that night, showing a basic disrespect to the memory of those who had died. I could understand in a way why he felt like that. As a shorthand means of conveying the enormity of the loss, half the squadron is not so wild after all.

V. The Bomber Boys

The winter of 1943-44 would see the most dramatic, terrible and costly period of Bomber Command's war. Having targeted the Ruhr, Hamburg, and a string of other cities, Harris, who had only been waiting for the opportunity, now at last turned his sights on the prize of them all – Berlin.

The difficulties of Harris accomplishing his long-declared objective of winning the war by bombing alone had always been colossal. The distances involved and the technical problems had been enormous. With the focus now shifting to Berlin as prime target, the problems increased exponentially. The city was sited in 'Fortress Europe' behind hundreds of miles of defences placed in the occupied countries and Germany. Added to the very considerable threat posed by the enemy were those posed by serious bad weather. Berlin was a 1,200 mile round trip, under risk of decimating attack virtually the whole way, and the campaign had had to be deferred until the onset of winter because only then would there be sufficient cover of darkness.

The Battle of Berlin commenced on 18th/19th November. From that very first night when one 97 Squadron crew was shot down, the squadron would with deadly regularity lose one or two crews on every operation. Seven or

fourteen men would just disappear off the station, their fate unknown for
many weeks, perhaps years – some still not known yet, half a century later.
Other crews came home with seriously wounded or dead men on board,
their aircraft beaten up, gaping holes in its skin, an engine out of action, the
controls so badly affected that landing the kite at Bourn was as dangerous
as everything that had gone before. Yet once this terrifying ordeal was over,
as likely as not that crew would be back on ops the following night.

Any operation was acutely stressful, but those to Berlin were, by
common consensus, the worst of all. Before such a raid, the air was electric,
yet there was a sort of massive brooding calm underneath all the frenetic
activity. Joan Beech, who worked in Bourn's Met Office and later described
her time there in *One Waaf's War*, wrote of the moment when all the
preparations came to fruition:

> We could hear the aircraft revving up at their dispersal points
> and then one by one taking off, labouring to get their weight
> off the ground before they ran out of runway. Soon the fading
> sky would be full of bombers from neighbouring airfields and
> others further north, all on their way to the same distant target
> . . . It was an awe-inspiring sight to stand in the dusk outside
> the office, watching and listening to the boys going out on
> what we all knew would be a hazardous and dangerous
> mission, from which at least some of them would not return.
> When they had gone and the noise of the engines had faded
> away, all would be quiet for a few hours and most people on
> night duty could relax . . .

The time that the planes would return was known to within an hour or so. If
a plane was not back by the later time, the hour at which its petrol ran out,
it might be that the crew had landed away at another aerodrome. But if no
phone call came through, the aircraft's absence could only mean one thing.

Those who had a particular interest in a late aircraft, perhaps with a
friend or a fiancée on board, would find their hope ebbing as they strained
to catch the sound of its engines faintly approaching through the night. The
airfield lay stretched out into the furthest shadows, an unbroken expanse of
grass and runway, the flare-path still lit, the red obstruction lights still
flaring, but an emptiness and nothingness over all which seemed a mockery
to those who waited. When the flarepath was finally switched off, it seemed
to the watchers as if all hope had gone.

For the aircrew who returned safely, the relief was enormous. Joan
Beech thought that the difference in their attitudes before and after
operations was very noticeable. Beforehand they were 'tense and quiet, and
no doubt very frightened if the truth were known, but on their return, if we
saw them at all, they would be relaxed and only looking forward to bacon
and eggs in the Mess – and then to bed'.

The chop rate was so high that, from an instinct of self-preservation, most ground crew who worked on the aircraft did not get that close to their crews. Bob Philips, a flight mechanic, said that one did not really have time to regret what had happened to the planes and the crews which went missing or crashed, 'before you could look round, there was another one'. All the same, 'it used to shake you when you lost your crew'. To sublimate the tension, he and his fellow mechanics took the greatest pride in their job and they did all they possibly could to make things go well for the aircrew – 'we got them through their ops'.

The vagueness of the fate of the aircrew increased the necessity for emotional distance. Joan Beech decided it was a mug's game to become involved with any of them; 'We saw so many of these bomber boys pass before us – we got to know them slightly and then they were gone'.

Bill Ford, who worked as an electrician on the Lancasters, believed that there was 'a tendency, due to the colossal losses, to keep a sort of distance from the aircrews – you would go onto your section the following morning and the aircraft you had been working on wasn't there – a week or two would go by and then that plane would be replaced by another, with another crew – there was never sufficient time to get to know anyone properly.'

To his mind there was a far closer relationship between the ground crew and the aircrew on the Mosquitoes which came into Bourn after 97 Squadron left, because the losses were nothing like as dreadful and because the Mosquitoes had only two crew – one might miss and mourn them just the same, but it was not quite so terrible as losing seven at one go.

Yet outstanding affection and loyalty there certainly was at times. Navigator Arthur Spencer remembers that the ground crew corporal in charge of the maintenance of his aircraft, J-Johny, refused to go on leave on the day appointed because 'we had only one operation left to complete our tour'. Leave was very precious to ground crew because they only got four weeks per year. Though it meant that every day he refused to go he lost an additional day, the corporal, a young married man, would not depart even though operations were twice cancelled. Eventually the crew did get away on their last trip and returned safely. The skipper, a young Canadian, Jimmy Munro, was so touched by the corporal's devotion that he managed to persuade his Flight Commander to agree a 48 hour extension to the man's leave, a most unusual concession for those days. Sadly, Jimmy Munro was to be killed before the month of November was out, together with the two remaining crew members, Ron Bennett and 'Weasel' Hill. All three had decided to continue after their 45th op; the two Canadians, Jimmy Munro and Weasel Hill, may have believed the then-current rumour that after 60 ops they would be repatriated.

The 19th November 1943, the same day that my father's crew reported to Wyton as junior Pathfinders, saw the safe return to Bourn, in the early hours of the morning, of 16 out of the 17 planes sent the previous night.

They had been part of a huge force sent on the opening raid of the Battle of Berlin, Harris's all-out attempt to win the war by flattening the German capital.

On the Lancasters' return, Bourn's ORB noted:

> 17 Lancasters detailed for tonight's operation. BERLIN was attacked in 10/10 cloud [total cloud cover] . . . viz. good-hazy. Explosions were reported but raid was scattered and no good concentration achieved. Owing to cloud crews saw little or nothing. Defences weak to moderate . . . 16 photos attempted. One a/c failed to return – F/S JOHNSON and crew. No news received at base, all other aircraft returned safely with little damage.

It was customary for pilots to fly as second pilot, 'second dickey', for two operations with an experienced crew before being sent out on their own. On his final trip out as second pilot, Pilot Officer Charles Owen, who had begun a terse diary of his operations, noted of this opening raid:

> Many fighter flares on route in, and we saw several aircraft shot down. There was a little cloud over the Big City, but hundreds of searchlights and very heavy flak. We overshot the target on our initial run, and so turned back and bombed against the stream. I did not like it at all, and made up my mind never to do it again if I could help it. Route out was very quiet, but we got a long way off track coming across France, and met heavy predicted flak at Aachen.

There was a second huge raid on Berlin on the night of 22nd/23rd – 97 Squadron sent 19 planes – 2 planes did not return, those of Flight Lieutenant Munro and Pilot Office McEgan. The Lancaster of Jimmy Munro, the young Canadian pilot mentioned above, was lost without trace on his 57th operation, and none of the crew, who had three DFMs* and two DFCs* between them, was ever seen again. Pilot Officer McEgan's plane, lost the same night, resulted in his death and that of two other crew members, and the four survivors becoming PoWs. The remaining Lancasters all returned safely, though some had suffered minor flak damage.

On the 23rd/24th Berlin was bombed again – Bourn sent 16 planes, Flight Sergeant Penny's did not return. All his crew were killed, but Penny became a PoW.

This crew had flown the previous night's raid, as had many of the other crews. The German defences were certainly sharper on this particular night. The ORB notes:

---

* Distinguished Flying Medal, Distinguished Flying Cross.

Weather was better although 10/10ths cloud, there were patches of visibility. Markers reported to be well concentrated – owing to cloud no details were possible, but the attack is considered very successful. Some incendiaries were seen through clouds. A good red glow could be seen for 20 minutes on route home. Fires were still believed to be burning from the previous raids . . . Many fighter flares and fighter activity. F/S PENNY and crew failed to return. All other a/c returned safely to base encountering bad weather and gales. Minor damage was sustained by some aircraft – F/L Riches had two engines shot up over the target, but the aircraft was brought back to base safely on the two remaining engines, the third cutting while still on the runway.

Those in authority were pleased with the opening stages of the campaign. On the 25th November, the ORB recorded the receipt of a signal from Harris: 'I have received the following message from the Secretary of State, which please convey together with my reply to all ranks'. The message is then given in full:

My warmest congratulations to you and to all ranks serving under your command on two crushing attacks upon the Nazi citadel. Berlin is not only the home of Prussian militarism and the capital of the Nazi government, but it is also the greatest single centre of war industry in Germany. Often before, your Squadrons have hit it hard. The most convincing measure of this success has been the huge deployment of the enemy's resources for its defence. Nevertheless your attacks these last two nights have reached a new level of power and concentration and have proved that, however much he may marshal his guns, searchlights and fighters, the enemy cannot match [the] skill and determination of your crews.

The reply from Harris, HQ and the Pathfinder Force begins:

On behalf of all ranks of Bomber Command, I thank you for [your] encouraging message. The Battle of Berlin progresses. It will continue as opportunity serves and circumstance dictates until the heart of Nazi Germany ceases to beat.

On the 25th/26th November, 97 Squadron took part in a raid on Frankfurt. 16 planes were sent, one did not return, that of Flight Lieutenant Brown. The entire crew was killed.

On the 26th/27th Berlin was attacked again – Bourn sent 8 planes, all returned safely. On the same night a further 10 planes were sent to Stuttgart and once again all returned safely. One of these aircraft had to turn back early, within a couple of hours of take-off – it was Squadron Leader Mackenzie's, and the early return was due to the sickness of the mid-upper gunner, Lang.

On the Berlin half of this night's operations was Charles Owen, flying for the first time as skipper in an aircraft with the call sign of K-King.

> First trip with my own crew, and the Big City at that. Usual flares and aircraft shot down on way in. Target was clear, and we could see fires burning from an attack the previous night. Hundreds of searchlights and very heavy flak, firing mainly into the cones. Flew over Hanover by mistake on return journey and was coned for seven minutes. Lost height from 20 to 13,000 ft. during evasive action from intense heavy flak. Several holes in starboard wing and roof of cockpit, and the bomb-aimer was wounded slightly in the leg. Also attacked by a fighter when coned, but only damage was six inches knocked off one blade of the starboard outer prop.

It was one of the very few times that Owen would get himself into trouble. His bomb-aimer soon recovered, and a few days later, after the necessary repairs, K-King was also back in service.

On the 30th, the planned operation was cancelled due to adverse weather conditions.

December that year was a wet and foggy month. It began inauspiciously at Bourn, when on the 1st, seventeen aircraft were detailed to attack Leipzig but once again the operation had to be cancelled due to bad weather. The order to scrub came through in the late afternoon after briefing when everyone had already psyched themselves up for the stomach-turning moment of departure.

On the 2nd, on the same afternoon that my father's crew arrived at Bourn, sixteen aircraft departed for Berlin. The Lancaster of Squadron Leader Garlick did not return, and Pilot Officer Coleman's limped back with flak damage and an injured flight engineer.

On the 3rd, the weather was once again rainy and misty, but the cancelled raid on Leipzig went ahead. Once again only sixteen crews were sent. Charles Owen was in fine form on return to Bourn:

> Change of target seemed to fox the defences. Very little fighter activity, as most of them must have been stooging around over Berlin. Target was covered by thin layer of 10/10 cloud, so searchlights were non-effective. Moderate heavy flak. Could see glow of big fires on cloud when leaving target area. Heard later that it was very successful prang.

Amongst those who missed this Leipzig operation were my father's crew. In particular, there is no record of Ted flying as second dickey in order to gain some operational experience before taking on the heavy responsibilities of skipper. The only second pilot recorded in the ORB for that night was Bill Coates, whose crew had trained alongside Ted's since July and like them had arrived at Bourn the previous day. Bill flew as second dickey with Flight Lieutenant Brill.

Nor were any of Ted's crew required to fill in gaps on other crews. George might easily have been asked to fill in for Pilot Officer Coleman's usual crew member, Maurice Durn, the twenty-year old flight engineer who had been slightly injured by flak the previous night. But instead it was a much older man, the thirty-four year old Dennis Moore, who took Durn's place. It was the most dreadful bad luck for Moore – Coleman and his crew, who had barely survived their previous trip, vanished without trace on this Leipzig operation and nobody would ever know what had happened to them.

John Arthurson, a navigator, remembers what a very bitter, indeed shattering, blow it was for him and the rest of Dennis Moore's regular crew when Coleman's plane did not return. This junior crew had arrived from Upwood only a few days before Ted's and would have their first operational flight together on the same night. Moore was a married man with children. His place on John Arthurson's crew would be taken by Maurice Durn once he recovered.

The 4th of December dawned fine and misty, but 97 Squadron was not required for operations because the full moon period so dangerous to the bomber crews was approaching. The station was stood down and instead the time was to be used for training. On the 5th of December, however, the weather worsened, with the early fair weather turning into thick fog; all flying practice was cancelled and ground training substituted. The foggy conditions continued for five days, with the ORB noting every day some variant of the phrase, 'No flying, weather unfit'. Ted's crew, newly out of training, were left in a nerve-racking state of inertia.

What to do with the aircrew when even flying practice was cancelled was always a problem for the Commanding Officer. Ground training could only take up so much slack. Once one had run out of lecture subjects or instructional films, and had used all the old stand-bys like dinghy drill, practice shooting, and aircraft recognition, inspiration was running short. Sometimes, in desperation, the CO might dragoon the aircrew into some domestic chore such as moving furniture. If all else failed, the crews could be sent on an educational visit, as indeed they were on 10th December, to the RAF engineering shops at Henlow.

One topic for lectures which brought an unwelcome reminder of the odds you were facing was that optimistically dubbed 'Evasion and Escape'. Little would be said, however, about how absolutely minimal your chances of evading capture were. For 97 Squadron, for the whole of 1943, only nine men escaped capture after bailing out or crashlanding in enemy territory, and eventually made their way back to England. Four of these were from the crew of Flight Sergeant Johnson, who were shot down by flak on their 29th operation during the opening raid of the Battle of Berlin. The Lancaster fell from 20,000 to 6,000 feet before Johnson regained sufficient control to allow the rest of the crew time to bail out. In doing so, he sacrificed his own life, as did so many of the bomber pilots. He had been a last-minute replacement for their usual skipper, an Australian pilot known as Snowy Jones, who had been barred from flying by the Medical Officer because of sinus trouble.

Another important part of the aircrews' ground training – and unfortunately a great deal more likely to be of use to them – was training in the basic techniques of first aid. Crew members might have to deal with lacerations, internal injury, concussion, severe fractures or even amputation after attack by enemy flak or fighters, or after a crash landing before any medical help arrived. These lectures were given by the Medical Officer and were based on the first-aid kits carried on the Lancasters. Only the simplest forms of treatment were covered, but they frequently meant the difference between life and death.

In the majority of cases which the crews might be called upon to deal with, shock was the most dangerous factor of all. Whatever the condition of the patient, he should be reassured and told not to worry; if his life was in danger, no one should tell him this as the news would only tend to increase the degree of shock. Aircrew were taught that warmth was essential, and that they should use whatever was at hand to maintain it. Clothing should never be removed from a wounded man unless it was necessary to apply a tourniquet or dressing, in which case the clothing should be quickly replaced. They were also taught how to give freedom from pain, by injecting the contents of one of the morphia ampoules included in the first-aid kit. As pain was often delayed by 20 to 30 minutes following the injury, instructions were that the injection should be given as soon as possible.

The weather began to improve on the 10th December, but it was not until the 11th that for only the third time since Ted's crew had left Upwood, they were able to get in some flying practice. Over the next three days, various training sessions were flown, including take-offs and landings, practice bombing, night flying, fighter affiliation, and split-second timing navigation incorporating the radar aids, Gee and H2S. 'Two night cross countrys and two a/c on dusk and dark circuits landing' are also mentioned in the ORB. Quite likely one of these aircraft was Ted's.

Because there were no raids, however, Ted did not get the chance to make the customary two trips as second pilot for a 'blooding' or familiarisation flight with an experienced crew. There is no record of him ever flying as second dickey. Perhaps the operations which might have been flown on 14th and 15th December would have given him a chance, but the weather was so unfavourable that not even flying practice could be carried out – once again all the crews were grounded.

During this long period of inaction, Ted, his fellow officer Sandy, and their five sergeants, would have gleaned all they could of what had been happening at the station before their arrival. It did not make a particularly comforting story, but they probably still only partially grasped the odds that they were facing. With the natural ebullience and physical self-confidence of youth, they probably thought – as so many other junior crews thought – that 'it' could never happen to them.

But it may well have been rather different for Jack. At thirty-one years of age, married, and of a thoughtful and reflective cast of mind, he probably had a far more realistic appraisal of just how lucky they would all have to be to survive.

The crew were very much the new boys on the station, and probably no one took much notice of them though my father was likely to stand out if there was any time for a bit of fooling around. There is a story that he used to tell my sister about playing the piano in the Mess. Though he did not say which Mess, had he done this at the Sergeants' Mess at Bourn it might have made an impression for he was incredibly good at it, jamming, horsing about, improvising, being silly – this might have made him stand out from the crowd. His fellow NCOs, depending on their mood, would either have told him irritably to shut up, or alternatively have found it exceedingly funny as he thrashed with hugely exaggerated arm movements up and down the keyboard, making the old piano thrum and shake. They may even have joined in in the singing of some ribald, drunken, mildly obscene RAF song. Someone might have taken particular notice of the baby-faced young man so strenuously acting the clown, seen the vulnerability of him and his crewmates. But no one I have spoken to about Bourn remembers a thing about them. Like so many others, they came and they went, vanishing too quickly, scarcely leaving a trace. Only the official records confirm for certain that they were there, for fourteen days in the winter of 1943.

The chop rate was so high and crews replaced so frequently that the chances of this one junior crew standing out from all the others were, in fact, virtually non-existent. Probably there really is no one left who remembers the crew as anything other than just a group of blurred white faces in the background. Such was the closeness of the seven men on a Lancaster that to a certain extent they tended to shun the company of outsiders. As Maurice Hemming, a flight engineer on the squadron at that period, said, 'One knew little if anything of other crews, they were replaced so often . . . Such was squad life: one lived, slept, played and operated as a crew, oblivious of those around you – one had to, to remain sane'.

To Ted's crew, the senior crews that they met in the Officers' and Sergeants' Messes must have seemed impossibly glamorous and battle-weary with their battered log books detailing the long tally of missions. 19, 20, 21, 22 – those must have been the really hard ones, getting towards the middle of the tour, when all illusions had been burnt off. Imagine having to go through the same number again before you finished your tour of 45.

The senior crews must in their turn have looked at the newcomers with a strange compound of sadness, cynicism and impatience, seeing the bright enthusiasm and the hopeless naivety, wondering how long they would last.

The worst period of the Berlin campaign was yet to come, but already the atmosphere at Bourn was becoming heavy and tense. As Joan Beech was to write, 'During the three winter months almost the entire squadron changed – well-known faces gradually disappearing and being replaced by new ones. It had a demoralising effect on us and we wondered how long this could go on.' With the mounting losses, the aircrews' attitudes were changing; 'there was none of the former exuberance if everyone returned safely, and just fatalistic shoulder-shrugging if someone was lost. You bought it or you didn't.'

Since the raid of 3rd/4th December, the bad weather had severely curtailed all forms of flying. By Thursday 16th, there had been a gap of almost a fortnight since the last operation, a respite for some, a nagging cause of nervous tension for others. But now the waiting came to an end. It was as if someone had decided that an attack on Berlin must take place whether the weather was suitable or not.

That someone could only have been Harris. From *The Pathfinder Force*, by Gordon Musgrove:

> Harris had gambled on the force getting back before the weather clamped down. At take-off, visibility was 2,500 yards and cloud base 1,200 feet with tops at 5,000 feet. This was hazardous enough but on return conditions had worsened: cloud base was 500 feet and getting lower by the minute.

Three

16th/17th December 1943

I. Preparation

The force which was sent against Berlin, codenamed Whitebait, on the night of 16th December 1943 was a very large one – 483 Lancasters and 15 Mosquitoes – around 3,400 men.

Much earlier that day, a Mosquito of 1409 Meteorological Flight had taken off for a reconnaissance flight across Germany, its mission being to assess the weather conditions that the bomber crews would face that night. The Met Flight planes were light and very fast, being unarmed for the extra speed and manoeuvrability. The Mosquito flew a circuitous route in order to avoid giving away the potential target to the enemy, and landed back in England shortly after midday. Its report was immediately transmitted to Bomber Command HQ, where it was used to refine the weather forecast given by Magnus Spence at that morning's nine o'clock conference in which Harris had decided to renew the attack on Berlin.

A second Met flight may perhaps have been made that same afternoon. This Mosquito would have returned shortly before take-off time. As the weather over the routes and the target, not to mention the return home, was absolutely critical to the success of a raid, the greatest care was taken to make sure that the forecasts were accurate. It was this three-tier system of forecasting which led to the not infrequent cancellation of bombing raids either in the early afternoon, after the first Mosquito had returned, or at any time in the hour directly before take-off when the second Mosquito came back. Such last-minute cancellations were always acutely stressful for the hyped-up bomber crews.

On this particular afternoon, contrary to the expectation of Bourn's Met Officer, the order to scrub the raid never came through.

At Bourn, preparations for a raid, destination as yet unconfirmed, had begun early that Thursday morning. It was still dark and chilly when the ground crew had struggled out of their warm beds and gone to breakfast at seven o'clock. By eight o'clock, they were out on the airfield. By now it was daylight but there were few signs of the sun appearing. The weather was cold, overcast and misty, with low-hanging clouds and hardly any wind.

Out at the dispersal points stood the huge dark Lancasters. Arriving in vans, on bicycles or on foot, a small army of men began to swarm around the aircraft. Ladders were propped up, wheeled scaffolding was pushed over, and inspection hatches gaped wide. Fitters, riggers, mechanics, electricians – each had their task to perform on one or more of the twenty-one planes. Because there had been nearly a fortnight's gap since the last operation, the planes were in excellent condition, and there was not the same tumbling frenetic haste that occurred when the Lancasters were operating on consecutive nights. All the same it was a scramble, with so many people working in the cramped fuselage, checking everything down to the smallest detail, making sure that the aircraft was 'on the top line' before the crew took it up for a test flight.

These test flights were known as night flying tests, NFTs. At half-past eleven that morning, Y-York, piloted by Pilot Officer Smith (always nicknamed Smithy), his navigator being John Arthurson, took off for the half hour test. Like Ted's crew, that night would be their first operation, and they were both excited and tense at the same time, 'wondering whether or not this would be "Go" and if so, where [the] first target would be'.

For security reasons, the destination would not be revealed until crew briefing that afternoon, but petrol and bomb loads were already known and were giving rise to frenzied speculation.

The aircraft which had been allocated to Ted's crew was JB176-OF-K, JB176 being the registration number, 'OF' being the squadron's code and K the aircraft's letter. K-King was a Mark III Lancaster, which had been completed at the end of August 1943 by the famous firm of A V Roe and registered with 97 Squadron on 6th September. She had already been on twelve operations, variously to Hanover, Mannheim, Munich, Frankfurt, Leipzig, Cannes, Ludwigshaven, and Berlin. When first delivered to the squadron she had been the favourite aircraft of a very senior crew of distinguished calibre and exceptionally high overall rank. The skipper of this crew was Squadron Leader S P Daniels, and his bomb aimer, Squadron Leader C M Dunnicliffe, was to be acting CO of 97 Squadron on the night of 16th/17th December. However, after this crew temporarily left the squadron, K-King was always flown by a different crew, which meant that by mid November she had become one of the reserve aircraft.

Her penultimate operation was the Berlin raid of 26th/27th November, on which she was flown by Charles Owen. His diary entry for that night has already been quoted – on the return journey, the crew accidentally strayed over Hanover, a mistake which very nearly finished them. In escaping, K-King suffered a fair amount of damage. She had to go in for repairs, and must still have been out of action when the early December raids began. Her thirteenth and last outing was to be with Ted's crew.

Shortly before mid-day on that fateful Thursday morning, K-King took off for the NFT. When Ted and George, his flight engineer, were happy with the plane's performance, and the other members of the crew were also satisfied that their equipment was working perfectly, K-King circled the airfield, came down to land, and returned to her dispersal for fuelling and bombing up.

Since early that morning, the handling crews had been out at the bomb dump in the south-east quarter of the airfield by the woods, sorting out the loads for the night. The area was hidden behind soil embankments ten feet high to tamp the blast in case of accidents but from the concealed Nissen huts there now regularly emerged a snake-like line of low trolleys drawn by a tractor. The ungainly train rumbled along the perimeter track from Lancaster to Lancaster, and at each aircraft the armourers unhitched a segment and wheeled it under the waiting bomb bay.

In the north-east corner of the airfield, other ground crew were filling and refilling the massive 2,500 gallon petrol bowsers and the oil bowsers, which held 450 gallons, and driving them to and fro from the dispersal points. On the long flight to Berlin and back, K-King would take off carrying not only 10,000 lbs of bombs but also the enormous weight of 2,000 gallons of aviation fuel stored in the six petrol tanks in her wings.

A hundred other vital matters were attended to. Armourers whose speciality was the guns fed the ammunition belts into K-King, and checked out the firing mechanisms and sights. Dozens of bundles of Window were stacked up in the front of the aircraft, ready to disrupt the German defences. (A radar-disrupting device of the simplest nature, Window consisted merely of millions of small strips of tinfoil, which George and Joe would throw out, bundle by bundle, whilst over enemy territory.) The photographic department loaded the camera which would hopefully assess the efficiency of Sandy's bomb aiming, and set it so that the shutter would open when the photoflash which dropped with the bombs ignited.

Only the crew took no part in the flurry of preparations. Once they had been warned that a raid was on and had completed their NFT, there was nothing to do but simply wait for the time to go by. All the crews had the same trouble in getting through that last hour or so before the briefing. Some tried to doze; others played games of billiards, cards, chess, or shove-ha'penny, a Bourn favourite; few could forget what the evening would bring. New crews, such as Ted's, Bill Coates's and John Arthurson's, who had never been on an operation before, were keyed up almost beyond endurance, not knowing what they would be facing and how they would acquit themselves. All the long months of training had led up to this particular day, and now, suddenly, it had come at last. For them it was a particularly feverish wait, as the minutes inexorably ticked past and the heavy white cloud lowered over the base, the station shut in upon itself by the damp misty weather.

Before the main briefing, the pilots, navigators and bomb aimers reported for pre-briefing, in which they were told they would be going to Berlin. This was mainly for the navigators' benefit, so that they would have time to work out a chart and flight plan.

Then at last, everyone assembled in the Aircrews' Briefing Room behind the Control Tower. 151 men would be flying from Bourn that night – there were four second pilots in addition to the normal crew compliment – and the room was very crowded and full of tobacco smoke. The Briefing Officer drew back the black curtain and revealed the giant wall map of Europe. The destination was marked with tapes, pins and arrows indicating the route to be followed. Also marked were the enemy defences which they would encounter, flak and searchlight belts. The junior crews now knew that their first flight would be to Berlin, 'the Big City'.

Those aircrew who had already been there several times groaned. Berlin was a very, very long way away, across hundreds of miles of hostile territory. But Berlin it was – there was no getting out of it.

Now the various section leaders spoke their piece, giving the latest information on navigation, gunnery, bombing procedures, alternative targets (two Lancasters, failing to reach the target, would drop their bombs that night on a Dutch island called Texel), air defences, signals, engine power settings, the route, the weather.

The attack would commence at precisely two minutes to eight with the dropping of the primary blind markers, and it would be over by twelve minutes past. At half past eight, a three-quarters moon would rise. To avoid the effects of the moonlight which favoured the attacking nightfighters, a quick direct route to Berlin had been chosen, with a long northerly return over the Baltic and Denmark after the moon had risen.

HQ's weather forecast for the English bases was for total cloud cover at dusk when the aircraft took off, the cloud beginning at 1,200 to 3,000 feet, with tops at 3,000-3,500 feet. Slight icing was expected near the cloud base. Visibility, it was estimated, would be two to four miles. An ominous rider had been added: 'These conditions will persist [but] if cloud base breaks up in East Anglia, visibility will quickly deteriorate to less than 2,000 yards . . .'. It was anticipated that there would be fog over the German airfields, thus preventing the fighters from scrambling, but it was the threat of fog over England at around the time the bombers returned which made Bourn's Met Officer say that he thought the raid would be scrubbed because of the possibility of the weather closing in early.

Squadron Leader Dunnicliffe, acting CO, now spoke the valedictory words, some variant of the time-honoured exhortation that the crews should prang the target and prang it hard. He wished them all good luck, and the meeting broke up. The wireless operators, gunners and flight engineers now went to their own sections for specialist briefings.

Then came the flight meal of bacon and eggs.

At around three o'clock, Ted's crew assembled at the crew room to dress in their flying gear for the sub-zero temperatures they would encounter. For Leslie in particular the clothing was very heavy, an electrically heated flying suit over his other clothes which, together with his stout fur-lined flying boots and gloves, made the diminutive Leslie waddle like an overstuffed teddy bear. Tony was also warmly wrapped up. Those flying in the front of the aircraft, where there was an efficient heating system, would not bother with heavy clothing mainly because it would be intolerably constricting. Instead they would fly in their usual RAF gear, supplemented by a white roll-neck sweater.

Over everything was worn the Mae West, or lifejacket, and the flying harness to which a parachute would be clipped in an emergency. Both lifejacket and parachute had to be signed for – they must be returned to Stores once the operation was over.

Now came the arrival of the transports to take the crews out to the dispersal points. Arrival at the planes was timed for approximately one hour before take-off, so that the crews could carry out their final checks before start-up.

At K-King's dispersal, Ted's crew jumped out of the flight van and, laughing and joking but with a distinct feeling of queasiness in the stomach, walked up to their Lancaster, well down on her undercarriage with the colossal weight of fuel and bombs. A metal-runged ladder led up to the main door near the tail, and one by one they climbed aboard and settled down in their own particular position.

At the front of the aircraft, Ted and George began to run through the long series of pre-flight checks. Jack stowed his and Sandy's parachutes beneath the chart table, then on top laid out in neat array his pencils, ruler, divider, protractor, forms, astro navigation tables, the detailed maps of the territory over which they would be flying, and the all-important flight plan. In the compartment behind him, Joe set down his flimsies printed with the radio frequencies and the colour of the day, then checked his radio and code books, and began a preliminary fiddle with the wireless and radio sets. Meanwhile, further down the plane, Tony and Leslie gave their perspex turrets a final polish and swung their guns and turrets around to make sure that the mechanisms were running freely.

The light was beginning to fade out of the sky and night to creep on. It was cold, and, although the thick clouds showed no signs of breaking up, mist was thickening at the corners of the airfield. Visibility had been poor all day – 3 or 4 miles in the morning, which had gradually reduced as the time wore on. The weather was almost ominously still, with only the lightest south-easterly wind.

Soon for most of the crew there was nothing left to do but wait around in the gathering twilight outside the aircraft. Nervous tension was building to fever pitch and yet there was still only inaction. Laughing too loudly at small jokes, smoking too many cigarettes, they waited for Ted and George to finish. There was one terrifying thought lurking at the back of their minds, scarcely glimpsed because they would not allow themselves to glimpse it – that in a very few minutes they would climb aboard, the door would be shut on them, the ladder would be dragged away, and the inexorable momentum of events which had brought them to this safe backwater would bear them away from it, up over enemy territory.

Start-up time.

One by one, the great engines were jump-started by trolley acc – first a crack, a puff of smoke, a series of coughs and bangs, and finally the full-throated roar. As more and more engines were started up, the air grew thunderous with noise and the very earth seemed to shake, the vibrations reverberating through the bodies of the bystanders, causing a massive uprush of adrenalin and nervous excitement.

Time for that last cigarette, that last pee – customary to take it against the wheel of the Lancaster for good luck. The last straggler climbed aboard as Ted as skipper signed Form 700, acknowledging that the aircraft was fully airworthy, and gave his thanks to K-King's ground crew. The door was closed, the chocks were dragged away, and the vast black aircraft ponderously began to move. Turning out of its dispersal point, it joined the twenty other aircraft moving in single file from their various dispersals towards the runway.

On the vast flat emptiness of the airfield the Lancasters stood out clearly against the darkening sky. This was the moment which always made the hearts of the onlookers miss a beat, the pride and magnificence of the squadron rolling slowly past to the uncertain night which lay ahead of them.

At the start of the runway, the chequered flight caravan waited, ready to show the green Aldis lamp which would let each aircraft in turn know when it was cleared for take off. Radio communications were not used in case they were being monitored by the enemy, and the Control Tower had no part in the take-offs save as a grim and silent presence overlooking the scene.

Once each pilot received his signal, he released the brakes and the engines roared up to full power. At first moving slowly, then faster and faster, massive vibrations shaking the frame, the aircraft hurtled down the concrete until at about 110 mph and three-quarters of the way up the runway, the four Merlin engines finally heaved the 30 ton load off the ground. As each Lancaster took off, they climbed away on different preallocated headings to prevent collisions. Shortly afterwards the navigation lights were extinguished.

Ted's aircraft left the ground at five to five.

Once true darkness came, it would be of the deepest densest black, due to the cloud cover and the blackout over the entire country. It was very close to the shortest day of the year, the winter solstice, when the human spirit is at its lowest ebb. Yet it was twilight as they took off and there was still some residual luminescence, enough to show them the land that they were leaving, a last shadowy impression of it before they ascended above cloud level. There lay the huge airfield with its stark geometric pattern of runways, the dark belts of woodland on the boundary and the huddled clusters of support buildings. Beyond, fading into the gathering obscurity, lay the dim mist-edged patchwork of fields, hedges, dykes, woods, ponds, farmsteads, a handful of tiny villages clustered around grey-stoned churches. Looking down, they tried to imprint the image forever on their minds – this faint departing view of a miniaturised crepuscular landscape might be the last glimpse of England they would ever see.

Once they had broken through the cloud cover and the thick white floor of the heavens sealed their view, it was as if they were divorced from the earth. They went on climbing steeply, intent on reaching their operational height of 20,000 feet before they crossed the Dutch coast. All around, in the still faintly illuminated skies, could be seen other aircraft of the same huge force.

The last glow of the setting sun was behind them as they flew out over the English coast. As darkness fell, their companions were lost to sight. Now it was just the seven of them on their own. Uncertainty had hardened to resolution; they were on their way.

II. Attack

Zero hour at Berlin was eight o'clock. The outward journey would take three hours.

It was pitch-dark now. Through the cockpit canopy, known as the glasshouse, Ted had an excellent view of the star-lit skies. His seat was fixed high, its hollow interior holding his parachute like a cushion. Close to him, next to a massive glowing assortment of switches and dials, sat his flight engineer, George, on a small low pull-down seat. Like all the crew, the pair wore leather padded helmets and oxygen masks, and only their eyes and cheekbones were visible in the dim luminosity of the instruments.

A narrow archway right next to George's seat led, via a very steep step downwards, into the nose of the Lancaster. When it came to the bomb run, this was the point from which Sandy would aim at the target, lying flat on his stomach looking downwards through the perspex blister, the Browning guns at rest in the position above him. Every so often as they flew on their way, he would use this same vantage point to search for landmarks in order to help Jack confirm the course that they were flying.

Jack sat directly behind Ted, seated sideways on. He had a long, green, leather-covered bench without a back, and a green metal desk, its right-hand edge smoothed off in a curve. The colour scheme was the same throughout the plane – a bilious light-green, designated 'Cockpit Green', for all the metal, a darker conifer green for the leather seats and for the few bits of leather padding which stopped the men from striking their heads on the many sharp protrusions.

Jack's work was lit by a pinpoint anglepoise light; a blackout curtain hung between him and Ted's seat, to stop the reflected glow from affecting Ted's critical night vision. After Ted, Jack had the most concentrated and difficult task of all – to keep the Lancaster on track through all the shifting variations of wind, course and speed. Bent over his charts, plotting their progress with pencils and ruler, he could not afford to let his concentration slip for a second. For much of the journey, Sandy would sit beside him, working the H2S set which gave a spectral plan of the ground over which they were flying.

Behind Jack sat Joe in his own little separate cubicle. He also had a metal desk and bench, this one facing forward towards the cockpit. At his right hand, affixed to the desk, was the Morse key. Before him, mounted on the wall, were the sets for receiving and transmitting messages, with their brightly coloured knobs, pointers and dials. His main job for the duration of the raid was a simple one – to listen to the half-hourly broadcasts from England. Even if no message was sent, a code number would be transmitted which he must dutifully enter on his sheets to be checked later by the Squadron Signals Officer. There was no question for the time being of him broadcasting himself, for a strict silence had to be maintained to base to avoid giving away information to the enemy. For the same reason, the crew kept chatter on the intercom to a minimum, their voices sounding strange and distant, very far off over the crackling of the static.

A thick metal door shut off the five men in the front from the two gunners. The only heat in the plane blasted out in Joe's compartment, roasting him whilst others felt the chill, particularly Tony and Leslie, a long way further up the plane.

There was a padded archway next to Joe's seat. A gigantic step up, a twist and a duck all at the same time, took you into the centre of the plane. There you slithered over the main spar, sheathed in smooth green-painted metal, and the second smaller hump in the floor just beyond it, into a low-ceilinged corridor. Here was the tiny room with a rest bed in which an injured man could be placed, strapped down in case evasive manoeuvres were necessary. Though massive-looking from the outside, K-King's interior was very cramped – all the more so because of the cluttering of numerous bits of equipment. If you were tall, you had to duck all the way down the centre; it was not until you had walked over the full length of the bomb bay that you could walk upright for a short distance with no fear of hitting your head.

Apart from Jack's lamp and the glow of the instrument dials, the interior of the aircraft was plunged in darkness. Occasionally pinpoints of star light could be seen. The aircraft skin, made of aluminium alloy, was very thin, and there was no padding or any other form of covering on the curved metal sides. Along these, looped up erratically, ran in full view all the wires and hydraulics. K-King's skeleton was made of risers and formers, intersected with holes on the same basis as a bird's bones, to give lightness at the same time as strength. The aluminium skin stretched over this skeleton was stapled down with a myriad tiny rivets, some of which were missing, thus allowing the pinpoints of light to penetrate. Condensation from the clouds also came in, and appalling cold.

Some distance down the fuselage were Tony's long dangling legs. Seated in his swivelling mid-upper turret, with his shoulders and head out in the night air encased by a perspex bubble, only the lower parts of his body were inside the fuselage. Here the space was full of equipment, including the snaking tramlines which carried the long linked belts of machine-gun ammunition to the Browning guns in Leslie's turret.

Leslie's position was beyond the main door. One first used the lid of the Elsan toilet as a step to the platform directly behind it. The plane had narrowed very considerably by now, and the ceiling was descending in height as you entered the tail. The last part of the journey was a slither through another fuselage door, then over a sort of narrowing metal bridge to the sliding doors which shut in the rear turret. It was over sixty feet from here back to the cockpit.

Leslie had the loneliest job of all, isolated virtually from take-off till landing. During all that period he would be searching the night sky. He had been taught that making visual sweeps from left to right, dropping his gaze a few degrees and sweeping back again, was the most efficient method and the least fatiguing and boring over long periods. His instructors at Night Vision School had also told him that the most effective way of seeing an object in the dark was not to look directly at it but slightly above or below it. Phantom shapes appeared now and then in the darkness as he watched hour after hour. To make it easier to see, a panel of perspex had been removed from his gun turret and this let in a relentless blast of icy air. The turret had no heating and was of an Arctic chill as he sat in what was virtually a tin can, searching millions of cubic feet of black hostile space. His electrically heated flying suit kept him warm, but because it took up so much room, there was no space in the turret for his parachute. This was kept in the passageway behind the turret doors. In an emergency Leslie would have to be very, very lucky.

The route this night was directly to Berlin across Holland and Northern Germany. The bombers crossed Holland at a point just above Haarlem and Amsterdam, and from then on flew a straight undeviating route to Berlin.

There was thick cloud and fog from the Dutch coast onwards and most of the nightfighters were grounded by the awful weather. Nevertheless, those few fighters which were in action picked up the bomber stream very early. At least 10 Lancasters were shot down just after they had crossed the Dutch coast or on the leg to Hanover, whilst another three fell victim to flak.

One of those shot down very early on was that of Warrant Officer W A Watson, from 7 Squadron of the Pathfinders. The Messerschmitt which targeted the Lancaster was from the heavily fog-bound base of Leeuwarden; it was the only fighter from that base permitted to take off that night, flown as it was by the ace Heinz-Wolfgang Schnaufer. The victim was plotted by radar, and doomed by the final visual sighting by Schnaufer. The entire crew were immolated. In the next few minutes, Schnaufer shot down another three Lancasters, before landing, out of ammunition, in atrocious conditions.

For most Lancasters, however, the fog and thick cloud provided ideal conditions of invisibility. The coastline was the last place where there were any breaks in the cloud and where the German beacons could be seen flashing beneath, the only ground activity most crews would spot before the target was reached. Others would report seeing searchlights en route, reflected on the base of the clouds, which were dipped to indicate the track of the bombers.

K-King crossed into enemy airspace at around half past five. There followed what seemed an interminable period of crawling at a snail's pace through the darkness before at some point the crew spotted the first of 156 Squadron's PFF route markers, hanging in the air seventeen miles north of Hanover. Eighteen miles north-north-west of Brandenburg came the second set of brilliant yellow markers. K-King was getting close now; it wouldn't be long.

Behind them another novice crew from Bourn, those on Y-York, had run into trouble. A fighter began suddenly to close in on them when Cliff Bradshaw, the rear-gunner, shouted 'Dive port' and Smithy the pilot took violent evasive action, the aircraft plunging hundreds of feet in seconds. The fighter lost them in the cloud and darkness. Y-York had gone off course and lost its operational height in the manoeuvre, and had to laboriously find its way back on track, but the crew had come out of it safely – it would be their only enemy encounter that night.

Close to Berlin a 97 Squadron plane went down. It was the Lancaster of Flight Lieutenant Brill. All eight of the crew died, including the unfortunate second pilot, Flight Lieutenant Handley.

Time over the target for 97 Squadron was two minutes past zero hour, and the barrage was already in progress. There was dense cloud covering the city, but the extremely powerful searchlights could be seen moving about on the clouds below the Lancasters. There were flak bursts all around, and numerous rocket projectiles, whilst the Pathfinders' flares – red Target Indicators, release-point flares of red with green stars, and pure green blindmarkers for the aiming point – went cascading down in myriads of sparks. As the attack commenced, photoflashes began to explode over the city as aircraft dropped their bomb loads. To the north of Berlin a long line of German fighter flares hung in the air, whilst 8,000 feet above the Lancasters PFF Mosquitoes dropped their own dazzling silver-white flares. Magnificent and terrifying, it was a dazzling spectacle.

K-King flew into this maelstrom at around 19,500 feet. It was Sandy's job to make sure that the five 2,000 lb High Capacity bombs on board were dropped on the aiming point flares. HC had a high blast effect but a minimum amount of penetration; the crew's bombs would blow in roofs and windows, and give the most destructive force of all – fire – the best chance to feed and grow.

Sandy asked Ted over the intercom if he was ready to commence the bombing run. This would be the most nerve-racking period of all, when Ted had to keep the plane flying straight and level for a given number of minutes, a very long time in such hazardous circumstances. When Ted okayed the run, Sandy began to give directions, counting down until they reached the aiming point – 'Thirty seconds – twenty seconds – ten seconds – steady – hold it – Bombs gone!' The Lancaster gave a lurch upwards as it was relieved of the 10,000 lb load. 'Bomb doors closed,' Sandy called Ted. As they sped onwards across Berlin, hundreds of feet below them their photoflash exploded, illuminating the scene for the aiming point photograph which would never be developed.

Even before K-King left Berlin's vicinity, Main Force was arriving in huge numbers to bomb the PFF flares. The entire attack would only last 14 minutes. Beneath the Lancasters, the central and eastern districts were being hit more than any other areas. A train was hit at the Halensee Station, killing 70 people. Considerable damage was being done to the railway system, and supplies for the Russian Front would subsequently be held up for six days. The National Theatre and a building housing Germany's military and political archives were engulfed in flames. Many houses were collapsing or on fire – by now, after the sustained bombing of the last month, more than one quarter of Berlin's housing was unusable. The total deathtoll for the raid would be over 700, including 279 unfortunate press-ganged foreign workers.

Due to the thick cloud, however, few if any of the results of the raid would be clear. Most of the returning 97 Squadron aircrew would say at debriefing that observation of damage was difficult owing to the cloud cover which had obscured Berlin. Their aiming point photographs would be equally non-committal.

On the far side of Berlin, where there was no longer the extreme danger of collision with friendly aircraft, Jack gave Ted an alteration of course so that the Lancaster could leave the area. Shortly afterwards, it made a right-angled turn to port for the Baltic, and at long last they were on the way home, leaving behind a sky lit up a dull bloody red by the fires burning so far beneath.

There was no sense yet in which they could relax. Window was still being dropped to confuse the radar systems, Leslie and Tony were still on full alert. Ted told Joe to stand in the astrodome and assist the two gunners in keeping an eye out for attackers. The astrodome was a circular dome directly over the w/op's compartment – a follow-on from the cockpit canopy, it gave an excellent all-round view. To use the astrodome, Joe simply stood on top of his seat, his helmet still plugged into the intercom point. Suddenly out of the darkness an attacker came looming, and he yelled to his skipper, 'Diving turn to starboard GO!' Ted kicked over the rudder and K-King plunged downwards through the sky. Even through the pumping adrenalin, Joe realised anew what an excellent pilot Ted was and was amazed that under his hands the heavy aircraft seemed to fly like a bird, with the most extraordinary lightness and manoeuvrability.

They had lost whatever had been following them. Together with the rest of the force, they finally shook off the remnants of the nightfighters by taking the northerly route home over Denmark. Searchlights could be seen on the clouds below as the enemy tracked the bombers as they flew home, but the flight back proved a quiet one. Jack and Sandy plotted their position with great care, getting a good fix over Denmark and the island coast lines, so that Ted could make the last two turns to port and at last set the aircraft on a direct course for England.

Once they were well out over the North Sea, Ted brought the aircraft down below the oxygen level of 8,000 feet, they removed their masks, and all could at last breathe a sigh of relief. There was no longer any need for strict radio silence. Joe, reverting to his role of crew clown, cracked a daft joke over the intercom and everyone exploded with laughter.

Their first, very dangerous, raid was over.

III. The Return to Bourn

At Bourn, those who were on duty at the station that night began to expect the returning aircraft from around eleven o'clock onwards. In Flying Control, the list of the twenty-one Lancasters which had departed for Berlin was chalked up on the wall display, together with their time of take-off, the pilot's name, and the letter of the aircraft.

Out on the dark airfield, the ground crew of the aircraft waited in the flight huts. They had watched the take-off some six and half hours earlier, after which they had settled down to while away the time with games of cards, many a brew of tea, and countless cigarettes.

Meanwhile, those aircraft which had survived the dangers of the night were droning steadily home across England. There was no Flying Control until you reached your own airfield; you just flew through the night hoping that none of the 450 other returning aircraft were on the same flight path. En route, you read the flashing Morse identification lights of other airfields until at last you came to your own. Then, and only then, would your pilot radio in for permission to land.

The drill was always the same when a kite reported in. If it was theirs, the ground crew would leave off their eternal games of cards and go out into the night to watch it come in. They would guide the Lancaster to its dispersal with glowing torches, wait for the engines' shut-down, put up the ladder and open the main door of the aircraft. The aircrew emerged, pale yet elated, into the night air. The ground crew handed out cigarettes, as there was a ban on smoking, not always strictly adhered to, during the flight. 'Had a good trip? Where have you been? Any damage or snags?' Then the crew bus would arrive to take the crew away for debriefing, whilst the ground crew attended to any urgent matters and then covered up the wheels, cockpit and engines with heavy tarpaulins.

Meanwhile the crews arrived back at the Aircrews' Briefing Room, which they had left so many tumultuous hours before. Drinking tea or coffee laced with rum, they gave their reports on what had happened that night, what the weather was like over the target, whether the supporting aircraft were early or on time, what level they had bombed at, what effects they had observed, whether they had seen any of their fellows lost. As the Met Office was right next door, sometimes as they passed by they would go in for a few minutes to tell the girls how right or how wrong HQ had got the weather forecast, in the latter case sometimes venting a little grumbling resentment. Then they would have a very late meal and go to bed.

That was a normal night's proceedings. On the night of 16th December 1943, the system fell apart. By eleven o'clock, the light mist of the afternoon had turned into a deadly peasouper of a fog, blanketing the country up as far as Yorkshire. At Bourn and Gransden Lodge, her sister PFF station three miles further south, conditions were amongst the very worst in the country. Visibility was dropping progressively with every minute that passed – by midnight, it would be down to 300 yards or less, and it took about 1,000 yards to stop a Lancaster. The problem was ironically exacerbated by the hundreds of coke fires burning in the Nissen huts, whose smoke could not disperse in the damp heavy air. Pockets of particularly dense fog collected in certain spots; at the cookhouse at Gransden Lodge, for example, you could not see the chimneys of that one-storied building even when you were standing right outside it. By the early hours of the morning, cloud base at Gransden Lodge would be at 100 feet and the fog would be meeting up with it. 405 Squadron, which was based on the station, would have as serious problems as 97 Squadron in trying to land their Lancasters – only five of the thirteen operating that night would eventually touch down at their home station.

With 21 Lancasters due to land within the space of about 90 minutes, Flying Control at Bourn would be stretched to the limit. Those anxiously awaiting the returning crews knew that there would be serious problems when they arrived. The airfield was covered in thick fog and pilots descending blind through the clouds would not break into even partial visibility until 250 feet. There would be little hope of them seeing the lights of the airfield circuit which ended in a funnel on the NE.-SW. runway. Nor would the angle of glide indicators be visible to ensure the correct approach – an amber if too high, a red if too low, a green if on the correct glide path.

Technical aids for landing in such difficult conditions were in their infancy. Gee, a radio navigational aid which was very accurate over England, would help the returning aircraft to locate their home airfield, but it was too imprecise to actually direct them down onto a runway. The only real facilities available to land in severe bad weather were FIDO and a system known as SBA.

FIDO, the Fog Investigation and Dispersal Operation, was at that time only operational at three airfields: Graveley six miles north-west of Bourn; Downham Market 35 miles to the north-east (the installation barely completed); and Fiskerton, close to Lincoln, 95 miles to the north. Only one of 97 Squadron's aircraft would land at Downham Market under very remarkable circumstances – it was to Graveley that at least six of the squadron's aircraft would be diverted.

FIDO was a very new system, which had only come into operational use at Graveley, the prime test site, in the previous month after a long series of trials and modifications. Conceived pre-war, work on the FIDO project had for a long while been leisurely in the extreme, and it was only in September 1942 that Churchill had given Geoffrey Lloyd, the Minister for Petroleum Warfare, a brief to get FIDO workable as quickly as possible. The official statement on FIDO, put out by Bomber Command shortly after the war ended and the need for secrecy had passed, summarises what had become a desperate situation.

> The electrical beam [SBA] could help the pilots to approach to within 100 or 200 feet of the runway but they were then still flying absolutely blind at over 100 miles an hour with the imminent danger of crashing the aircraft, and killing themselves and all their crew, because they could not actually see to land. Fog over British airfields [had become] more of a menace than flak over Germany . . .

FIDO was designed to disperse the lethal cloud and fog, but the mechanism by which it accomplished this was plain terrifying to the uninitiated. Vast pipes, carrying thousands of gallons of petrol, had been installed down all sides of the runway at Graveley. The pipes were pierced with holes, from which a fine jet of petrol spurted forth when the pumps were in operation. To fire up each section of the system, a man manually set alight to the first burner and then ran like hell when it ignited with a whoosh. The heat dispersed the fog and cloud, and the glow of the flames provided a flarepath.

The difficulties of getting FIDO to work had been formidable. The first ever night test of the installation took place in February 1943, in clear conditions, and was flown by the PFF chief, Bennett himself, in a Lancaster of 156 Squadron. He was coming on from trying out some new pyrotechnics at the bombing range at Rushford, and as he turned to leave the range he could already see the gigantic glow of FIDO through the darkness sixty miles away. As he approached, his first impression was that the glare would be blinding, but after a low trial flight along the length of the runway he landed without any problems. As he put it, 'I had vague thoughts of seeing lions jumping through a hoop of flames at the circus. The glare was certainly considerable and there was some turbulence, but it was nothing to worry about.' One aftermath to the test was that fire brigades from miles around turned up under the impression that the whole district was on fire. They were stood a drink in the Mess as an apology.

Bennett had the coolest of nerves and his nonchalance about FIDO was seldom emulated by his men. Describing another test later in the year, Pat Moorhead, a navigator with 35 Squadron, commented:

> . . . there was a very heavy mist and once airborne we could see very little of the ground, and circled round waiting for someone to strike a match. When they finally did, very little seemed to happen at first; and then gradually, the elongated rectangle of the runway began to show more clearly, with belching yellow flames and rolling swirling fog all around and above. The worst part was coming in over the flames at the end of the runway, and I remember wondering whether the undercart would melt or buckle or go up in flames – like entering the jaws of hell, and certainly different from a normal landing.

Considerably less daunting than FIDO but more difficult to use was SBA, Standard Beam Approach, which was installed at all the base airfields, including Bourn. Referred to as 'landing on the beam', SBA employed signals emitted by beacons in line with the main runway. These beacons sent out a code to the pilot which showed if he was straying off course, dots to one side, dashes to the other, and just a steady note if he was right on track. The pilot first picked up the sound from the outer marker of the airfield and, once on top of it in 'the cone of silence', checked his altimeter to determine his angle of approach to the runway. He then passed on to the inner marker for a similar procedure. If his height and speed were correct, it was okay to land – blind, for he still could not see the runway in front of him.

The theory was fine but the practice infinitely more difficult – the planes which would try to land that night, in such appallingly low visibility, would be travelling at around 100 miles per hour, a speed which took them right across the airfield in little more than 30 seconds. The margin for error was exceedingly small and each failed attempt brought an increase in danger. SBA approaches had been practised by *some* of 97 Squadron's aircrew during training, but such exercises could not possibly repeat the conditions of coming home from a very long raid, exhausted, having burnt up most of your petrol.

There was also the considerable additional pressure of having twelve or fifteen other aircraft stacked up at different height slots on the circuit, all running short of fuel and all wanting to get down as quickly as possible. With Gransden Lodge with its own orbiting aircraft a mere three miles away, there was also an ever-present risk of collision though each squadron was flying a different circuit.

Flying Control at Bourn, which had been contacted by each plane as it returned, had followed established practice by transmitting the routine landing information together with instructions to join the stack already milling around overhead. One of the most crucial pieces of landing information being given out that night was the airfield barometric pressure, known as the QFE – the aircraft's on-board altimeters would be set to the reading on the ground at Flying Control, thus allowing for local pressure changes.

Each new returning aircraft was also allocated a position, 500 feet higher than the previous one. Each would only be brought down 500 feet at a time as the lowest aircraft in the stack landed. Meanwhile, all the other crews could do was circle and wait. Many people on the ground that night recall how eerie and discomforting it was to hear the sound of the planes circling endlessly, or roaming blindly through the fog, searching in vain for another airfield on which to land.

For the crews who came down out of the illusory safety of the sky, it was to be a terrifying experience as they tried to locate the runway with or without the help of SBA. The density of the cloud and fog obliterated the flare paths, hid the landing lights, blanked out the moon and stars, and left no reference point in the impenetrable murk but the dull red glow of their plane's exhausts or the distant twinkle of the navigation lights at its wingtips. The blackness made it appear as if the aircraft was scarcely moving at all as they sat in virtually complete isolation in its dimly lit, petrol-stinking, heavily vibrating interior. Their sole contact with the earth was the radio transmitter, and the disembodied faraway voice of Flying Control coming intermittently through the crackles of the static. Meanwhile, the petrol gauges just fell lower and lower; in the end all you could do was take that chance . . .

As the inevitable crashes began to occur, crews still in the air sometimes saw, even despite the thickness of the murk, the sombre burning glow of crashed aircraft as they descended below cloud cover. This added to the appalling stress that all the pilots and crews would experience that night.

The first safe landing at Bourn was at twenty-five past eleven, some six hours and twenty minutes after the last of the Lancasters had departed for Germany. Pilot Officer Snell came in twenty-five minutes before anybody else. His plane landed apparently without incident, but the next plane to land, at ten to twelve, seriously damaged its starboard pin and rudder on landing. The plane was too far down the runway when it touched down, but the skipper, Flight Lieutenant Wilson, somehow managed to turn the aircraft aside just as it ran out of landing space. The Lancaster hit a transformer violently, sideways on, the point of impact being just above the tail wheel. The rear gunner, Sergeant Pleydell, narrowly escaped injury when the tail section was ripped off on the port side and twisted back at right angles to the main fuselage. By the time the aircraft had finally jolted to a halt, Pleydell had decided that enough was enough. In his hurry to get out of the Lancaster, no doubt thinking with good reason it was likely to catch fire, he used his axe to hack his way out of the gun turret.

Charles Owen, whose plane had left at the same time as Ted's, came in at five past twelve. There were severe technical malfunctions in his transmitters and navigational aids, but his navigator, Bill Shires, and his bomb aimer, Nigel Leak, were good enough to get the aircraft home. Owen noted later in his diary:

> Trip was generally quieter than usual. 10/10 cloud over the target and rather less flak than usual. W/T and 'Y' and 'G' packed up on way home, so homed across North Sea on D/F Loop, which luckily was not jammed. Homed onto base on SBA beam, breaking cloud at 250 feet to find fog, rain and visibility about 300 yards and deteriorating. R/T then packed up, so after circling for ten minutes at 200 feet, landed without permission in appalling conditions. Six other aircraft landed at base, three landed away, three crews bailed out when they ran out of fuel, four crashed when trying to land, and one was missing. Quite a night.

His figures for the fate of the aircraft are not quite correct, but his last comment speaks volumes about the aircrews' general attitude.

Owen had been fortunate to get back to Bourn so early – Flying Control was soon swamped by the large number of returning aircraft. John Arthurson, the navigator with the novice crew on Y-York, remembers that there was a lot of trouble with SBA that night, 'the system was not working well'. When his pilot Smithy contacted Flying Control, he was instructed:

> to circle at a height of several thousand feet, which meant there were probably about eighteen other Lancasters waiting to land. It soon became evident to the crew listening on the intercom that the fog was no clearer than at five o'clock as pilots using the SBA were having difficulty and 'going round again', which meant minutes before the next plane could be called up for landing.

Using SBA was a lengthy process, and required a very high standard of flying skill. If the approach was not exactly right, the pilot would open up the engines, go round and try again, which took at least five minutes. In the end, John Arthurson's crew, believing their chances of landing safely were minimal if they continued to wait, went off to try their luck elsewhere.

Squadron Leader Cawdery's plane was now circling in Number 1 slot, waiting for clearance to land. Cawdery, very unusually, was a prewar pilot, of about 31 years of age; most of his contemporaries were either dead or had already finished their tours. His crew were all youngsters, of 19 to 21 years old, and they used to get joshed for the age of their skipper – 'What on earth are you flying with an old man like that for? What right has he to still be alive?' However, they were to be amongst the few who would survive their Pathfinder tour. On this night, their luck was in as usual.

Arthur Tindall, the wireless operator, remembers this night as their 'longest trip ever to Berlin'. By the time they landed at Bourn, they had been in the air for 7 hours 45 minutes.

It was 12.35 when the crew landed after their third attempt at SBA. It was not actually the pilot, Cawdery, who was flying but the second dickey, Flight Lieutenant Clarke. He had been the crew's instructor at No 14 OTU, and he had come to 97 Squadron to do his second tour – as was customary, his first trip out was made as second pilot. Cawdery had handed him control sometime before the end of the trip, so that he could get some practice. Clarke muffed the first two attempts to land using SBA, and then offered to let Cawdery take over the controls. Cawdery with supreme coolness of nerve replied, 'No, you've got the practice in now', and at his last attempt Clarke landed the plane without mishap.

Only two other squadron aircraft would land safely after them, that of Flight Lieutenant Mansbridge, and that of Flight Lieutenant Pete de Wesselow, a precise immaculate patrician sort of fellow, whose Lancaster – like Cawdery's – belonged to B Flight.

As for Cawdery's crew, they all realised that they had been extremely fortunate to get down at all. As they arrived at the debriefing, the dreadful losses to be incurred that night were already beginning to be suspected though people were still hoping that some of the missing aircraft had been able to land elsewhere. After debriefing, the crew went for a meal and then, utterly exhausted, to bed. The following morning, they would be told by their ground crew, amongst other news concerning the night's events, that their Lancaster had much less than 50 gallons of petrol in it when they landed. Lancasters used about a gallon of petrol for every mile flown – the crew had survived by the skin of their teeth.

In all, only eight of Bourn's twenty returning planes managed to land at their home airfield, their approach to the runway made through swirling damp and fog, with the lights of the flarepath half-obliterated. As these Lancasters touched down and finally came thundering to a halt, those on board were deeply grateful. As the ground crew opened the door, and the raw night air, tainted with smoke from the camp fires, came rushing in, nothing could be seen a few yards beyond the aircraft but a solid wall of mist. Their legs stiff from long inaction, their ears ringing from eight hours of thunderous noise, yet they could still hear the noise of their comrades' aircraft roaming around overhead, until even the sound of those last stragglers died away and ceased.

Less than ten minutes after Cawdery's landing, just before quarter to one in the morning, there came the terrible thump and scrape of a plane crashing on the northern perimeter of the airfield. It immediately caught fire. The fire tenders and ambulance went racing out to it. It was F-Freddy, the Lancaster of Squadron Leader Mackenzie, a small reserved Scottish lad of 27 years old. Mackenzie was killed immediately, as were his flight engineer and bomb aimer, both of whom were with him in the front section of the plane. All four survivors got out of the plane or were dragged clear before any of them suffered serious burns.

The survivors were immediately taken to Station Sick Quarters, which had a small but well-equipped casualty ward with provision for shock treatment in the form of heat cradles, oxygen supply, and transfusion apparatus with ample serum and plasma. The Medical Officer diagnosed that Marshall, the navigator, had a fractured tibia and fibula, and shock, and Keith Kirby, the rear gunner, had internal injuries and shock. Hunter had lacerations of the scalp and Lang abrasions and lacerations of the face. The appalling fractures were splinted and the burns and lacerations dressed, but as soon as possible Lang, Marshall and Hunter were sent on to Addenbrooke's Hospital in Cambridge in one of the station's ambulances. Kirby, because of his injuries, was taken to the specialist RAF hospital at Ely, where he was discovered to be suffering from a fractured spine.

The following morning, Mackenzie's aircraft could be clearly seen by the side of the main road near Two Pots Farmhouse, charred, bent and twisted, and scarcely recognisable as a plane. A thick fog still shrouded the surrounding countryside. It would not clear properly until 10 o'clock that night, but by then all of 97 Squadron's missing Lancasters had been located.

My father's crashed and burning aircraft had been found at two o'clock in the morning of Friday 17th (the full story of its discovery will be told shortly). Two other aircraft had also crashed in deserted farmland but were not discovered until several hours later. The first had crashed attempting to land at Gransden Lodge, where conditions were no better than at Bourn. Pilot Officer Kirkwood and all his crew died of multiple injuries. There is no record on the accident card of a fire starting on the ground, but this seems to be an omission as the relevant part of the card has not been filled in. The Lancaster went down just past midnight, apparently in a last desperate attempt to locate the airfield but instead crashed into Hayley Wood close to the perimeter. It was only found at quarter to eight on the Friday morning, with the entire crew dead around or inside it. They had only been posted from 207 Squadron to the Pathfinders on the 27th of November.

Flight Sergeant Scott's Lancaster came down one and a quarter miles north-east of Graveley, at an unknown time. The wreckage was not found until just after seven o'clock the following morning. After crashing, the aircraft had caught fire. There was no one to help and there were no survivors. It was the Australian pilot's second operation; he was only twenty years old.

Five of 97 Squadron's diverted aircraft were to land safely, one at Wyton, three at Graveley before FIDO was lit, and one at Downham Market at half past one in the morning, the very last 97 Squadron plane to land that night. It carried the crew who had been all through Silverstone, Wigsley and Upwood with my father's crew – their friends and rivals, Bill Coates, Stanley Nuttall, William Chapman, John Baldwin, Frank Thompson, Bertram Nicholas and William York.

The crew's survival was due to an astounding feat of flying by their twenty year old skipper. Their Lancaster, N-Nan, had been hit by a friendly aircraft's incendiaries, dropped down from the skies above them during the raid. Hit on the port wing, turret and amidships, N-Nan burst into flames. Ordering his crew to put on their parachutes, Coates threw the aircraft into a violent dive to try to shake off the incendiaries. This toppled the D.R. compass gyro, upsetting all the instruments connected to it, but fortunately the fires were completely extinguished and N-Nan climbed back to a safe height of 21,000 feet.

Shortly afterwards, in an entirely separate incident, the Lancaster was hit by flak. The propeller tips of the starboard inner engine were broken, and one large fragment flew off, slashing through the fuselage of the aircraft and severing the hydraulic pipelines. A second fragment shot off backwards and damaged the tail plane. The starboard outer engine was also badly hit, and both starboard engines had to be shut down. By now N-Nan was so badly crippled that it looked impossible that the crew would ever make it home. Losing height constantly, they limped back over Occupied Europe, and by a miracle made it to Denmark and set course for home.

Twenty miles past the Danish coast, N-Nan began losing height so rapidly that Coates told the crew to take up ditching stations. A SOS was sent, but the chances of survival in the freezing waves of the North Sea were so minimal that no one would have wanted to take the ditching option. Somehow Coates and his Welsh flight engineer, Bertram Nicholas, managed to coax the aircraft into maintaining a height of 5,000 feet if they flew a steady speed of 120 knots. In time the SOS was cancelled, and eventually, to the most profound relief of everyone on board, N-Nan made it back to England.

Even here there was an additional problem to surmount, for the crew were first carelessly directed to Marham, which then sent them on to the FIDO installation at Downham Market.

Like other airfields Downham Market was suffering from the weather, and, though cloud base was higher than Bourn's at 400 feet, visibility was still very poor. The aerodrome was suffering from very serious congestion – at one point there were thirty-six aircraft waiting to land. Even damaged aircraft were forced to wait, such as that flown by Pilot Officer Crombie of 514 Squadron which had lost one of its port engines. (On requesting priority to land, Crombie was told by Control that others below him had bigger problems. He was eventually to get down safely with, as his flight engineer put it, 'just about enough fuel to fill a cigarette lighter'.)

Most of the instruments on N-Nan were unusable. The undercarriage had to be lowered using the emergency air system. After the very harassing and tense five hours that the crew had experienced, they must have been extremely nervous as they approached the airfield through the all-enclosing blackness. Then the unrelieved gloom began to give way to a pinkish diffused glow like the dawn, and suddenly they could see the FIDO flarepath burning brightly along all sides of the runway. Negotiating the bucketing turbulence caused by the rising hot air, Coates came down over the flames and landed the aircraft perfectly without any further damage after eight and a half hours in the air.

It is said that the crew carried him from N-Nan on their shoulders like a conquering hero. Doubtless that is exactly how they felt about him, but the real reason why they carried their skipper was because he could no longer walk; his feet had been jammed against the rudder bar for so long that for the moment Bill couldn't even stand up.

IV. Graveley

Graveley had only had its first operational landings using FIDO on 19th November, less than one month before. Though on that occasion things had gone well, on 16th/17th December, for some unknown reason, FIDO was not actually lit until twenty to one in the morning long after the situation had become critical.

Perhaps it had been considered that conditions were so bad at Graveley that lighting FIDO would not help, but it at least had the potential to provide additional assistance on a night when fog and cloud were at their most deadly and hazardous. Several aircraft managed to land safely before FIDO was lit, but it is a virtual certainty that their SBA landings had consumed time which Graveley Flying Control could not afford to waste. The four Lancasters which crashed on or close to the airfield that night all went down around the time that FIDO was lit, and all the losses were apparently due to the pilots being forced into fatal actions by petrol shortage.

The Fog Dispersal Report for Graveley for that night, signed by Group Captain S W B Menaul, the Station Commander, gives a vivid idea of the difficulties the pilots were facing. Horizontal visibility was not too bad at 1,200 yards, and there was only a very light wind. It was vertical visibility which was the problem, with fog thickening as the night wore on, and eventually combining with smoke pollution to form a dense curtain which rose to the very base of the thick clouds themselves. In a second report for the night, signed by a Major J Rogers, the Duty Officer, the comment is made that whilst horizontal visibility was maintained between FIDO's burners, 'vertical visibility was so bad as to make approach impossible'. Given the dry language generally employed in such reports, this comment says much about the horrors of trying to land that night.

As at Bourn, conditions deteriorated by the minute. FIDO was lit at 00.39 (some fifteen minutes after the order to do so, there not being enough staff for a rapid light-up), and did not reach full burn until 00.53. No aircraft were to land safely during the burn, and the installation was finally closed down again at 01.43, after an astonishing 24,500 gallons of petrol had gone up in flames. As the burners were turned off, they glowed for a brief while, then cooled to blackness, and were lost from sight. Horizontal visibility plummeted and within minutes was down to only 300 yards.

The Fog Dispersal Report gives the reason for lighting the installation as being 'to assist aircraft who could not land on the normal flarepath', but FIDO did little to ameliorate the situation because pilots simply could not trace the burning flarepath from above through the fog and cloud. Mr Swanston, a tanker driver on duty that night, was later told that those crews who did manage to locate the airfield could only see 'one bank of light, one big red glare', not the sharply illuminated oblong which should have defined the runway.

It was a strange feeling to be on the station that night, for conditions were not too bad on the ground with all the lights on but only 20 or 30 feet up there was dense mist. Mr Swanston recalled, 'You could hear all the planes flying about and they just couldn't land – it was terrible'. Yet many did not realise just how grave the situation had become. Isabel Burton, then a WAAF M/T driver, wrote many years afterwards, 'I will always remember walking back to the WAAF site through an eerie pink fog with droning aircraft above and hearing the odd thud, never dreaming that aircraft were crashing around us – we presumed the thuds were distant guns or bombs falling'.

RAF Graveley had been on complete stand-down that night, the Halifaxes of 35 Squadron not being required for operations. A dance had been arranged in the Sergeants' Mess, but late in the evening the music was stopped and it was announced over the tannoy that all FIDO personnel must report for duty immediately. Don Pawley, an airman who was home on leave from another station, took his sister back to The Three Horseshoes at Graveley, where his family lived. As they stood outside the pub, they could hear the aircraft circling the airfield, and some they could almost see because they were so low.

> The Fido was increasing then and was clearing the fog and we could see a Lancaster through the trees beyond the football pitch. It was very low – and then we heard the crash. My brother Charlie and I had a good idea where it had crashed and we knew how to get to it. We ran up through the village and across the fields to the scene of the crash. We were the first people there.

Though it was almost one o'clock in the morning, they could see well enough because of the diffused glow of FIDO through the fog, and because little bits of the aircraft were burning as it lay in shattered pieces on the ground. A terrible sight met their eyes. The aircraft, D-Donald, had only been 50 feet high when abruptly its petrol had run out, the engines had cut, and it had been forced to land. The Lancaster had run across a potato field on Ingles Farm and might well have stopped safely had not the deep ditch of the farm's boundary lain in its path. The aircraft's front wheels dropped into the ditch and the body of the plane was catapulted right over with appalling force. The tail section broke off, the main fuselage broke into two large pieces, and dozens of smaller fragments were hurled away. As Don Pawley ran up to this scene of devastation, he saw in amongst the debris the bodies of the crew, who had been hurled out of the plane when it hit the ditch.

Five of them had died instantly. The pilot, McLennan, was still alive, but he was unconscious and spurting arterial blood. His leg was almost completely severed. Don Pawley tried in vain to stop the bleeding with his thumb. His brother, Charlie, who was a driver at Graveley, ran back to get an ambulance and a doctor; Don Pawley stayed with the mortally wounded McLennan. At that moment he believed that all of the rest of the crew were dead. Then suddenly out of the mist, staggering and dazed, there emerged the rear gunner. His name was Clair Nutting, and he was a Canadian like McLennan and four other members of the crew. Many years later, in 1987, he wrote about his memories of the crash:

> My own recollection of events after the crash is dim. We were stacked up over Graveley trying to get down and after one unsuccessful attempt to land on the beam, I think we went round to come in again. We were very low, perhaps no more than 50 feet off the deck.
>
> When the aircraft crashed and the tail broke off, I was strapped in securely, braced against the guns. When my head struck the gun-sight I was knocked out. I recall climbing out over the guns. Further on, the aircraft was burning. Various fail-safe devices were blowing up.
>
> It seems to me that I could see in the fog the airfield perimeter lights through the trees. Weighed down by my flying gear I remember my boots sinking in the mud as I went to look for the others in the crew. I found two. One was dead. The pilot, McLennan, was alive and when I went to move him I saw the bare bone where his leg was all but severed at the knee, so I left him. The next thing I remember was going in to hospital with McLennan in the back of a van. He died, I was told, shortly after we got there.

Not long after McLennan's crash – at twenty past one in the morning as recorded on the accident card (there are various timing discrepancies concerning this crash) – a Lancaster from 97 Squadron crashed on Graveley airfield itself. It was that of Squadron Leader Ernest Alfred Deverill, who had been posted back only 11 days before from 1660 Conversion Unit at Swinderby, where he had been acting as an instructor. The Berlin op that night was the first raid of his third tour. A highly dedicated man, he had flown so many operations that he could easily have missed this last tour.

27 year old Deverill had once been a 'Halton Brat' – that is to say, a pupil of No 1 School of Technical Training at RAF Halton, where apprentices and boys were trained to become technical staff to service and repair aircraft. Deverill had outstanding natural ability, and overcoming all the usual conventions he had remustered as a pilot in 1938. He had flown over a hundred sorties, most of them for Coastal Command, before he once again bucked the norm and became an officer, having worked his way up from the very bottom of the ladder. There is no doubt that he was a superb pilot. For his bravery and persistence he had won the Distinguished Flying Medal, and the Distinguished Flying Cross twice. He was posthumously to be awarded the Air Force Cross.

Deverill had been one of the stars of the early days of 97 Squadron at Woodhall Spa. He was on the famous Augsburg raid of 17th April 1942, when 97 Squadron had garnered a sheaf of honours. A daring and in the event very costly experiment by Harris using the then new Lancasters, the raid had been a daylight operation to Bavaria to wreck the engine assembly shop within the MAN diesel engine factories. The operation was dogged by ill-luck and, though serious damage was done to the factory, only five of the twelve Lancasters reached home. The raid proved once and for all that even the magnificent new Lancasters could not be used in daylight raids. Deverill got his plane back to England only after it had suffered appalling damage. Y-Yorker had been hit in numerous places; it had lost an engine, the hydraulic pipes had been ruptured, the gun turrets put out of action, and at one stage the hydraulic oil caught fire, burning a large part of the fuselage. Y-Yorker was a write-off for any future operations, though it was patched up and used for training at Wigsley until the following year, when it broke up in the air over Hertfordshire.

Deverill's aircraft on this December night had a call-sign of P-Peter. A Public Records Office document, *Flying Control Historical Record – Graveley*, gives an account of the night of 16th/17th December 1943 and the last moments of a P-Peter. No squadron is given but it must be Deverill's plane as it was the only one of the crashes at Graveley that night which occurred on the actual airfield itself. The account, in its very terseness and brevity, conveys only too strongly the horrors experienced:

> At 2110 . . . Graveley was told to stand by for diversions. The Drem lighting was switched on at 2257 and a visitor was landed. Just after midnight four aircraft were overhead and one of them crashed N.E. of the airfield. At 0016 W-William landed. J-Jig, D-Dog, R-Roger, H-How and O-Orange were stacked overhead. R. H. and O. had been given permission to land but nothing happened . . .
>
> There was no fog [as yet] below the cloud, but Group ordered Fido to be lit as a marker, and while it was being lit H-

How landed safely. Then Y-Yorker came up on radio but two-way contact could not be established. At 0051 P-Peter and J-Jig were instructed to divert to Wyton and Warboys as it was thought that conditions were better there. C-Charlie said he had only 15 minutes petrol left, he was told to go to Warboys.

At 0057 an aircraft crashed to the West of the airfield, then S-Sugar was told to go to Warboys. Meanwhile P-Peter returned saying 'There's no future at Wyton, can I have a crack at your Fido?' He approached almost at right angles to the runway. Just as it looked as if he was going to touch down he opened up and then his engines cut and he crashed into the bomb dump and burst into flames . . .

While all this was happening S-Sugar said he could not get in at Warboys so he was told to stand by as another aircraft was landing. At 0151 it was reported that two aircraft flying at about 20 feet had crashed North of the airfield. The wing tip of one hit a haystack.

Thanks to the fire party and the armament crews, the blaze on Deverill's Lancaster was quickly brought under control, preventing a catastrophic ignition of the bomb dump. When the rescue team finally got into the aircraft, they found only one man alive, Warrant Officer James Benbow, the mid-upper gunner. He was taken from Graveley SSQ direct to RAF Hospital Ely, suffering from second degree burns of his face and hands, and compound fractures of the tibia and fibula.

P-Peter had run out of fuel just as they were about to land. Deverill, aware that he was nearly out of petrol, had gambled on coming in at the correct angle. The approach was wrong, and at the very moment which he tried to correct the mistake, his petrol ran out and the engines cut. Of all the terrible incidents on that night, this seemed the most tragic and unjust. Bourn's departing Commanding Officer, Group Captain Fresson, was to particularly remember Deverill and this crash and to say of it many years later, 'I have always thought that this was the worst of bad luck'.

V. Y-York

Some time around one o'clock that night, two 97 Squadron crews, despairing of being able to land safely, took the enormously difficult decision to abandon their Lancasters. This was absolutely a last resort, as abandoning the planes was a very serious business given the value of a Lancaster in wartime and the cost of building it, £59,000, never mind the loss of all the expensive equipment on board. Yet the navigator of one of the planes, John Arthurson, remembered more than fifty years later that not the slightest blame or criticism was ever directed at the two crews which took this option. The other catastrophes of the night put the matter into perspective, and Bourn's Station Commander and Commanding Officer were only too aware that without this drastic action there could have been another fourteen fatalities.

The ORB gives 12.35 as the time when Pilot Officer Robert Leo Mooney and his crew abandoned S-Sugar 'owing to weather conditions making landing too dangerous'. This crew was at first reported as missing, lost at sea. Eventually, however, they all turned up safely and it was accepted that the aircraft, flying on George, the automatic pilot, had followed the correct heading out to the North Sea where its petrol finally ran out and it crashed into the waves. The accident card specifically records the reason for the abandonment of S-Sugar as being lack of petrol.

No time is given for the abandonment of Pilot Officer Smith's Y-York, but the take-off time and duration of flight give ten past one in the morning. 'On return to base, fog and low cloud made landing dangerous so crew baled out from 7,000 feet. All landed safely.' John Arthurson and his crewmates always thought that their Lancaster had crashed in the North Sea, just as Mooney's, and it was only many years later that John Arthurson discovered that it had actually crashed three and a half miles north of Orford in Suffolk, at Iken Common, about six miles short of the coast. After they had jumped, the Lancaster had only flown an additional fifty to sixty miles before crashing to the ground.

It will be remembered that the crew of Y-York had originally abandoned the stack at Bourn for fear that they would never land. The flight-engineer, Maurice Durn, had told his skipper that at the very slow rate they were descending down the stack, the plane would run out of petrol before they got a chance to try SBA. Smithy, the pilot, agreed that the situation was desperate, and put out a call to 'Darky', the SOS system for helping aircraft in distress (Darky was also used for all R/T communications when FIDO landings were being made). Y-York was then directed to Graveley, which they had to find by dead reckoning, that is to say by flying a certain course at a given speed for a fixed length of time.

The crew had been told that at Graveley a rocket flare would be fired to fix Y-York's position. The thickness of the fog and the cloud made detecting this flare a forlorn hope. As John Arthurson wrote:

> This flare was not seen by any member of the crew, nor [was] a second one, and so the pilot descended and with wheels and flaps down started flying low, in the fog, looking for a place to land. The bomb-aimer was in the nose of the aircraft giving instructions, 'Up a bit', 'Down a bit' etc, amid exclamations of relief at something or other just missed.
>
> Suddenly Fido . . . loomed out of the murk and a runway between its burning rows [was] glimpsed. The crew cheered and the pilot did a turn which should have brought the plane round and lined up with the runway, but it came upon the runway sideways, and ensuing turns failed to find it.

The fog and cloud were so heavy that even the bright flames of FIDO disappeared as soon as one had flown a short distance away from them. Having seen that blazing path to safety once, the crew simply could not locate it again. The tension in the aircraft was by now terrific. At last Maurice Durn said that there was only enough petrol left for fifteen minutes more flying. John Arthurson was the first one to voice the obvious suggestion, 'Let's get up and bale out'. Hearing him on the intercom, Cliff, the rear gunner, and Gordon, the wireless-operator, strongly agreed.

> The skipper said he was loath to take this decision just then, but after a further brief time of fruitless searching agreed. The pilot asked to what height he should climb and [I] said, 'Make it seven thousand feet so that if any chute doesn't open its owner won't know much about it'. The pilot quickly climbed the plane to this height heading east towards the North Sea and after telling which exit each crew member was to use gave the order to abandon the aircraft. The bomb-aimer, navigator and flight-engineer left by the front hatch and the wireless-operator, rear gunner and mid-upper gunner by the rear door. With the automatic pilot in control, the pilot checked that all had gone, returned to the front and left by the front hatch.

When John Arthurson jumped out of the plane, he found himself in the moonlight. Above the low cloud and thick fog, the skies were clear and starry and there was a bright three-quarters moon. Y-York disappeared, flying like a ghost ship into the night, the roar of her great engines gradually receding. John Arthurson's parachute opened and after the initial jolt he just seemed to hang there, seemingly suspended on a level with the moon, stationary and unmoving. Time had lost its value, it was as if he hung there forever. Then suddenly he went through the cloud into the cold air and fog, and almost instantly, so it seemed, landed with a very hard thump on the ground.

Recovering his breath, he took a few moments to orientate himself to his situation. He had landed in the mud of a ploughed field. It was pitch-dark, cold and very foggy. Realising he must get moving, he took off his parachute and harness, and rolled them up under his arm to carry them back in deference to standing orders.

Like a blind man, he felt his way through the darkness until he came to a hedge. He followed the hedge, walking along beside it, not knowing where it would lead. Soon he became fed up with carrying the parachute, and thinking to himself, 'I'm not carrying that any more', stuffed it without ceremony into the hedge.

He continued walking until at last he came to some huts on the edge of Graveley's airfield. Going into one of the huts, he woke someone up who, startled and appalled, exclaimed 'Where did you come from?' and John

Arthurson pointed at the sky.

Eventually a WAAF driver arrived with a van to take him to SSQ, where he found his flight engineer, Maurice Durn. Both of them were very shaken by what had happened but otherwise perfectly okay. The MO came in, asked if they were hurt, and checked them over. Then he made them go to bed for twenty-four hours, as was standard policy for an unscheduled baling out.

All Smithy's crew landed safely, but the rear-gunner's story is rather special. Though so much was grim and terrible about that night, it was not without its more farcical moments, and none more so than the events which befell this rear gunner, Cliff Bradshaw, who was severely concussed when he baled out of Smithy's plane. The story was written down by John Arthurson shortly after the war, under the title: *Truth is stranger than fiction – A Rear-Gunner's Story*.

> . . . When the rear-gunner jumped he caught his right foot between the door step and the fuselage, enough to swing him underneath the plane and he thinks his head hit the tail wheel and he was knocked out. From now on events for him became, at best, somewhat hazy, but he does recall the stars being one second 'above' and the next 'below' him. He does not remember pulling the rip-cord, but the parachute did open for he descended safely and on nearing the ground, and still swinging, his heels hit a fence (between two fields he found out later) and he fell heavily on to hard ground on his shoulders and again bumped his head.
>
> When he 'came to' he heard several aircraft flying around, could see the glow of one or two fires in the fog – probably crashed aircraft, as many did that night – which convinced him that he was still in the target area, Berlin.
>
> All aircrew were told that the Germans drew a circle of about ten miles radius around any crashed plane to search for missing crew . . . and so were instructed to get as far away as possible as quickly as possible.
>
> With this in mind, Cliff set off to escape, but first he ripped off all badges and rank, buried his heavy flying suit, flying boot tops, parachute and harness under leaves in a nearby ditch. Before leaving this spot he cut a rough square off the parachute and made a neckerchief, checked that he had his escape kit (maps, money and ingenious items such as button compass etc), rubbed earth on his battle dress and set off to get away from the area. He walked mainly on the opposite side of a hedge to a roadway. He made detours round any houses and walked for what seemed a very long time.
>
> By now he was very thirsty and needed a drink badly and on

hearing some hens in a shed, got out his penknife to kill one to suck its blood, but couldn't get into the shed as it was locked, so continued his walk. Later on, deciding that he was dying from lack of liquid, he prepared to give himself up and finally knocked at a farmhouse that loomed up.

When a voice from inside, at this early hour of the morning, (the crew baled out about 1 a.m.) called, 'I'm coming, what do you want?', and proceeded to open the door, Cliff was taken aback in amazement and said, 'What, you English?', whereupon a middle-aged woman with a younger one behind, grabbed him and pulled him inside saying, 'Got you, a German spy' and called her husband, the farmer.

Cliff, protesting his German nationality, said he was an English airman and the young woman asked to see his 1250 (twelve fifty). This was the form number of RAF identity cards and the rear-gunner became more confused than ever, thinking he was being cleverly interrogated by an English-speaking German, not knowing she was a WAAF on leave, the daughter of the house.

However, after further discourse, and most welcome cups of tea, the family were convinced of Cliff's true identity and called the police, who knew of several bale-outs following the previous night's operations. Cliff was collected by the police who delivered him to his Squadron where he was put to bed in Sick Quarters.

Still suffering the effects of amnesia Cliff began to wonder about the rest of the crew and again decided he was in Germany and 'escaped' from Sick Quarters. He told some tale to the airman on sentry duty, who thought, 'drunken aircrew, so early in the day', and managed to get out of camp. This was the first of his escapes and he was found and returned to Sick Quarters. Later he heard a Medical Officer mention the word 'shot' and point towards him. On reflection, he thinks the doctor was meaning an injection of something to make him sleep. But he 'escaped' again and this time was picked up near a railway siding in Cambridge, hoping to jump a lift on a railway waggon.

Time lacked any pattern for the next two days, but after rest and sleep he was feeling 'normal' when he was handed over to the skipper with these words from the M.O., 'And take this German off my hands'.

VI. The Loss of K-King

On returning from Berlin probably around midnight my father's plane, K-King, joined the stack at Bourn. Like the other 97 Squadron planes, it circled waiting for permission to land for a very considerable time.

Listening in on the intercom, the crew overheard the Control Tower chatter that their skipper Ted was monitoring, and knew that they were in for a very long and anxious delay.

The aircraft which was at least two, possibly three, slots below them in the stack was Squadron Leader Mackenzie's. Bourn's call sign was 'Crestwave', and eventually, at about twenty-five to one in the morning, K-King's crew overheard the operator speaking to Mackenzie, 'Hello F-Freddy, hello F-Freddy, Crestwave calling; you have permission to pancake [land]'. Mackenzie would then have started his landing run, calling 'F-Freddy, Funnels' as he descended towards the runway, which again the crew on K-King would have overheard. The standard procedure for the landing aircraft was to let Flying Control know the moment it was safely down. Instead there came that horrific crash on the edge of the airfield, in which three crew members including Mackenzie were killed, immediately followed by F-Freddy catching fire. The time of the accident would later be precisely recorded on F-Freddy's accident card as 00.42.

By this stage of the night, the situation at Flying Control was fraught in the extreme. Weather conditions were deteriorating and aircraft were on their last petrol reserves. The rate at which petrol was burnt in a Lancaster rested on a host of factors – wind speed, aircraft speed, engine performance, and so on – as well as the accuracy of the course the navigator had plotted. It was also affected by a pilot's decision whether or not to deliberately conserve fuel on the homeward journey by trimming the aircraft to fly for maximum endurance. Bill Coates's Lancaster, the last of the squadron's planes to land, was to scrape into Downham Market, on two engines, at half past one in the morning, having spent eight and a half hours in the air. By contrast, Cawdery's plane, which had landed at Bourn at 12.35, was virtually out of petrol. Other 97 Squadron planes were to run out of petrol between one o'clock and twenty past.

At a quarter to one in the morning, directly after Mackenzie's crash, Flying Control must have been faced with the most terrible dilemma. Nobody knew exactly what had happened to F-Freddy or the reason why it had crashed. They did not know what wreckage or debris might still be on the runway. There was surely only one option that Flying Control could have taken – they must have told the orbiting aircraft that they had to keep circling whilst the true situation was established.

Yet a mere eight minutes later two aircraft landed at exactly the same time. This may, of course, be an error in the ORB – there are several timing discrepancies in the records. (The most significant is that between the ORB and K-King's accident card. The latter states 1.57 as the crash time, but in fact, in line with the timings on Scott and Kirkwood's cards, this has to be the time at which the wreckage was located.) It is also possible that, out of these two aircraft, Flight Lieutenant Mansbridge's did not land at Bourn at all but at some other airfield. Apart from Bill Coates's plane, the ORB does not record the identity of the aircraft which landed at alternative airfields, and though the words of Mansbridge's report – 'Low cloud at 400 ft. at base made land very dangerous' – suggest he did come in at Bourn, it might also possibly mean he landed elsewhere – it is impossible to tell from the highly abbreviated report.

What is certain is that the very last Lancaster to land at Bourn that night was captained by Flight Lieutenant Pete de Wesselow. Belonging to B Flight, he was welcomed by Cawdery's crew on his entrance to the B Flight debriefing room. It was always understood by Arthur Tindall, Cawdery's w/op, that de Wesselow's was the only Lancaster which landed at Bourn after theirs. Apart from the special case of Coates's Lancaster, it was in fact the very last 97 Squadron aircraft to land safely anywhere.

From a privileged and wealthy background, cosmopolitan in outlook and speaking several languages, De Wesselow had transferred to the RAF from the Brigade of Guards. A man of cool self-possession and very high flying skills, de Wesselow was certainly the type of captain who could have defied an order from Flying Control had he deemed it necessary. If Flying Control had told the remaining aircraft to keep orbiting or to find themselves another airfield, Pete de Wesselow had the experience and the inbred self-confidence not to listen to what they were saying now that the critical moment was approaching when he would have no petrol left.

Either Ted followed Flying Control's directions more scrupulously, or he had the misfortune to be above de Wesselow in the stack and thus even before the crisis point had been reached had finally accepted, with a sickening jolt, that he was not going to get the chance to land at Bourn. Did he radio Flying Control then and tell them he had virtually no petrol left? Did Flying Control respond by telling the crew 'just to get themselves down', as Ted's brother Jim recalled many years later?

It is impossible to establish exactly what happened next but it is certain that it happened very quickly, because at approximately the same time that de Wesselow was landing, K-King hit the ground.

In the moments directly following Mackenzie's crash, K-King was descending rapidly through the clouds. Due to the murk, the crew could see nothing whatsoever of the ground but it is entirely possible that they saw the refracted glow of F-Freddy burning as they made their terrifying approach to land.

The extreme danger they were in must have been pressing dreadfully on all their minds. K-King was within minutes of running out of petrol. George, the flight engineer, who had been nervously watching the dials for an hour, told Ted that they had virtually nothing left.

By now the crew had been in the air for very nearly eight hours. They had survived their first very dangerous operational flight, but the exhilaration had long worn off. They were bone-weary and longing only to get down and go to bed. They had not eaten for ten hours apart from some sandwiches, dried fruit, and chocolate. Their flasks of tea or coffee were empty. The smokers amongst them, including Joe, would have been dying for a fag. But in the last few minutes all these minor physical discomforts had been obliterated by the growing realisation that they might not get down out of that fog alive.

Jack, the navigator, and Sandy, the bomb aimer, would have been the two who, prior to the crash, were trying to pinpoint exactly where the aircraft was. Sandy had himself qualified as a navigator, which took some of the responsibility off Jack, but nonetheless the pair of them were under the most intense pressure to fix their position as quickly as possible. The last moments of the flight must have been spent frantically looking for a place to land. It is even possible that Jack and Sandy were specifically looking for the Hay, because if you had to chose any place in the surrounding countryside to put down a Lancaster in an emergency, this would be exactly the place that you would chose.

The Hay, as already stated, was an extremely large and very noticeable area of flat land, free of trees, ditches, or other obstructions. In daytime it was easily seen from the airspace above RAF Station Bourn, and it was well known that the place had been used as a flying ground in recent years. Some Lancasters had apparently landed there as an exercise during the summer dry spell, some four or five months earlier. However, though the best option in Bourn's locality for an emergency landing, the Hay was very far from ideal. There were no lights to guide an incoming aircraft and, due to the damp and rainy winter, the ground conditions were likely to be extremely bad.

The problems of landing there may well have been discussed, but, if so, the crew voted to take the chance anyway. In truth, they had no other choice – the option of baling out had long ago disappeared.

Ted brought the Lancaster down below cloud level. They were now only 100, then 50 feet off the deck. Visibility was 150 yards or less, and as the huge Lancaster shot across the countryside at around 110 mph, the swirling mists rushed up to part before the windscreen. Ted must have been acutely aware of the appalling gravity of their situation, but he was calm and level-headed by nature and the paramount responsibility which fell upon him, the skipper, kept his natural fear in check.

As K-King made her final descent, the white vapours parted and the anxiously watching crew saw a hedge looming obliquely in front of them. A semi-wild hedge of thorn trees and a few other native species, it was neither a particularly high nor a particularly solid obstacle. The plane took a chunk out of it with one of her wheels and carried on regardless. Moments later, she landed perfectly, beginning a 300 yard run up the muddy field. Then the undercarriage collapsed. The body of the aircraft hit the ground where an obscure and little used footpath crossed the Hay. Once down, K-King slid forward with huge velocity, breaking up and catching fire as she went.

The crash site was deserted farmland, far from human habitation. The horrifying dangers of this situation were exactly the same as had snuffed out Kirkwood and Scott's entire crews, all of whom were to be found dead in or around their burnt-out aircraft when the dawn broke. However, in K-King's case, there was one different factor. Against the most extraordinary odds, at dead of night, in dense fog, in a lonely expanse of ploughed mud, a man just happened to be passing that way on a bicycle.

That man's name was Sidney Matthews. He was a South African, a member of Bourn's ground crew, and by the most bizarre and improbable quirk of chance he was actually the flight mechanic for K-King herself.

Sidney, like the other erks at Bourn, had a reasonably happy working life, but very little leave and certainly not much in the way of personal freedom. Like all ground crew, he bent the rules a little, but on this day something had for once persuaded him to step seriously out of line. Some time in the afternoon of the 16th, probably around five o'clock just after K-King had set off for Berlin and there would no longer be any likelihood of fixing late-developing faults on the aircraft, Sidney had taken one of the better bikes on the camp and had absented himself without leave. He had a girlfriend in Cambridge whom he particularly wanted to see, and for her he was willing to make not only the eight mile trip into Cambridge, but the far more tiring return late at night so that he could be back in his sleeping quarters before midnight. The city lay below Bourn, in the Cam 'valley', and it was a shallow climb all the way back – too much like hard work except to the very keen and committed. However, the advantages of using a bike on this as on all illicit occasions was that it kept you clear of the bus and railways stations where Service Police tended to hunt for their prey.

As long as Sidney did not get into trouble in Cambridge, managed to avoid all predatory SPs, slipped back into camp without being detected, and was on time for the work the following morning, there probably would have been no repercussions from his escapade. Had he failed to return by 23.59, his mates at his hut would either have assumed he had a sleeping-out pass or would have known that he was breaking Standing Orders and would have covered for him. Only at work the following morning, when the roll was called, would concealment have become impossible. His immediate section superior was just as unlikely to cause trouble. Such men were generally corporals who slept in the hut with the men and were considered 'one of us'. Had Sidney's nominal superior known of his plans, the most authority he would have been likely to assert would have been to tell him to keep clear of public places, and to mutter some dark warnings against the whole idea.

Sidney had no intention of getting into trouble and had probably aimed to get back well before midnight, but either his girlfriend or the fog detained him and he was an hour late, and still a mile and a half from the airfield, when K-King went down.

It must have been around twenty to one when Sidney turned down the farm track which began at St Mary's Church at Hardwick. He bumped down it until it dwindled off into the narrow footpath which led straight across the Hay in the direction of the airfield. There was not a sound to be heard out on that vast, empty, fog-shrouded plain, and the only light came from the wavering feeble beam of his bicycle lamp. His progress was slow, but at last he reached the boundary hedge of the farm, got off his bike, lifted it over the gate, and climbed over after it.

He was just remounting when, out of the dense stillness of the foggy night, to his amazement he heard the thunderous roar of a Lancaster approaching. The kite was far too low, only twenty or thirty feet off the deck, and it appeared to be coming down right over his head. The sound grew absolutely deafening. Then despite the murk he thought he actually saw it, delineated by its navigation lights, an immense black monster scarcely discernible through the fog, seen for an instant, then in an instant disappearing into the murk and mists of the Hay.

Moments later came the terrible, splintering, grinding sound of the impact as the aircraft came down off its undercarriage. The body of the Lancaster hit the ground on the footpath he had just crossed, smashing down with terrific force and shattering the very heavy metal castings of at least one of the engines. In the same instant, the tail broke off and was left behind as the fuselage continued its inexorable momentum forward, jolting violently and catching fire as it went. The propellers of the four massive engines were still turning and went hacking into the ground, spraying debris everywhere. With a vile shearing noise, the Lancaster shed dozens and dozens of fragments of her metal skin, which were twisted and contorted in ghastly shapes by the terrible force to which they were subjected. The perspex windows shattered to bits, showering hundreds of pieces over the field. Only the centre part of the plane remained relatively intact. This was where all her strength lay, in the massive reinforced floor of the bomb bay and the main spar between the wings. The immense weight of this centre section, and the adhesive nature of the heavy soil, slowed the Lancaster fairly quickly to a halt. She ended up close to the southern boundary of the Hay. Gouged behind her through the earth was a 350 yard long trail of debris and bodies, with fragments of wreckage burning here and there.

Probably one or two of the crew had been killed immediately. Others, including Ted, had been fatally injured. All five dead would later be recorded as having suffered 'multiple injuries'. Those pieces of crumpled aircraft skin could cut like so many jagged, saw-toothed knives – they could cause the most terrible lacerations, sever arteries, amputate limbs.

Someone, maybe two men – who is uncertain – apparently managed to get away from the wreckage at this point. They were mortally injured but still able to move. Instinctively, in a daze, hardly knowing what they were doing, they just wanted to get clear.

Joe, who had been knocked unconscious, was still inside the fuselage, trapped in twisted metal from his waist downwards. He had no head or chest injuries, no injuries to his vital organs, but severe fractures of both legs.

The main body of the plane was on fire, but in the initial moments after the crash it was not burning very fiercely. There was plenty of flammable material around – rubber, paper, hydraulic fluid, oil, spilt petrol – and the flames quickly spread. Shortly they reached the ammunition belt for one of the guns. They set off the bullets, which began to whine and ping through the air. One of the bullets ricochetted through the fuselage and hit Joe in the arm, breaking it and immediately exiting. The shock was enough to bring him round. He did not realise that he had been shot, but he could hear the bullets popping, flying in all directions, set off by the encroaching fire.

He had no idea what had happened immediately prior to the crash, and he was never to remember it. All he knew was that the plane had come to a halt and that there was a perfect stillness. He was sure that he was on the ground. He did not feel any pain, but only a sort of incredulous amazement that after eight hours in the air, with incessant deafening noise and pitching motion, at last the sound of the great engines had stopped. Everything had a strange, preternatural stillness. Despite his terrible situation, a calm almost euphoric passivity enveloped him.

It was beginning to get hot. He could feel the metal which trapped him becoming warm and little cinders beginning to settle on his face, which stung so that he had to move his head to shake them off. He was in the most extreme danger. Yet he could do nothing to help himself and he was too shocked and dazed to panic.

The same acute shock had overwhelmed Sidney Matthews for a moment. Too stunned to move, he just stood there stupidly, holding his bike, looking back into the darkness of the field he had just crossed which was now strewn with the wreckage of the aircraft. It must have been all too obvious that he himself had only just escaped death.

Then the obscurity was pierced by the light of the burning debris, and awakening with a horrified start from his daze he hurled aside the bike as if it impeded him, vaulted back over the gate, and ran as fast as he could towards the trail of wreckage. Lit by the lurid light of the flames, the scene was appalling, indescribable. It did not seem possible that anyone could still be alive. But then suddenly, staggering out of the darkness, weighted down by his heavy flying boots in the sticky mud, there appeared the rear gunner, Leslie. He was shocked and disorientated, blood was trickling down his face from a small cut on his cheek, but otherwise he was perfectly all right.

There was no time to waste if they were going to get anyone out of the aircraft. They began to run up the field along the path of the debris until they reached what was left of the fuselage. With the utmost courage, disregarding the bullets whining and crumping all around, putting their own lives in the most extreme danger, Sidney and Leslie climbed into the shattered Lancaster.

Though semi-conscious, through his daze Joe heard voices. The sound of these voices became louder and now he knew that there were two people with him but he was too muddled to realise who they were. One voice said, 'I'll get his arms and you get his ankles'. Together those two men pulled him out of the wreckage and laid him down on the ground by a hedge, some distance from the plane.

Then the pair of them went back into the burning aircraft for Ted. They brought him out with difficulty, for he was a big man and Leslie for one was very slight, and carried him to safety by the shelter of the hedge. It was a most brave and heroic action but it was all for nothing. Very soon afterwards, cradled in Sidney's arms, Ted took his last breath and died.

The death of his tall, dark-haired, kind, easy-going skipper must have been the most terrible grief to Leslie, but he buried his feelings in taking care of Joe. The ground was extremely cold, and knowing that someone in shock must be kept warm, somehow he obtained a parachute. Though my father wrote in his memoir that it was his parachute, aircrew never wore parachutes during the flight, only the harness to which the parachute was clipped in an emergency. The sole exception was the pilot, who, because he would always be the last one to abandon the aircraft, had his parachute affixed to his harness – sunk in his hollow seat, it doubled up as a seat cushion. It was almost certainly Ted's parachute, brought with him as they carried him out of the aircraft, that Leslie used to keep Joe warm.

Pulling the rip cord so that the parachute bloomed out in the misty night air and sunk down gently on the ground, Leslie gathered up the fine white silk and wrapped it closely around Joe. Joe was beginning to be a little more aware of what was happening now. By the flickering light of the fire, through the strange haze which seemed to cloud his senses, he slowly realised that it was his crewmate who was tucking the material around him. Leslie was asking him how he was, trying to reassure and comfort him. Joe could see that Leslie had blood running down his face and in his turn asked him wonderingly if he was okay, but Leslie laughed it off, saying it was only a cut.

Also lit by the firelight, Joe could see Sidney Matthews whom he only knew very slightly. He was too dazed to think how odd it was that Sidney was there but just accepted his presence unquestioningly.

Sidney and Leslie now conferred as to what they should do. With the immediate need for action past, Leslie was sliding into a state of shock. Though he was wearing a very thick warm flying suit, he was beginning to shake a little as if he was cold. It was best for him to sit down on the ground with Joe. Sidney said that he would go and fetch help; after all, he was the only one who knew exactly where they were. Besides which, Leslie knew the rudiments of first-aid, unlike Sidney who as a member of the ground crew had never been taught such things. Sidney told Leslie he wouldn't have the stomach to give Joe a morphine injection, he hadn't a clue how to do it, and it would be much better altogether if Leslie stayed to take care of Joe – he would be back with help as quickly as possible. Realising the sense in this, Leslie agreed.

Sidney left the pair of them and ran back to pick up his discarded bike, then headed straight on for the airfield itself, knowing that he could bring the ambulance back with him from SSQ. It was about a mile and a half to SSQ, half a mile back to Hardwick, but there can have been no doubt at all in Sidney's mind which he should head for – he knew where he could find highly skilled medical help together with the necessary emergency equipment, and he went to get it.

It took Sidney perhaps twenty-five minutes to get to SSQ. As soon as the ambulance was ready, he got in beside the driver and they began the journey back to the Hay. It was official policy that in no circumstances should an ambulance set out until the exact location of a crash was known, either through an eye-witness or through Flying Control. The station's ambulances carried grid reference maps and had a wireless link, and the drivers had a thorough knowledge of the local countryside, but on such a night as this an eye-witness like Sidney meant the vital difference between saving or losing a critically injured man.

With Sidney gone, Leslie, using the first-aid kit from the Lancaster, tried to give Joe a morphine injection for what he could clearly see were terrible injuries. In the first-aid classes, Leslie had been told he should give the injection as soon as possible and that was what he thought he should do, even though Joe said he was not in any pain. Leslie had a hard job convincing Joe that he needed the jab, because Joe, slightly preposterously, argued with him and said he did not want it because he was terrified of needles. Nevertheless, eventually Leslie succeeded in injecting his reluctant patient. Then Joe asked him to pull him further away from the aeroplane because he was afraid it would explode if the fire reached the petrol tanks. Leslie thought they were quite safe, but he did what Joe asked and dragged him on the parachute to a greater distance. He sat down next to him on the ground, and the pair of them looked back at the last convulsions of the aircraft, racked every so often by loud explosions.

The fire was burning very fiercely now. It was cremating any crew member left inside the wreckage. The air was filled with the dreadful stink of the conflagration. In the centre of the fire, the temperature had reached such high degrees that the aluminium was running down like water. A fine drizzle drifted through the air, the tiny droplets absorbing the orange-red glow of the flames. Beyond this awful zone of light, the ineffably dreary and comfortless landscape seemed to stretch away forever into the mist and darkness.

It seemed as if they were miles and miles from anywhere. Sidney was an awfully long time coming back, and Leslie began to worry about what to do if he did not return. He had only the vaguest idea of where he and Joe were, and if he had to leave him might wander blindly for hours through the unknown terrain in order to find help. He was very afraid that Joe might die from his dreadful injuries. It must have been the most terrible experience for this young Londoner, only twenty years of age, as he sat on the cold ground and comforted Joe, or consumed with anxiety, grief and restlessness, wandered a little distance away before returning to the side of his injured crewmate.

The agonising wait seemed never-ending. Leslie, in desperation, thinking that Sidney had got lost or that the return party could not locate them in the mist and the darkness, blew the whistle which all aircrew carried, attached to the collar of their uniform. He took the whistle off his collar and put it to his lips, and the sound rang out into the night air, thin but piercing, a most eerie, metallic and haunted music. Musically acute as Joe was, the sound seemed so unutterably strange to him that he would never forget it, and it would echo in his mind for the rest of his life.

Then at last, at long last, at two o'clock in the morning, a whole hour after the crash, people began to arrive. Amongst them was a group of senior officers, and Leslie to his amazement recognised the Pathfinder chief, the great Bennett himself, who had come to see the terrible losses of the night first-hand.

Bennett was in his thirties, a very powerful figure and a man of supreme confidence and ability, and yet when he looked down at Joe, a mere sergeant of twenty-one who appeared still more immature with his baby-faced features, he was moved enough to give him his own coat. It was very cold, and my father, who did not realise who Bennett was until Leslie told him afterwards, was very grateful when the shadowy form of this unknown senior officer took off his uniform greatcoat and laid it gently on top of the parachute in which he was already wrapped.

Two ambulancemen had also arrived, one of whom managed to severely disconcert the patient by saying 'I think we'll have to cut this off', meaning his trouser leg, but which Joe took to mean his leg itself.

After a brief consultation concerning his injuries, they loaded Joe into the ambulance. The decision had been made to take him to the civilian hospital of Addenbrooke's. Another of the medical staff, in the meantime, had also examined Leslie. It having been ascertained that Leslie was not suffering from concussion but only from shock, he was permitted to have his wish and accompany Joe to hospital, on condition that he returned to SSQ with the ambulance afterwards.

The station's ambulance drivers had been trained to drive their vehicles over rough muddy cross-country areas without inflicting too much suffering on their patients, but even so Joe was for the first time aware of the pain of his injuries as the ambulance began to jolt over the rough and uneven surface of the Hay. Soon they reached the stony farmtrack up to Hardwick, which was just as bumpy and agonising. Another few minutes, however, led them out onto Main Street in Hardwick, which shortly joined the main road to Cambridge.

The six and a half mile ambulance journey from the muddy field to the centre of the city took about half an hour. At around three o'clock, they at

: Joe Mack (inset and third from right,
[b]ottom row) during initial RAF training in
[the] summer of 1941.

[Bo]ttom: Pathfinder chief Donald Bennett
[add]resses a PFF bomber crew – in the
background can be seen a typical wartime
airfield which could easily be Bourn. On
the far left is Geoffrey Lloyd, Minister for
Petroleum Warfare, greatly involved in the
development of FIDO.   *(IWM)*

Top left: Joe just after joining the Pathfinders (their hovering eagle badge is on his pocket), November 1943.

Top right: The control tower at Bourn, summer of 1942, with the Duke of Kent.

Middle: 1943, Grange Farm barn in the north-east corner of the airfield, one of the few surviving farm buildings. The picture shows petrol bowsers Popeye and Big Ben, and a mixed group of armourers and electricians (Walter Bushby third from left).

Bottom left: Bombing up – the load in the foreground is of target-indicators. OF-J crew members (L to R) Peter Burbridge (b/a), Ron Bennett (m/g), two ground crew unknown, Weasel Hill (r/g) Ron Swetman (f/e).

Bottom right: On a dispersal at Bourn, Jimmy Munro's Lancaster OF-J, with signatures of some of the crew, summer of 1943.

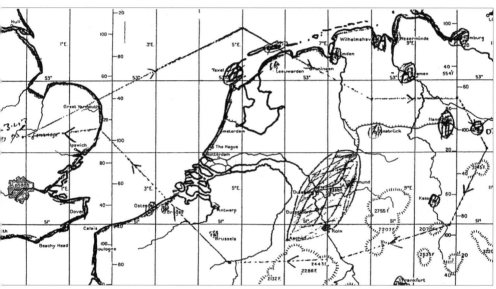

op: Giving an unforgettable impression of the huge size of a Lancaster, M-Mother with the ground crew of C Flight, March 1944, shortly before 97 Squadron was taken out of the Pathfinders and C Flight moved to Downham Market.

Above: Navigator Bill Shires' route map for 14th/ 15th January 1944, showing the route taken from Bourn (just to the west of Cambridge), to Brunswick. Note the scribbled over areas, showing concentrations of heavy flak, especially over the island of Texel.

(Charles Owen's papers, IWM)

Right: Pathfinder Stations. Huntingdon Area, December 1943.

■ Upwood (Training Centre)

■
Warboys (156 Sqd)

PATHFINDER STATIONS

HUNTINGDON AREA, DECEMBER 1943

All squadrons flying Lancasters unless otherwise stated. There were also four Mosquito squadrons, two at Marham in Norfolk, one stationed at Wyton and one at Oakington

HUNTINGDON
PFF H.Q. ● ■ *Wyton (83Sqd)*

■ *Oakington (7 Sqd)*

■ *Graveley (35 Sqd, Halifaxes)*

Bourn (97 Sqd) ■ ● **Highfields**
● **Hardwick**

●
■ *Gransden Lodge (405 Sqd)*   **CAMBRIDGE**

THE CREW OF K-KING

Top left: Ted Thackway, photograph taken September 1939, just after joining the RAF – this photograph is said by his family to be the best likeness of him.

Top right: Ted just after qualifying as a pilot and becoming an officer, early 1943.

Bottom left: Leslie Laver just after he qualified as a Rear Gunner and around

the time he joined the crew at Silverstone OTU, July 1943.

Bottom right: Sandy Grant, the only Canadian on the crew; this official photograph was taken just after he qualified as a navigator and before he embarked for England in April 1943.

(National Archives of Canada)

Top left: Tony Lawrence with his fellow trainee aircrew just after he joined the RAF, May 1943.

Top right: George Grundy just after he qualified as a Flight Engineer and around the time he joined the crew at Wigsley CU, September 1943.

Bottom: Jack Powell (second from right, back row) with a group of fellow navigators, circa winter 1941.

Top left: Jack Powell with Agnes on their wedding day, 24th December 1937.

Top right: Jack.

Bottom: B Flight 97 Squadron, September 1943.

AIRCREW FLYING ON 16TH/17TH DECEMBER 1943

Top left: Y-York with crew shortly before r actually on the memorable 16th December (L to R) Gordon Townend w/op), Smithy (pilot), Jimmy Wilson /a), John Arthurson (nav), Harry teward (m/g), Maurice Durn (f/e), Cliff radshaw (r/g).

Top right: John Arthurson and Cliff Bradshaw at Bourn.

Bottom: William Darby Coates, 'Bill', (far right) who won the DFM – in training in Canada late 1941.

Top: Ernest A. Deverill (front row fourth from right), after being decorated for his part in the Augsburg raid, 1942. *(IWM)*

Above: Charles Owen's crew and ground crew. *(IWM)*

Right: McLennan (third from left) with 405 Squadron at Gransden Lodge. Also shown (L to R) Buck (not on trip), L. H. Cornwell (f/e), Morrie Martin (not on trip), Eric Halliwell (w/op), G. R. Schneider (b/a).

p left: Tony Lawrence in the summer 1943.

p centre: Leslie with his girlfriend, *ris*.

p right: Peggy Lawrence as a Land Girl, *14*, around the time she visited Joe at *y* Hospital.

Middle right: Leslie in Air Training Corps before joining the RAF.

Bottom: Ted's brother Jim marries Ted's 'Jill', December 1944. The youngest brother John is third from left. Behind him is Jim next to Jill. Elsie and Grandpa Wrightson on far right.

LESLIE LAVER'S LAST CREW

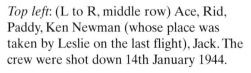

Top left: (L to R, middle row) Ace, Rid, Paddy, Ken Newman (whose place was taken by Leslie on the last flight), Jack. The crew were shot down 14th January 1944.

Top right: 'Steve', the pilot.

Bottom left: Paddy, the navigator, who stayed with his pilot to the end.

Bottom right: Ace, after capture by the Germans; his RAF number hangs aroun his neck.

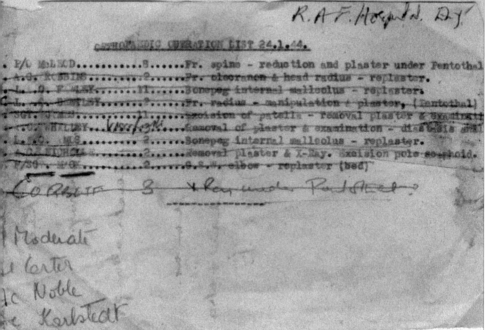

Top: Ely Hospital, Ward III from the gardens, 1943.

24th January 1944, Flight Sergeant Mack (Joe) ninth on the list.

Bottom: Armstrong's Operation List from

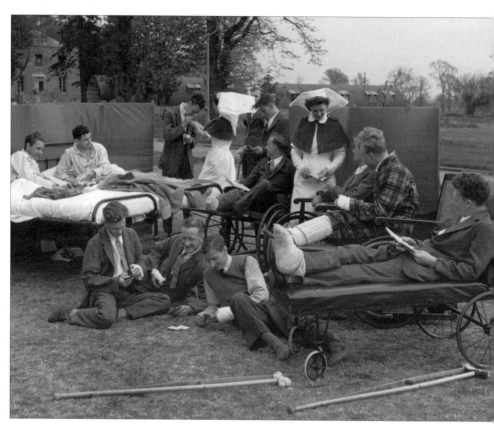

Top: Sister Mac in the garden with patients, Ely.   *(IWM)*

Bottom: The famous dancing classes at The Leas.

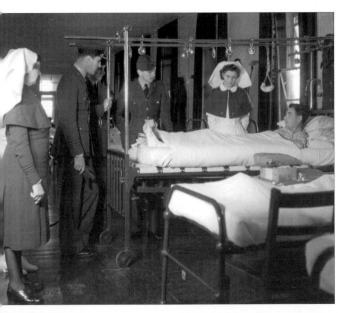

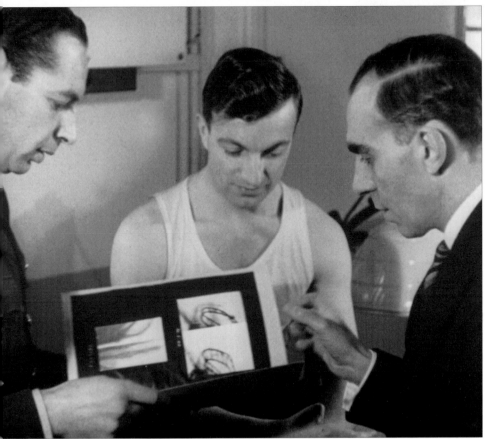

left: (L to R) Miss Jackson (Matron),
tain G. P. O'Connell, (CO), Squadron
der Guest (M.O.), Wing Commander
my Armstrong (Orthopaedic Surgeon),
er Mac, unknown patient.   *(IWM)*

Top right: Daddy Dawes in the gym.
(IWM)

Bottom: (L to R) Harold Cantor, unknown
patient and Reginald Watson-Jones.
(IWM)

Top: The Leas Boys.

Bottom left: Bill Gadsby, S-Sugar's W/OP.

Middle right: The Leas 1943. The centre figure is David Page, Rehabilitation Instructor.

Bottom right: Grave at Fonteinsnol, Tex (either Bill Gadsby or 'Jack' Skinner before reburial at Den Burg). The sunlit crater in the background is where S-Sug crashed.

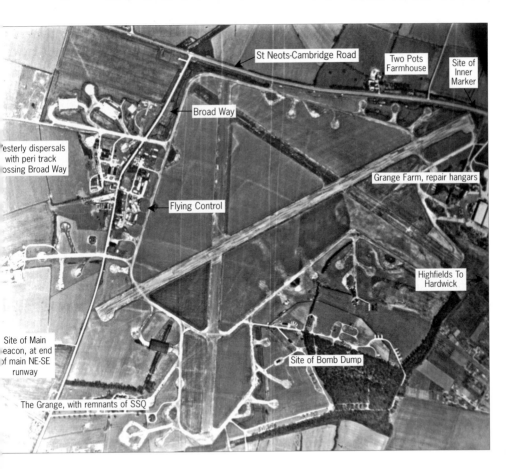

The following labels appear on the aerial photograph:

- St Neots-Cambridge Road
- Two Pots Farmhouse
- Site of Inner Marker
- Broad Way
- Westerly dispersals with peri track crossing Broad Way
- Grange Farm, repair hangars
- Flying Control
- Highfields To Hardwick
- Site of Main Beacon, at end of main NE-SE runway
- Site of Bomb Dump
- The Grange, with remnants of SSQ

RAF Station Bourn about ten years after the war ended, and already beginning to melt back into the landscape.

The most important buildings of the camp are still clustered around Flying Control. The main road onto the airfield leads up behind it, from the entrance by Great Common Farm where once stood the checkpoint manned by Service Police.

The faint pod-like shadows on the airfield itself are the old dispersals, now broken up but still showing through the crops. The bomb dump has disappeared beneath the new trees of the Bucket Hill plantation.

Bourn Grange is approached via an avenue of trees from Broad Way. The Grange is the cluster of buildings nearest the airfield; to the left of it is what remains of SSQ – the mortuary and ambulance garage have gone, but a ghostly goblet shape marks the old driveway which led up to them.

Opposite SSQ, on the other side of Broad Way, faint white rectangles mark the former Site No.7, containing airmen's, sergeants' and officers' quarters. The Sergeants' Mess was at Site No. 2, further down Broad Way, just below SSQ but not quite visible on this picture. Sidney Matthews' sleeping quarters were probably at Site No. 2, or another even further towards Bourn village.

The crash site of K-King is to the east, beyond Highfields and going towards Hardwick, approximately the same distances as from Flying Control to the end of the short NW-SE runway.

Top: The Hay, September 1997, looking back from the spot where Sidney Matthews passed through the field gate. K-King crashed onto the ground behind him, half way between here and the truck in front of the barn. After ploughing across the field, the Lancaster ended up some distance behind the van on the right of the picture and burnt out at this spot.

Middle: Bourn Grange today, from the airfield – SSQ was on the far side by Broad Way.

Above: The Sergeants' Mess and other wartime buildings, 1994.

last reached Cambridge, its deserted streets veiled in mist. Their destination was Trumpington Road. At the very end of this road stood The Leys, a large school built in fanciful Victorian Gothic, with several collegiate-style buildings, including a chapel. The school was now a commandeered annexe for Addenbrooke's Hospital.

Unlike the rather grand front entrance, the two small side doors of The Leys faced onto Trumpington Road itself. Each was reached by a flight of ten stone steps leading to an arched stone doorway like a church's. It was almost certainly to one of these side doors that Joe was brought, for he would always remember how awkward it was for the men to get the stretcher up the 'very difficult stone steps'. Once he was inside, safely in the charge of the medical staff, there was a painful parting as Leslie said goodbye to him, fervently wished him luck, and disappeared to return to Bourn with the two ambulancemen.

Joe was now examined by a civilian doctor and civilian surgeon. His left leg was in very bad shape, with the two bones which form the upper part of the knee joint having been sheered off by the impact of the crash. The wound was full of aircraft debris, as were the deep abrasions he had received in his buttocks. Because of the trauma it would cause an already dangerously injured body, the doctors decided to defer treatment of the left leg for the time being, merely immobilising it by putting it into a temporary Thomas's splint. Plasters, however, would be applied to his other fractures, those of his right ankle and right arm, the latter being the gunshot wound inflicted by one of the stray bullets set off by the fire.

After the preliminary examination, Joe was taken to the operating theatre. He asked a nurse there, 'What became of the others?' She did not want to tell him so she laughed it off, saying, 'They all . . .', before pretending to be distracted by something else.

Up till now it would appear from his written account that Joe had been comparatively alert and wide awake. However, soon after his arrival in the theatre, his condition took a very serious turn for the worse. What caused his collapse was shock, the clinical state in which the blood pressure becomes very low or unrecordable. This condition causes rapid deterioration of the functions of the vital organs – brain, liver, kidneys, and finally heart. Joe's bleeding from his wounds would be the major cause for his state of shock but probably two other factors were involved – dehydration related to the long dangerous Berlin flight and 'crush syndrome' caused by massive muscle damage. At that period, medical knowledge on shock was incomplete and it had not yet been realised that severe bleeding can occur within the strong fibrous compartment which surrounds each muscle group. The subsequent anaemia is difficult to recognise and needs the measuring of the blood haemoglobin, a laboratory test which in late 1943 would have taken an hour or more even in an emergency.

Joe would have been given intravenous infusions of serum and plasma from which the red blood corpuscles had been removed, perhaps even as early as the ambulance arriving at the Hay. This would have increased the circulating volume of fluids and perhaps raised his blood pressure a little but it would not have increased at all the oxygen-carrying haemoglobin. Joe must have got worse and worse until belatedly the medical staff realised that he also needed a blood transfusion. Such a blood transfusion also took some time for the laboratory to test and cross-match before it could be given safely. Joe must almost have died before this corrective measure was started and even then his pull back from death would be a slow one.

Up at the crash site they were still searching for missing members of the crew. The search lasted all night. Before it was light, Bob Plane, the 14 year old boy who lived at Hardwick, got up to go to work. At six o'clock, he left for Wood Farm, a dairy farm where he milked the 28 cows morning and night. It was very dark, even more than unusually grim for a midwinter's morning. The fog was thicker than ever. He could not see his hand in front of his face, and it was so difficult to pick his way that once he stumbled into a ditch even though he knew the way so well.

Then all of a sudden, booming out at close hand through the mist, he heard voices calling, 'Is anyone there?' and saw torches flashing. It gave him a terrible fright because it was so close by and so unexpected. Bourn's ground crew were out, searching for the missing crew members – they had not been able to find them because of the fog and darkness.

Much later he heard the story of what had happened. People from RAF Station Bourn used to go and drink at The Chequers, the local pub which was kept by his aunt, and they 'used to talk a lot about that night, they were very down and depressed about it'. They said that some of the crew had wandered away from the plane and died of shock. They were huddled – separately – in bushes and ditches, trying in vain to keep themselves warm. 'It was a cold horrible foggy night, near to freezing if not freezing . . .' They became disorientated due to the fog and the darkness, and died separately, each man on his own, within walking distance of help and warmth.

As the five bodies were located, they were transported back to the mortuary at Bourn, on the west side of Station Sick Quarters. SSQ was built on what had once been the side lawns or pastures of Bourn Grange, between the house and the road. There was a second prefab site next to it, an overflow across Broad Way, which included amongst many other buildings some officers' and sergeants' sleeping quarters. It is possible that Ted, Sandy, Jack, Tony and George, had slept the previous night in those very huts, a mere stone's throw away from where they now lay in darkness on the cold mortuary shelves.

The bodies of Donald Mackenzie, John Pratt and William Colson, all killed in the F-Freddy crash, had also been placed in the mortuary. All the bodies were examined beforehand, perhaps washed and laid out. An off-duty WAAF who had gone down to SSQ to offer her help was overwhelmed by the sight – SSQ seemed to be overflowing with bodies. There was nothing she could do – there were simply no casualties to treat.

The mortuary at Bourn would never normally have had to cope with such a number. Though the squadron regularly lost 7 or 14 men on each operation, their deaths almost always took place far away, in Germany, Occupied Europe, or the North Sea. Those who lost their lives so close to home on this particular night were burned, gashed or mutilated in the most horrible ways. Their appalling injuries and the sheer numbers of the dead brought home to those at SSQ the brutal nature of the war in which they were all engaged. Perhaps it is a sign of the stress that everyone was under that night that the Medical Report is littered with errors, including the erroneous recording of injuries and men's service numbers.

Of all 97 Squadron's crashes, involving 35 men, the only one to sleep in Bourn SSQ that night was Leslie Laver. He is recorded in the Medical Report as having 'received slight abrasion of cheek with shock'. Terribly wearied, overcome by all that had happened, the poor lad must have been half dead on his feet.

They cleaned up the slight scratch on his face. They put him to bed, gave him something to make him sleep. It must have been four in the morning by then. The last things he saw in his mind as he lay in the narrow bed in the darkness were vivid, constantly unrolling scenes of the crash. Despite his weariness, he still tried to make sense of the events of that dreadful night, the sight of his fellow crew terribly mutilated or dead, the rescue of Joe with Sidney Matthews, the muddy field lit by the fiercely burning plane. From out of the dense black of the foggy night, he had at last seen help arrive, Bennett arrive, the senior officers arrive, and he had at last escaped that hateful desolate place by driving away with Joe in the ambulance. Then the brightly lit hospital rooms in Cambridge, saying goodbye to Joe, fervently squeezing his hand, wishing him good luck, and returning all alone, the only one who was left, to the place which all seven of them had flown out of in their Lancaster less than twelve hours before. These swirling images must have run through his mind until at last, unutterably weary, he fell asleep.

The next morning, he was given forty-eight hours survivor's leave. He went home to his house in South London, to the old familiar scene of warmth and normality, to his mother Jenny and his brother and sisters.

97 Squadron's ORB in the meantime was recording that he had been posted to the ground crew of RAF Station Bourn, the station being considered a separate entity to the squadron. In this decision there was an element of compassion, of allowing Leslie to get over the dreadful shock he had experienced. But there was also a brutally pragmatic reason and that was that he had lost his entire crew. For the time being he was absolved from flying – that is, until another crew lost a rear gunner.

Four

Aftermath

I. Black Thursday – The Reckoning

The night of 16th/17th December 1943, in which my father's aircraft and so many others were lost, was a serious blow for Bomber Command, though the losses now seem comparatively modest compared with the horrendous toll which was exacted by the enemy in January, February and March of the following year.

Black Thursday, as the day was soon called, saw the loss of twenty-five Lancasters during the Berlin operation but a further thirty-one lost due to the fog over England, crashed or abandoned when their crews baled out, or in the case of two unfortunate crews collided over Lincolnshire. Other aircraft – Stirlings, Halifaxes and Lysanders, variously on gardening, training or Special Duties flights – also crashed due to the fog. In total, Bomber Command suffered 327 deaths and lost 70 aircraft on this day. Chorley's masterly reference work, *RAF Bomber Command Losses* (1943 volume), lists ten pages of horrendous crashes, deaths, injuries, and amazing escapes for 16th/17th December. The death toll for the bad weather crashes in England was close to 150, not counting those who later died of their injuries. 97 Squadron's losses were the heaviest of all.

Altogether, twelve Pathfinder Lancasters were lost because of the appalling weather. Only 7 Squadron had no bad weather losses, though it can have been of little consolation as they had lost four crews on the Berlin raid. 83 and 156 Squadron lost one plane each; 405 Squadron lost three out of the thirteen planes flying that night, one near Marham (where three of the squadron's other Lancasters landed safely) and the other two at Graveley. The PFF dead were two from 83 Squadron, six from 156 Squadron, fourteen from 405 Squadron, and twenty-eight from 97 Squadron, fifty men in all.

Black Thursday saw the worst bad weather landing casualties in Bomber Command for the whole of the war. They were also by far the worst that 97 Squadron ever experienced. The official details are recorded in Bourn's ORB, and, though studiously dry and matter-of-fact, the account makes harrowing reading.

21 a/c detailed to attack <u>BERLIN</u>. Good concentration of bombing in early stages falling off later. No results seen only reddish glow . . . Many fighter flares and scarecrow flares . . . One a/c F/Lt Brill and crew failed to return – no news heard since. On returning to base a/c encountered bad visibility over England and the Squadron had a disastrous night in a/c losses and 28 aircrew being killed.

The following is a brief summary of the return. 8 a/c landed safely at Bourn, and 3 at Gravely [*sic*]. 1 a/c landed at Wyton. F/S Coates, after being hit by another aircraft's incendiaries and having two engines put out of action on the same side by flak, put out a ditching signal when not far from the Danish coast. With great skill he flew the a/c back on the two engines and landed safely without further damage at Downham Market.

Two crews, P/O Smith and F/O Mooney the captains, baled out over Ely and Wyton. All the crews were uninjured but one a/c is missing and untraced.

S/L Mackenzie DFC crashed at Bourn on the edge of the airfield. Three were killed, S/L Mackenzie, F/O Colson, P/O Pratt, the remainder are either in hospital or sick quarters.

F/O Thackway and crew crashed near Bourn airfield, killing all except Sgt Mack who is in hospital and Sgt Laver who escaped uninjured.

S/L Deverill DFC DFM and crew crashed at Gravely all being killed except for W/O Benbow who is in Ely hospital.

F/S Scott and crew crashed at Gravely all being killed.

P/O Kirkwood and crew crashed near Gransden all being killed.

Total loss of aircraft 8. Airmen killed 28. Injured 7.

With the as yet unconfirmed deaths of all Brill's crew, 97 Squadron had lost over a quarter of the 151 men who had flown out that night.

Why had it happened? Why had everyone in Bomber Command been so unprepared? There had been several occasions in the past when serious losses had been incurred as a result of fog. FIDO had been designed to be a large part of the solution, but FIDO at Graveley did not land a single aircraft safely that night. Though weather conditions were so appalling that it is probable that an earlier lighting of FIDO would not have made much difference, still it is one of the most baffling questions about Black Thursday – why had the order to light up been given so late? By the time FIDO was finally on full burn – at seven minutes to one in the morning – 405 Squadron had already lost two aircraft, whilst 97 Squadron had lost three and was to lose another four within the next quarter of an hour or so.

Graveley's Station Commander, Group Captain Menaul, commented on his report, 'After light up conditions inside the installation were good but the pilots could not see it from above cloud. The aircraft which crashed . . . were short of petrol and it must be presumed that they ran out before an attempt to land could be made.' Knowing full well that petrol reserves were low, why had Gransden Lodge and Bourn not diverted their aircraft earlier?

In old age, Ted's brother Jim would look back on this night and with good cause still feel extremely bitter about the loss of his much loved brother. He remained very angry with the RAF that the Lancasters of 97 Squadron had not been instructed to land elsewhere but had been kept at the base 'milling about', having been told 'just to get themselves down'.

The cruel truth is that the system as it stood at the end of 1943 simply could not cope with the influx of 450 Lancasters in severe bad weather, all needing to land more or less at the same time. The only true blind landing aid was SBA, and it was hopelessly cumbersome when heavy aircraft had to get down in a hurry. Pilots were forced into drastic, and often fatal, actions by the long delays they endured whilst their petrol dwindled. By the time certain aircraft were cleared for landing, they were absolutely at their last reserves and the margin for error was non-existent. It is not surprising that many pilots forewent the use of SBA, as they were simply not in a position to spend the time required to line up on the beam – they had to get their Lancaster down, come what may. What speaks so clearly and movingly for their sense of duty is that so few of them abandoned their aircraft. It was a matter of pride to bring their kites home, and probably many of those who died thought that they had both the luck and the skill to do so. Others may have been loathe to jump into what was the complete unknown. Nobody was keen to trust their lives to a parachute – a common joke was 'You can't take it back to Stores and complain if it doesn't open'. They would be jumping into what was in effect an unmapped lightless void, with the countryside beneath totally obscured by cloud, fog, night, and the black-out. In such circumstances, it may just have seemed safer to stay with the aircraft. Yet those who chose to abandon their planes and jump were, in fact, the ones who correctly assessed the level of risk.

Given the weather forecast that night, the inevitable conclusion is that the raid should have been cancelled. The Met Officer at Bourn had stated that he thought that it would be, but the order to scrub never came through. Operations had not been flown for almost a fortnight, and at the top of the chain of command there must have been great pressure to resume them. Harris took a gamble that the weather would not be as bad as was expected, but in the event it was very much worse. Sending the force out that night was a huge tactical blunder, but no commander whose operations so closely depended on the weather could hope never to make such a mistake.

Shortly after the war, Harris was to write in his study of the campaign, *Bomber Offensive*, that amongst the very worst strains of his command had been 'the continuous and fearful apprehension about what the weather may do'.

Meteorology is an inexact science; in fact it is still in the condition of being an art rather than a science. This being so, and our climate being what it is, I should have been able to justify myself completely if I had left the whole force on the ground, if I had done nothing whatever, on nine occasions out of ten . . . The whole of the responsibility, the final responsibility, for deciding whether or not to operate falls fair and square on the shoulders of the Commander-in-Chief and falls on them every twenty-four hours. For all he knows he may lose the whole of a very large proportion of the force by weather alone, to say nothing of enemy action. It is best to leave to the imagination what such a daily strain amounts to when continued over a period of years.

There was apparently no detailed enquiry into the night's events, and no blame ever attached to Harris. There was a war on, and the real villain was Hitler, who had necessitated the planes going out in the first place. The bad weather was just put down to dreadful bad luck.

Meanwhile, resources continued to be poured into the FIDO project, and it was hoped that shortly the system would be able to cope better with extreme weather conditions, so that there would not be a repetition of that disastrous night.

Nor was there. FIDO, though a crude and eccentric creation, eventually fulfilled all that its developers had promised. Soon there were 15 installations in Britain, stretching from Carnaby on the Yorkshire moors, to Manston on the Isle of Thanet in Kent, to St Eval in Cornwall where the main problem was seafog. FIDO would enable 2,500 Allied planes to make safe landings in fog during the last years of the war. But in December 1943, it just wasn't ready.

Hoping for further clues as to how each of 97 Squadron's planes had met its end, I obtained the accident cards for all seven from The RAF Museum at Hendon, only to find that the paucity of information was on a par with the usual surviving wartime documentation. There were file numbers logged on each card, so evidently a far more detailed dossier had been compiled for each crash, but my enquiries at the MOD and the Public Records Office failed to produce any of these files. The Air Historical Branch at the MOD informed me that the files are probably no longer in existence, explaining, 'Unfortunately, original Court of Inquiry records relating to RAF accidents were not retained in any systematic way, and most have long since been destroyed'.

From the accident cards themselves I learnt nothing new about the seven crashes, save that it was confirmed that all of them had involved a fire, with the possible exception of Kirkwood's plane. What was utterly startling, however – and then caused me the deepest disgust – was the terse sentences about the cause of the crashes written on each card.

They had most evidently been filled in as a batch, with virtually the same phrasing and remarks on each of them. The comments had been made by Bourn's Station Commander and Commanding Officer, each backing up the other's judgement, and they contradicted the assessment already given in 97 Squadron's ORB that the losses had been due to bad visibility, fog and low cloud.

Instead, all the accident cards were inscribed with the same thing, 'E of J' – Error of Judgement. No blame was to be placed on the landing aids and facilities, or on the training program of RAF Station Bourn or the training units which had preceded it – instead the entire responsibility was to be dumped squarely on the shoulders of the seven pilots.

The report for K-King is representative of the whole (I have filled in the abbreviations for all the quotations from the cards):

> Aircraft crashed into ground in conditions of low cloud and bad visibility attempting to locate airfield. Commanding Officer: SBA landings should have been practised. Station Commander: Error of Judgement in bad visibility. Aircraft crash one of twelve – subject of special report.

'One of twelve' refers to the total Pathfinder losses that night. Despite all efforts, I have been unable to locate this special report, destined for Harris and ultimately Winston Churchill.

For Scott's plane, the one which had crashed near Graveley with the loss of all the crew, it was much the same – 'Aircraft crashed near airfield. Station Commander: Error of Judgement in bad visibility and low cloud; should have used SBA.'

For Kirkwood's plane, in which all the crew had died near Gransden Lodge, there was no attempt at fairness – 'pilot's Error of Judgement in bad visibility'.

For Mackenzie: 'Aircraft attempting to locate airfield crashed in low cloud and bad visibility . . . Error of Judgement in bad visibility'.

For Deverill, the highly decorated Squadron Leader whose plane had run out of petrol at Graveley, the following disgusting travesty was entered: 'Aircraft crashed attempting to locate airfield in conditions of bad visibility and low cloud. Station Commander: pilot not using beam – pilot Error of Judgement in bad visibility.'

If Deverill was not using the beam, it was because he knew full well the appalling nature of his crew's predicament and that he had to land as quickly as possible, having been delayed in the air for so long whilst other aircraft were landing. The slur on his competence is unforgivable. It also directly contradicts the ORB's statement that the loss of P-Peter had been due to 'very bad visibility and low cloud'.

Deverill might have chosen to abandon his Lancaster. It would have cost the plane but probably would have saved the lives of himself and the five of his crew who died. Those pilots who did abandon their planes were commented on more lightly: concerning the loss of Y-York, the card reads 'abandoned due to bad visibility and shortage of petrol . . . primary cause bad visibility, secondary failure to use SBA'; for Mooney, 'poor visibility. Short of petrol . . . contributory factor was pilot's failure to use SBA'.

Both these last two cards stated that the SBA training of the pilots would be concentrated on from then onwards. But whose responsibility was it that SBA had not been practised in depth before? It was the responsibility of the Commanding Officer and the Station Commander.

The Commanding Officer on 16th December was Squadron Leader C M Dunnicliffe, but though he had been on the station for some time he had only officially taken over from Group Captain N H Fresson on 15th December when Fresson was posted to RAF Snaith. Dunnicliffe was well-liked and a very capable officer, but his was only a temporary caretaking appointment – Wing Commander E J Carter would succeed him as CO three weeks later, on 7th January.

Group Captain N H Fresson, nicknamed 'Presson Fresson' after the RAF's unofficial motto 'Press On Regardless', had not been much liked by his men. For five months, from July to November, he had combined both the Commanding Officer and Station Commander's jobs until Group Captain J L Airey, DFC, had assumed the latter on 24th November. Perhaps the heavy strain upon Fresson had led to the neglect of SBA practice, but it seems far more likely that SBA had been seen, in the context of the war as a whole, as something that the pilots would just have to muddle through.

In the ORB details of flying practice for the five weeks prior to the 16th, there are only two mentions of SBA being practised, one in early November and one on 1st December. Of course, such training may have taken place on other occasions and not been noted down, but it seems obvious from the comments on the accident cards that none of the pilots had recently had such training.

So far as the new pilots are concerned, it is actually very hard to see when they would have been able to practise SBA. To take the example of my father's skipper, Ted, since he had arrived at Bourn there had been at the most five days when weather conditions permitted any sort of flying. It is highly unlikely that Ted's officers would have told him to practise SBA at the expense of other vital parts of his flying training – after all, the lives of the crew were infinitely more likely to be imperilled by their coming flights over enemy territory, and what is more they had a job to do and their commanders intended them to be able to do it properly.

Arthur Tindall, the wireless operator on Squadron Leader Cawdery's plane, personally did not remember that his crew had *ever* practised blind landing, and he says that they had a night exercise the following night after Black Thursday, or at least very shortly afterwards, in which they had to go through the procedure exhaustively.

Y-York's crew, having picked up their new plane from Wyton on the 19th (Wyton was the airfield to which all new PFF Lancasters were delivered for their final modifications and test flying), were also ordered to practise SBA, which they duly did on 22nd December from six in the evening onwards.

The comments on the accident cards were grotesquely unfair. A more balanced appraisal was given by 405 Squadron, stationed at Gransden Lodge a mere three miles from Bourn. The two squadrons had shared the same appalling local weather conditions that night, their fortunes had been interlinked, and the summation given by 405 Squadron's CO related to exactly the same set of circumstances. The squadron's ORB noted that its three lost aircraft had crashed 'owing to poor visibility and lack of petrol'. On the accident cards, the identical comments read that the crashes had been due to 'pilot's inexperience and very poor weather for night landings. SBA training to be stressed.'

Higher up the chain of command, none of the comments made on what had happened that night mention pilot error – it would obviously have been quite farcical to do so given the number of planes involved. Air Marshal Sir Edgar Ludlow-Hewitt, Inspector-General of the Royal Air Force, wrote with impartiality that the accidents were partly due:

> to the lack of any pre-planning and practice of a scheme for homing in bad weather and neglect of SBA. The system should not be regarded as obsolete because it is to be replaced by GCA. The night was ideal for SBA, but many stations ordered aircraft to break cloud over the sea and try to come in under the low cloud, which resulted in accidents due to aircraft flying into high ground and congestion over airfields at low altitudes.

Sir Archibald Sinclair, the Air Minister, reported to Winston Churchill that 'exceptionally bad weather conditions with drifting masses of very low cloud' had developed at the base airfields 'some twenty minutes before the bombers returned, resulting in 34 crashes. Fortunately, from these, sixteen entire crews are safe and also a number of individuals.'

The aircrew on the stations, or those who had survived the crashes and were now recovering in hospital, came up with their own explanations for the catastrophe. My father suffered from partial amnesia after the crash but in his memoir he wrote that what had probably caused it was the thick fog 'coupled with the fact that the altimeters were very primitive and had to be set according to the atmosphere pressure'. He wrote that he had radioed the base for the new altimeter reading whilst they were still in the air, and 'when I received it I was suspicious of it but I had no option but to pass it onto the skipper to make his approach to land'.

Why had he had no option but to pass it onto his skipper? Why had he not voiced his misgivings? It was his duty as well as the natural response of someone who wished to get down out of that fog alive. But in fact, the whole passage is extremely confusing, as all other sources have indicated that it was the pilot who was given the QFE directly over the radio and that the wireless operator had nothing to do with it.

The Lancasters' altimeters were set to the QFE transmitted by Ground Control as they circled awaiting their turn to land. Well, whoever took the message on K-King that night, my father certainly appears to have believed that the altimeter reading was at fault. However, at least nine other Lancasters (including one from 405 Squadron) landed safely at Bourn and none of those crews left any record of having been given the incorrect QFE. Charles Owen's private diary entry for 16th/17th December, whilst describing the dangers he and the squadron encountered, makes no mention of such a dreadful error.

The theory about the altimeter may well have been something that my father picked up in Ely Hospital as rumours began to circulate there about the losses of Black Thursday, brought into the hospital by the survivors' RAF visitors. Dark mutterings about incorrect QFE seem, in fact, to have been rife. In Martin Middlebrook's *The Berlin Raids*, there is a statement by a Flight Sergeant Ron Buck, a rear gunner (though he was not at that time with 97 Squadron as detailed in the book). His plane had been descending normally when Ron Buck, to his horror, suddenly saw the ground rushing up at them and screamed over the intercom to the pilot, Pete Drane, to pull up, which he did and instantly soared back into the night sky to overshoot the airfield. 'Pete Drane came on the intercom and told me we couldn't have been on the deck; he had 300 feet on the clock when I shouted. It turned out that we had the wrong QFE and I believe that many others did the same that night, but they never lived to find out.'

The crashes at Graveley were also being blamed on incorrect information. This time it was suspected that the angle of glide indicators had still been set at the steeper angle necessary for the Halifaxes of 35 Squadron and this had led the diverted Lancasters to crash. This, however, seems to have had as slim a factual basis as the QFE theory, because all the Graveley crashes had occurred off the airfield except that of Deverill and he had approached the runway from an incorrect angle.

Rumours such as these reflected the fact that, due to the stringencies of wartime secrecy, very few people had a full grasp of what had happened. The appalling weather conditions that night, together with the huge number of incoming aircraft, had certainly been sufficient in themselves to explain the crashes without resort to any other factors. However, faced with the extent of such terrible, pointless losses, it must have been easy to believe that human error had compounded an already desperately grave situation.

II. Aftermath

97 and 405 Squadrons were devastated by their losses. As Gordon Musgrove wrote in *The Pathfinder Force*, 'The next day there was a

numbness at Bourn and Gransden Lodge. Everyone moved about as if waiting for someone to wake them from a nightmare.'

At Bourn, sorrow was universal. Les Hammond, one of the ground crew, remembers that everyone at the station was 'totally shattered'; he was too new to know anyone well but the grief was shared by everyone. 'Initially we were going to lynch the Met man' (that is to say, Magnus Spence at Bomber Command, not the local chap). Later, however, they calmed down and accepted it as one of those things which happened in war, 'just one of those terrible things'.

A most unenviable task was the gathering up of the effects of the forty men who had been killed, were seriously ill in hospital, or had been recorded as missing. Someone had to go to their rooms and their lockers, and remove any small personal belongings. Nobody owned very much – there was no room to keep it – but the paucity of the collection did not make it any less poignant. The numbers involved seemed overwhelming.

One of the items for which the searchers were looking was a will or any last letters to the dead man's friends or family. Someone searched Ted's belongings for the former, and, evidently not finding it, noted on his service papers, 'No will in pay book'.

The Station Commander, Group Captain J L Airey, made preparations to sign 28 death certificates. Telegrams telling of the fate of the men, followed by individual letters signed by the Commanding Officer, Squadron Leader Dunnicliffe, were sent to the next of kin.

A happier duty for Airey and Dunnicliffe was recommending Bill Coates for the immediate award of the Distinguished Flying Medal, a very great honour for such a junior pilot. On 22nd December, Dunnicliffe wrote a glowing report of the heroic flight home after incendiaries and flak had crippled the Lancaster, N-Nan. 'By his devotion to duty, prompt obedience of orders and superb captaincy, Flight Sergeant Coates saved his aircraft and crew.' This opinion was seconded by Airey. 'This NCO put up an outstanding show which thoroughly deserves the award recommended by his Squadron Commander.'

The recommendation was accepted and cited in the *London Gazette* three weeks later, on 7th January, the account of the award concluding 'In harassing circumstances, this airman displayed great skill, coolness, and resolution'. The DFM ribbon would be pinned on Bill Coates by Bennett himself in front of the entire squadron.

Dorothy Halliwell was 15 when the telegram arrived which told of her brother Eric's death; he had been with the 405 Squadron crew which had crashed on Ingles Farm at Graveley.

> When the telegram came my mother knew what it was but she couldn't read through her tears. All it said was that Eric had been involved in a crash. My father tried to find out more but

men were coming down in their hundreds and we never got
anywhere. We later found out that his plane had run out of fuel
near to the air base but we never knew where . . .

It was not until half a century later that she found out when a local man,
Colin Stocker, set up a memorial at Ingles Farm and an article in a paper
said that he was looking for relatives of the crew of D-Donald.

Colin Stocker still lives in Yelling. Though nothing is now left of the
wartime airfield, he remembers the days when Graveley could be seen on
the skyline, beyond the huge treeless fields. The presence of the RAF
absolutely spellbound the local youth and in Yelling, as elsewhere, a whole
generation of country boys, living in small hamlets which at that time had
scarcely changed for 200 years, grew up with all that charisma and drama
just on the horizon. Colin had seen amazing sights – 50 to 100 American
Flying Fortresses overhead, going to or returning from the raging battles in
Europe, a plane coming in on fire, or one with a large part of its wing shot
away, distress flares being fired from approaching aircraft which let those
on the ground know that there were injured or dying men on board, and
FIDO itself, lighting up the village as bright as day.

The local folk had been totally bemused by the strange goings on in their
midst. At night when FIDO was first lit, palls of evil-smelling black smoke
billowed everywhere, then as the burners settled down, 'you could see all
the village as clear as anything – you could see to read a newspaper'.

Colin said he sometimes regretted he had not gone away into the RAF
as he had wanted to, but had stayed all his life with the family businesses
in Yelling. Whenever he said this to his friends, they were always very
happy to point out that if he had gone away, he would not be nearly so rich
as he was.

What happened at Ingles Farm in the aftermath of the crash was
representative of the way the RAF dealt with such incidents. They were
usually on the scene within half an hour, and once they had arrived no
civilians were allowed near the wreck. The authorities were particularly
sensitive about Pathfinder aircraft because of the additional top secret
equipment which they carried. The guards at Ingles Farm erected a small
tent, so that they had somewhere to brew tea and shelter from inclement
weather. I asked Colin Stocker who the guards were and he laughed hugely
and said they wouldn't have been the Yelling Home Guard, because 'they
were no good' – they were RAF police.

Colin Stocker's uncle, Herbert Reed, was the manager of Ingles Farm in
the war years. On the Friday morning of 17th December, Uncle Herbert
went into Colin's father's shop in Yelling to say that a Lancaster had
crashed on the family farm, down in the 47 acre field. Colin was then only
fifteen years of age. He at once went up to have a look. It was soon after 10
o'clock in the morning, but still so foggy that he could not see the Lancaster
from his vantage point. Standing by the cattleyards at the farm, there was

nothing to be seen but a dense wall of mist – 'I couldn't see my hand in front of my face it was so thick'. In the early afternoon, the fog had cleared sufficiently and he went back to the farm and could then see clearly. The plane had run across their land, met the boundary ditch, and catapulted over onto the neighbouring farm, Home Farm, which belonged to a Mr Ashcroft. The sight made Colin very sad, and he made himself a promise he would never forget that day and the men who had died, and that one day he would have something put there to remember them by.

The guards disrupted the farm's business. Uncle Herbert was not best pleased. He was a perfectionist, and, gazing at what was left of his newly prepared potato field across which McLennan's plane had run, grumbled, 'Look at the mess he's gone and made of it'.

The guards remained there for a few days, until the largest pieces of the Lancaster were taken away on the low-loading lorries known as Queen Marys. After this, five or six RAF men combed the fields for remains – 'it was like the scene of a crime' Colin said, a line of searchers moving slowly forward, combing every inch of ground. The wreckage was not strewn over a wide area but was in a relatively compact area, some of it in Uncle Herbert's potato field, whose neatly banked up rows were now even more comprehensively trashed.

When the salvage operation was completed, the tent was taken down and the guards left. But despite the exhaustive search, pieces would keep turning up over the years, thrown up by the plough after it had buried them for decades, small fragments of perspex and contorted metal, twists of aircraft skin, nothing spectacular, yet an ever-present reminder of what had happened that night.

A similar process of clearance took place at the Hay. Somebody in officialdom saw the wreck of K-King on 17th December and noted that it was Category E, Salvage only. Category E was known as 'reduce to produce' – the aircraft would be cannibalised at the same time as scrapped. K-King had cost £59,000 to build, and she had clocked up only 138 hours including test flying and training. What pitiful remnants were in a state to be recycled would go back into the war effort.

By 28th December, the salvage operation was completed. The largest pieces had been cut up and taken out on Queen Marys, the Hay cleared by hand of whatever was left. Part of what the salvage crew missed now sits on the table next to me.

Normal squadron life resumed quickly at Bourn. Around noon on the 17th, all the surviving aircrew were summoned to the Aircrews' Briefing Room, where coolly and factually Squadron Leader Dunnicliffe outlined the losses and the number of survivors, and reassured his men that replacement crews and new aircraft would be arriving in due course.

The ground crew at Bourn were deeply shocked by the loss of the aircraft which they had tended so carefully and what each one represented in the toll of aircrew lives. Whereas on 16th December, 97 Squadron's strength had been 29 aircraft, now it was only 20. Eight had been lost altogether and one was so seriously damaged that it would never fly again. It seemed a miracle, though, the ground crew agreed, that they had not lost the lot. Walter Bushby and the other erks who had seen the dense fog the previous night found it incredible that any of the skippers could have made a safe landing.

One important visitor to Bourn in the aftermath of the crashes was Bennett. He is noted in the ORB as giving 'a long and interesting talk to all flying personnel' on 21st December, almost certainly as a morale-boosting exercise as only the following day, on the Wednesday, the twenty-eight fatalities from the Squadron were to be buried.

The survivors got the standard 48 hours survivor's leave. Leslie left immediately, travelling out of Bourn on the Friday on a weekend pass. He went home to his family in Upper Sydenham, South London. He must still have been in deep shock after the devastating events of the previous night, his feelings in turmoil as he walked up the steep hill to the house and the family he had left only nine months before. By the time the door was opened, however, he had steadied his composure, and neither his mother, his brother, nor his sisters would read in his face anything of the nightmare he had just passed through.

No 47 (now 49) Panmure Road was a decorative Victorian house, one of a semi-detached pair subdivided into four maisonettes. It was here that Leslie had grown up. Because Victorian architecture was so unfashionable, Jenny, his mother, had got her house with its large sloping garden at a very low rent. It was a cold house and most uncomfortable to live in, though it had its charms – tessellated floors and stained glass amongst them. Moreover, once the Blitz had begun, the family had been very glad of their old house which was extremely sturdy and stood up to the bombing far better than the gerry-built modern houses further down Panmure Road. There was a large wine cellar in the basement and this was what they had used for an air-raid shelter until an Andersen shelter could be built in the garden.

As the house stood on very high ground, the back rooms had a panoramic view over south London, across Dulwich College grounds towards Crystal Palace and Norwood. As the Blitz had worsened, the family could see plainly what damage was being wrought every night. There were huge anti-aircraft guns on railway tracks in the College grounds and, with the sound of the German bombers droning overhead and the bombs falling, the noise had been absolutely terrific. Leslie's older brother, Wally, whose health had kept him out of the war, would always remember some service pals who were home on a weekend pass telling him that they were leaving that Saturday afternoon. 'But you're not due back till Sunday,' Wally objected. 'We going back to base – we can't stand all this bombing – at least we've got something to fight with there.'

South London had suffered appallingly during 1940-41. None of the

family would have had the slightest qualms about Leslie giving the
Germans a taste of their own medicine, but no one had wanted him to
become a rear gunner in the very hazardous way of life in Bomber
Command.

Leslie was the youngest of the family, he had been a most endearing little
child and they had all made of him something of a pet. One of the most
prized anecdotes about him as a very small boy was the time he had draped
a large towel round his shoulders, placed a paper crown on his head, and
walked around the house, aping the priests at the local Catholic church,
singing hymns with nonsense words but the correct tune. He had been quite
serious about it and naturally his family thought the whole thing hilarious.
Even now that old story was still being told. Though Leslie was a young
man now, it was hard to overcome the old habit of looking on him as the
baby of the family. His mother in particular was very fond of him.

Only Dorothy still lived at home with Jenny, but the married children
(apart from Cyril, who was in the Army and had been captured at El
Alamein in 1942) gathered together at their mother's once they heard that
Leslie was back. Wally would always remember the severe shock all the
family received when they learned for the first time, as they sat together at
the round table in the dining room, that Leslie had been on operations and
had actually been over Germany only two nights before.

> Just before he died, he came home on leave for the weekend.
> On the Saturday we were sitting at the table, all talking about
> different things, family things. Then the conversation all went
> quiet. Just as it did so, Leslie said something I might have
> missed otherwise – he said 'What a load of shit came up at us
> over Berlin the other night'. My mother said 'What's that, Les?'
> 'Nothing, Mum, nothing.' 'You've been over, haven't you?'
> 'Yes, we've been over.' Well, it was a shock to all of us; we
> didn't know he was flying [on ops]. It came out of the blue and
> we were really shocked.
>
> That weekend, that was the last time I saw him.

Leslie never told his family about the terrible aftermath of his Berlin flight.
He told them nothing about the crash, nothing about the loss of his crew,
and nothing about the rescue of Joe with Sidney Matthews. He kept utterly
quiet about the recent events which must have been so horrific and
traumatic to him. Perhaps it was something which at the time he felt that he
could only share with his fellow airmen, because only they would have
truly understood what it meant. Besides, like all service people, he had had
it drummed into him not to say anything to civilians, even to his closest
family. But, more than anything else, his silence was probably due to his
realisation of just how shocking and upsetting the revelation would be. He
had already seen his mother's appalled reaction to the statement that he had

been over Berlin. Probably he just could not bring himself to say anything further. Instead, he took his baby nephew, Michael, from his sister Jessie, smiling and laughing, 'Isn't he lovely?', and with everyone petting the baby the subject was changed.

On the Sunday night, still keeping the matter secret within his own breast, Leslie returned to Bourn. None of the family was to know what had happened to him on the crash night until I managed to get in touch, over half a century later, with his now seventy-nine year old brother Wally. Once Wally had got over the shock of hearing what had happened to his brother, he became very interested in the story. When I asked him what would have happened if Leslie had told his family, he said laughing, 'We probably would have killed him'.

Back at the airfield, Squadron Leader Dunnicliffe told Smithy, the pilot of Y-York, that he must take out the flight van with Cliff, the rear gunner, to collect all the equipment that he had ditched during his 'escape'. Eventually, after some trouble, they managed to locate it through a farmer who knew where it was. John Arthurson's parachute was also searched for but never found. Just as none of his crew were ticked off for abandoning their aircraft, so John Arthurson was never reprimanded for losing his parachute, and whoever found the parachute 'got a nice piece of silk'.

All the Y-York crew were deeply conscious of how lucky they had been. They went through the customary little ritual of gratitude – 'it was the done thing to give the WAAF who packed the 'chute which saved one's life ten shillings'.

One of the much prized emblems of a baling-out was a nonsensical but delightful badge of a caterpillar, a minute jewel of a thing, gold with ruby eyes, with the name of the recipient engraved on the back. The caterpillar was a silkworm, and symbolised the fact that the man's life had been saved by a parachute made of silk. On 23rd December, at Bourn's squadron office, a Flight Lieutenant Hind wrote to the Honorary Secretary of the Caterpillar Club at Irvin Air Chutes of Great Britain Ltd, based at Letchworth in Hertfordshire, listing all the names of Smith and Mooney's crews:

> Dear Sir
> I am pleased to inform you that the undermentioned aircrew personnel of this Squadron saved their lives when baling out near Cambridge on the night of 16th/17th December 1943, using Irvin parachutes. I should be pleased if you would make them members of your club and forward the brooches to this Unit for distribution.

It would be April 20th 1944 before the pins arrived, with a letter saying that Mr Irvin would be most grateful 'if you will present these fourteen Pins to the above with our compliments and the hope that they bring them Good Luck'. There was a sad irony about this, for Mooney and all his crew had been dead for four months, hit by flak when returning from Berlin on New Year's Day.

Smithy's crew were allowed to go home for Christmas on their special forty-eight hour leave. The Medical Officer at Bourn, still rather concerned about the rear-gunner, said that Cliff must be seen safely home to his family in the Midlands by John Arthurson. Cliff said that he did not dare go home, as his mother would be too shocked by all that had happened, and he persuaded John Arthurson to let him go south to his married older brother instead. Much against John Arthurson's better judgement, he agreed and he was mightily relieved when Cliff returned on time. By 29th December they were operating again and flew many more 'nightmare trips though none ending like that first one'. All but Harry Stewart, the mid-upper gunner, and Maurice Durn, the flight engineer, were to survive the war.

Harry was killed on 25th April 1944 when flying as a replacement with another crew. Maurice Durn had been so shaken by his flak injury, the loss the following night of all his original crew, and the bale-out which followed on his next operation, that he never flew with Smithy's crew again. He disappeared off the station, but it is evident that at some stage he recovered his nerve because he was flying again with 97 Squadron at Coningsby the following year, when he had the misfortune to be involved in a terrible mid-air collision on 23rd June. The squadron were on a formation flying exercise over Lincolnshire when the Lancaster flown by Edward Perkins drifted to starboard and, in an attempt to regain position, struck the tail of the Lancaster of Henry Van Raalte. Van Raalte's aircraft immediately went into a steep dive and plunged into the ground, killing the entire crew instantly. The other plane crashed shortly afterwards, only one man escaping by parachute. So deeply was the wreckage of Van Raalte's plane embedded that human remains were discovered in it fifty years later when it was excavated by the Lincolnshire Aircraft Recovery Group. One of those on board had been Maurice Durn.

For Harry and Maurice, like so many others, surviving Black Thursday had only been a temporary reprieve.

Bob Philips, the engine mechanic for F-Freddy, Mackenzie's crashed plane, has a most vivid memory of the aftermath of the crashes for he and some of his fellow ground crew were detailed to go to Cambridge City Cemetery and dig a grave 36 feet long, six foot deep and six foot wide.

> There was no doubt about it, it was not an easy job. We were there all day and sometimes we looked around us, or walked around and saw the graves. We saw that most of them were in their twenties, and it really brought the war home to us. There were perhaps 20 of us there digging, we were brought our meals

and there was a great big tea urn . . .

It was not just our station who were digging – we had sent some of our blokes, other stations like Wyton had sent their blokes – it seemed that everybody in the Air Force was at the cemetery that day.

The coffins would later be placed there, shoulder to shoulder, in a line, amongst them Mackenzie himself, next to two members of my father's crew – Sandy, the only Dominion crew member, and Tony, my father's friend.

Geoffrey Gilbert, in a different squadron of Bomber Command but with a family home near Bourn, recalls that the night of 16th/17th December was much talked about afterwards and that people always remembered the huge number of coffins which left Bourn for burial. Bob Plane of Hardwick remembered it being said that they took the coffins along the road to Cambridge on low-loading lorries, Queen Marys, because so many had died. Other squadrons were also sending their dead. Yet despite the extraordinary nature of this mass burial at Cambridge, it was not mentioned in the local newspapers, no doubt because the story would be so bad for morale. Nor would any information ever be printed about the crashes in the fog, despite the wrecks which still littered the local farms; the usual cloak of wartime secrecy had descended to hide the disaster in which Bomber Command had lost 150 men.

On Wednesday, 22nd December, Bourn's ORB notes of the funeral of its men:

> Today S/L Mackenzie, Sgt Lawrence and six dominion aircrew who were killed on the 17th December were buried at CAMBRIDGE, the Station Commander, Squadron Commander, some officers and aircrew NCOs attended. The twenty other personnel were conveyed to their various home towns for burial, a representative of the Squadron was in attendance in each case.

Nancy, Ted's close friend, never forgot the senior RAF officer who came back to Harrogate with Ted's body 'with orders not to leave the coffin'. He did not leave the coffin for a moment – even when the grieving family gathered in the sitting room prior to the funeral, he was still there – it was not until Ted was safely underground that he left.

Ted's friends and family had been shattered by the news of his death. In particular, Jim, was utterly distraught for he had idolised his brother. It was he who had told Nancy the dreadful news, hardly able to get the words out, standing on her doorstep, 'I've come to tell you Ted won't be coming back, he's been killed'. Jim had followed his brother into the RAF, though he was not aircrew but ground crew, working as a fitter, and in his grief he was unable to comprehend why Bourn station had let his brother down. 'There wasn't enough help for them. There wasn't enough help. If our Ted had been coming in on my station, we would have got them down.' Jim said he had seen too many aircrew taken out of crashed planes, and he desperately wanted to see Ted, to make sure that it was all of him in the coffin and that they had not just made up the weight with sandbags. But the officer kept in strict attendance, and none of the family saw Ted's body. Nancy wrote: 'We all knew the reason for that, even though we were told he only had a tiny mark on his temple'.

At last the coffin was born out of the little house and loaded onto the waiting hearse. The funeral was held at the local church, St John's, where Ted had once been a choir boy. Later that day they buried him at Killinghall, a couple of miles away, in the village in which his mother had grown up. Grandpa Wrightson, a retired quarryman, still lived in one of the row of tiny stone cottages on the Ripon road. He was now churchwarden for the church of St Thomas, and one of his duties was to look after the graves. Perhaps it was due to him that his grandson's grave is so prominent, right by the main door of the church. His is the typical War Graves headstone, inscribed with the RAF badge. Underneath the family's tribute has been carved: 'Greater love than this no man hath'.

Some time after the burial, Jim was told by the RAF – far too late – that he could have looked in the coffin if he had wished.

Jill, Ted's last girlfriend, was on Christmas leave when he was killed. Knowing nothing of this, she returned to Scampton with a dress and a coat to be married in when Ted had his next leave. Shortly after her return, she took some dry cleaning into Lincoln on the Scampton station bus. One of the other passengers was a pilot officer whom she knew slightly, and it was in the brief laconic parlance of the time that he told her, 'Ted's bit the dust'. Jill was utterly devastated. For confirmation she got in touch with their mutual Lincoln friends, and heard the worst possible news that she could have when the Musgraves told her, 'We buried him last week'. Through the Musgraves, it was arranged that Ted's mother, Elsie, should come to Lincoln to meet Jill for the first time. Not long afterwards, Jill suffered a minor nervous breakdown through grief and shock, and was sent home to Liverpool. Ted's brother Jim obtained leave and visited her there. In comforting one another and coming to terms with their loss, they were to fall in love.

Ted's errant wandering father, George, had come back for his oldest son's funeral and stayed at the family home a further year, before dying from a heart attack in November 1944. One month later, Jill married Jim. Ted's portrait was to hang in their house for years afterwards. Their daughter was scared of it when she was little, for her dead uncle's fine dark eyes seemed to follow her everywhere.

Ted's flight engineer, George Grundy, was buried at Undercliffe, in the

Eccleshill district of Bradford; his favourite sister, Joyce, was shattered by his death. It long remained a memory in the family that when the undertaker had collected George's body from the railway station, he exchanged some brief words with the guard on the train. He was told that when the train had started on its journey, the guard's van had been full of RAF coffins. The guard had found the whole thing harrowing and was distinctly upset about it.

Navigator Jack Powell was buried at Wakefield Cemetery. His coffin was sealed when it arrived back at his home town. Once again, the relatives were told it would be best for them not to look inside. They did not.

Two days later, on December 24th, the sixth wedding anniversary of Jack and Agnes, this notice appeared in the *Wakefield Express*:

> In grateful and proud remembrance of Jack Powell . . . who lost his life on active service . . . his devoted wife Agnes, relatives, friends and colleagues render tribute to a loving husband and a loyal friend who lived to serve his fellow-men.

These are not just conventional pieties but show deep feeling for a man who had been very highly respected and deeply loved.

Almost exactly three years after Jack's death, Agnes remarried, as close to the date of her first wedding as possible for that time of year was always acutely depressing for her. Her new husband was thirteen years younger than she, and as this was socially unacceptable in those days both fibbed about their age on the wedding certificate.

John Allott repaired railway engines and was a very different sort of fellow to the meticulous, clever and ambitious Jack. John would never make any money to speak of and Agnes would always be poor compared to her time with Jack, but John was a kind man and very laid back, and the marriage was a happy one which produced a daughter, Judith.

Agnes never forgot Jack, and an unexpected mention of him could make her burst into inconsolable tears. Yet John was never jealous of her first husband but held his memory in great respect. Each year, close to Christmas, Agnes would take a wreath up to Jack's grave. For the headstone, she had chosen the words, 'At the going down of the sun and in the morning we will remember them'. The Cemetery, in its Victorian heyday a place of some splendour, became more and more tumble-down as the years passed, but at each anniversary Agnes or John would take the wreath up to the grave until old age brought infirmities and neither could manage to go there. Before his death in 1998, John Allott expressed a strong wish to be buried in the same grave as Jack. Agnes too wanted to be buried there, all three of them in the same grave. She is still alive but sadly now suffering from Alzheimer's.

Tony Lawrence and Sandy Grant were placed side by side in Cambridge

City Cemetery. Leslie must have been at their funeral, one of the 'aircrew NCOs' attending.

So it was that Tony was the only English member of the crew whose body was not taken back to his home district for burial. For some unknown reason, Peggy had her son buried not at Shurlock Row but in the military cemetery, with a poignant inscription placed on the gravestone, one of the very few gravestones in the place to carry one. It is thought by the family that this epitaph was selected not by Peggy but by Tony's strong-minded grandmother, Mabel, who had been so involved in his upbringing.

My father saw Tony and Sandy's graves in 1993 when his sister Daphne took him back to the cemetery a year before he died and he had already grown very weak and feeble. It must have been the most poignant and tearful moment for him, the man who had lived for half a century beyond the crash standing face to face with those tall white markers, so simple, stark and moving, with the familiar names engraved upon them.

Shortly after that visit, I and my brother Rick went to see Dad. At that stage I knew next to nothing about the true facts or indeed that only two of the crew were buried at the cemetery. I recorded in my diary what my father abruptly told us, quite out of the blue:

> *March 21st*
> . . . suddenly father off into a long speech about looking for some graves. I hadn't been paying attention – don't know how he got there – but apparently Carole [our stepmother] or one of his sisters had driven him out to a cemetery to look for them. Rick made a crack which I knew was tactless – so did he – then we made some more to cover up the first one. Dad not to be deflected. Determined, talking clearly and firmly for the first time the whole day, he spoke of going hunting for these graves. And they found them. 'The 17th December 1943, that was the Day of all Days, the Fateful Day'. When the bomber crashed and everyone was killed except for himself and one other man. The graves were of the rest of the crew, buried together side by side – 'my best friend was there'. All this was said with an intensity and genuine force which one never sees in him nowadays.

I was taken aback, embarrassed and unsure of how to act, this story had come with no warning whatsoever. Dad *never* spoke about such things. Though as children we had often heard the story of the aircrash, he had long ceased to talk about his time in the RAF and anything to do with it had become a taboo subject. I had heard nothing about the aircrash for perhaps twenty-five years, and yet all of a sudden he was compelled to tell us about this visit to the graves, was so strengthened by the need to tell that his often slurred speech became distinct and comprehensible.

Dad seemed on the verge of becoming deeply upset, and somehow or other Rick and I got him off the dangerous subject and back onto our usual trivial bantering level. Now I wish I had taken the opportunity to ask him more, but at the same time I doubt I could have done that – it would have just seemed too cruel. It was obviously a raw and painful wound to him, and the possibility of him breaking down was very real. Dad was so weak and frail by then that it seemed best not to upset him further.

I went to the cemetery myself four years later. It was a visit which was full of grief.

We had been warned that the cemetery was hard to locate but we found it easily enough. It was large and rather patchy in style, with many variable coloured gravestones, all of different heights, jumbled about any old how. In the distance could be seen one or two rather crudely carved angels pointing upwards at the heavens, but other than that the place had very little romantic atmosphere. Houses had gradually crept close around the perimeter, something like a factory was close by, and the boundary hedges were not high enough to block out the surroundings and ensure a feeling of repose and quietude.

The cemetery was still very much in use, with a fresh grave, as yet without its headstone, lying covered in flowers close to the main path. This was the civilian quarter; the war graves began with a small outcrop running along a neat hedge by the main path, in amongst which was a boy of sixteen years old. But the main war cemetery was completely separate, in its own hedged enclosure at the far end of the site, lying on the left as one walked up the main path. There one stepped out of the jumble and chaos of the civilian section into a grassy court of the starkest and most austere beauty.

There is no doubt that it is an awful moment walking into this place. The grass is emerald bright against the bone white of the graves, which are all the same height and size and set in geometrically precise rows. Close up they are handsome to look at, puritanical but elegant and deeply moving. No squadron names are given but there is a beautifully carved badge for each man: for Tony the RAF eagle; for Sandy the emblem of the Royal Canadian Air Force. In the centre there is a large altar-shaped stone, which reads 'Their Name Liveth for Evermore'.

'Their Name Liveth for Evermore' – one has heard and read this phrase a thousand times, but still it carries the most immense emotional charge. Impossible for the tears not to come – each of these austere graves represents someone's life, someone's son, someone's brother, someone's lover, someone's best friend. You weep for those who were left as much as for those who had gone. At the senseless waste of it and at the unbearably touching nature of the sacrifice.

Most tombstones carry only the badge they were proud to wear, their rank, their work – pilot, air gunner, air bomber – their name, the date of their death, and a simple cross. In a very few cases, the relatives have added something, some few words of their own, within the allowed maximum of 20:

For Tony Lawrence, his age and the lines:

> Death doth hide
> But not divide
> Thou art
> But on Christ's other side

And for McLennan, the Canadian pilot fatally injured at Ingles Farm:

> I have fought a good fight
> I have finished my course
> I have kept the faith

The sheer enormity of the losses of that night becomes all too physically obvious as you look down at the graves and the names. Though the cemetery contains other victims of the fog of 16th and 17th December 1943, there is one row in which 23 (now 21, two have been exhumed) – are buried in one long terrible line. There is but one solitary interloper in the row, a man named Meridew, who died on December 11th.

The first grave is that of Pilot Officer C J Kinross, a New Zealand captain lost on 16th December from 75 Squadron. The plane had been on a mine-laying operation and crashed on return at Biddington Farm, at Sutton in Cambridgeshire. It is probably his two crewmates who have been exhumed and reburied elsewhere, no doubt taken back to their homelands – Flying Officer Jenkin, a New Zealander, and Sergeant Emmerson, an Australian.

The next grave is that of Squadron Leader Donald Forbes Mackenzie, killed on the edge of the airfield at Bourn. On his right lies Sandy Grant, and, by Sandy's side, Tony Lawrence. Beyond Tony is the 97 Squadron crew of Flight Sergeant Scott, who crashed at Graveley with the loss of everyone on board. The four Dominion crew are buried side by side, Scott, Irvine, Foxcroft and Hope. Beyond them is Flight Sergeant Crossgrove, the New Zealander killed in Squadron Leader Deverill's crash, in which all except James Benbow died.

Beyond Crossgrove lie McLennan and his navigator, Flying Officer Sheppard. Their two crew mates are buried separately further down the row, Warrant Officer Schneider, and Sergeant Roobroeck. Another 405 crew, that skippered by Flight Lieutenant Allan, intermingles with them – Flying Officer Stamers, Pilot Officer Collier, Sergeant Strang. The last of the 405 crews lost that night, captained by Flying Officer Drew, lie together, Flight Sergeant Mienert, Flight Sergeant Saunders, Warrant Officer Dobson, and Sergeant Bessent, only eighteen years old.

At the end of this poignant row of deaths from that disastrous night lies Flight Sergeant Tankard, of 83 Squadron, an Australian injured in a crash at Wyton, who died in Ely Hospital in the early hours of the morning of 17th December from his terrible head injuries.

All lie very close together, with only a few inches between each grave. The earth around the headstone is dark and freshly turned, and in it there grow a few small flowers.

III. RAF Hospital Ely

Joe's collapse in the operating theatre at Addenbrooke's in the early hours of the morning of 17th December was so dramatic that he was unconscious for nearly two days. (The arithmetic of the story in his memoir is not quite right, but there is no doubting the severity of his condition.) Some time on that Friday, his parents travelled up from Hertfordshire to be with him. In the first few hours after their arrival it must have looked very much as if they were going to lose him. When he at last regained consciousness on the Saturday evening, their relief must have been enormous.

> . . . [by] that time I had been unconscious for the rest of the night, all the next day and up until 8.45 pm [the following] night, a total of forty-four hours and when I gradually came to, I vaguely recognised Mum, and my first words were, 'Hello Mum, I've got a sore arse!' And indeed I had, because a portion of wrecked aeroplane had become embedded in my bum and it must have been very sharp.

If his parents were shocked by his appearance, they tactfully gave no sign of it. He was deathly pale, evidently extremely ill, and his face was covered with small superficial burns where the red-hot cinders from the fire had landed on it. There was no question of them going back home again – instead they found a hotel in Cambridge, so that they could stay close to him during those critical first few days.

His half-sister, Monica, came up on 20th December three days after the crash, to see Joe and to verify his condition for her parents. She was a fully trained doctor, and it is her letters to her husband, Michael, a Medical Officer caught up in the terrible war in Italy, which are the main surviving source of information about Joe's injuries. (The extracts were provided for me by my uncle Michael, as understandably the letters themselves are considered deeply personal and private.)

> [Joe] was just about as bad as he could be and still alive . . . he has no injuries to head, chest or abdomen, but the rest of him is in plaster. He has got a compound T-shaped fracture of his left femur with half the aeroplane in it; Pott's fractures of right ankle and puncture compound of right humerus. His chief trouble apart from shock was that he nearly bled to death before he was found.

'Before he was found' should, of course, read 'before medical help arrived'.

The commandeered school, The Leys, was not particularly well suited to its wartime role, being according to Herbert Bailey, another wartime patient, 'most depressing, with high windows, churchy windows. It was very dark and gloomy in there – it was not the best place to get better in and if I had stayed there, I don't think I would ever have got well.' At some date which he could not later recall, Joe was transferred from this dark gothic place to a proper ward at Addenbrooke's Hospital.

By Christmas Day, nine days after the crash, he was strong enough to be observant of what was going on around him though scarcely able to join in. The ward had been decorated and 'the Sister was wheeled into the ward in a wheelchair by two or three nurses who were obviously tipsy'. A special Christmas meal was served at lunch time, 'but I couldn't join in any fun or eat anything because I felt too ill'. It was traditional for these Christmas meals to be served by the senior doctors. A long table would be placed down the middle of the ward, with a small Christmas tree upon it, and those patients who were well enough sat at the table whilst those who were not watched from their beds.

A couple of days later, Joe had recovered enough to take in some details of his fellow RAF patients. There was a tall lanky man by the name of Brie who was suffering from dreadful frostbite in both hands, and a young man who had been on the run from Service Police 'because he was out late at night when he should not be, and in trying to escape, had been hit by a train and had lost an arm and a leg'. These two patients are the only ones whom Joe describes in his memoirs, though he writes several more paragraphs on his nine months of medical treatment.

Soon he was well enough to be transferred to the specialist RAF hospital at Ely. His admittance is noted in the hospital's ORB on 30th December, the very last entry for the year 1943. His rank is given as Flight Sergeant – his injuries are noted as 'fractured femur and humerus. Abrasions.' The Pott's fracture of the ankle is not mentioned.

At the time of Joe's admittance, RAF Hospital Ely had been open for some three and a half years. S C Rexford-Welch, in his three-volume tome, *The Royal Air Force Medical Services*, summarises why the hospital came into being:

> During the period of expansion which preceded the events at Munich in 1938, it was planned to set up numerous RAF stations in the Fens area which, owing to the flatness of the country and the complete absence of geographical features likely to impede flying, was particularly well suited to aerodrome construction. It was a foregone conclusion that a hospital of some considerable size would be needed to serve these stations.

The hospital was thus founded specifically to cater for the RAF casualties anticipated in the forthcoming war. Construction began in early 1938, but on the outbreak of war in September 1939 the hospital was by no means ready and instead a temporary annexe was commandeered – The Grange at Littleport, five miles north of Ely. Les Mitchum, an Orderly Clerk GD (General Duties), was the first RAF man into what would become known as the Littleport Annexe, which was taken over on the very first day of the war. It had been the Transport and General Workers Union convalescent home, and he recalled the chaos and mayhem of that first day – 'as we moved in, they were moving patients out'.

The Grange was a handsome Victorian building with flamboyant rounded turrets, but its charm was soon rather impaired by the usual proliferating gaggle of Nissen huts. Supposed to be a temporary measure, it in fact remained in use throughout the war as did so many other makeshift sites. It was to cater for any dermatological cases, treat patients with infectious diseases, or problems of the eye, and was used as Ely's overflow convalescent centre for both surgical and medical cases.

Ely Hospital was a very different place, a flagship hospital, designed and built for permanency. It was regarded with justifiable pride when it opened in August 1940, with its facilities not yet quite completed. Rexford-Welch writes:

> The construction of this hospital merits special mention since it was perhaps the most modern and well-built of all the RAF hospitals, although RAF Hospital, Wroughton, was later constructed on similar lines. It is a two-storied brick building, designed in the shape of the letter H, with the wards running out at right angles from the cross stroke. Viewed from a distance the most striking feature is the large area of window space; the pleasantly rounded glass windows of the wards all face south to obtain the maximum amount of sunshine and all have solarium facilities.

The hospital had many distinctive features, including a main corridor said to be a quarter of a mile long and a most handsome modernistic staircase. Nor had the design of its grounds been neglected – large and beautiful gardens surrounded it, containing many specimen trees and shrubs donated by Kew Gardens, though the lawns which were supposed to set them off had mostly been sacrificed to the 'Dig for Victory' campaign.

When first opened, the total number of beds in the hospital was 230. However, further accommodation was added later, particularly in the run-up to D-Day. By 1944, the authorities had learned their lesson about pre-planning and erected many additional Nissen huts in the grounds in anticipation of a flood of casualties, but most fortunately they were never needed.

The hospital had a high repute and was one of the best equipped Service hospitals in Britain. It was the hospital to which all the injured or sick RAF men were brought from the 40 RAF stations within a 50 mile radius of Ely. Besides departments of general medicine, it had a physiotherapy and burns centre. For the latter it was especially renowned. It was a tragic feature of life in the bomber squadrons that the most dreadful burns were often sustained by aircrew, either on operations or in accidents back in England. The standard treatment for burns at that time was saline baths, for it had been observed that those who came down in the sea had a better prognosis than those who did not. Saline baths were a horribly painful process. Tom Williams, an orthopaedic patient, himself badly smashed up, with one leg amputated and in danger of losing the other, remembered how sorry they had all been for the burns cases and how terrible it had been when they had to take those baths – 'it was agony for them, poor devils'.

Wing Commander George Morley was the Burns Specialist at Ely, and he had been trained by the famous Archie McIndoe, of the Queen Victoria Hospital at East Grinstead. McIndoe himself came to the ward once a month, to see who had recovered enough for plastic surgery – 'You, you and you, down to East Grinstead!' Then would come a horrendous series of operations; some men had as many as 30 or 40.

Ely was very much a military hospital, and kept the same RAF Form 540 which was filled in for the bomber squadrons. However, all the patients who are listed on these forms, still surviving at the Public Records Office, are very serious cases. Ely was not confined to such patients, and the hospital also treated many minor injuries, minor health complaints, or carried out comparatively minor operations, but these must have been documented under a different system.

Though the surviving ORB is not particularly detailed and seems to have been somewhat erratically compiled, one can still trace the progress of a few of the injured of the night of 16th/17th December 1943. The first entries are for the 17th itself. Flight Lieutenant Allan, the Canadian pilot from 405 Squadron who crashed near Graveley, is on the DI (Dangerously Ill) list with a fractured skull. (He was transferred later to St Hughes Hospital, Oxford, and died there on 28th December.) From Bourn, it is noted that Keith Kirby, of Squadron Leader Mackenzie's crew, is on the DI list with a fractured spine, whilst James Benbow, the sole survivor from Squadron Leader Deverill's crew, is less ill despite severe burns to the face and hands and a fractured leg – he is placed on the SI (Seriously Ill) list.

Deaths are also very briefly noted. Flight Officer McLennan, the Canadian captain of the Lancaster which crashed at Ingles Farm, killing all the crew except him and Clair Nutting, survived only long enough to be admitted to the hospital where he died of multiple fractures. Flight Sergeant Tankard of 83 Squadron, the Australian injured in a crash at Wyton, died only four hours after he was admitted from a fractured skull and brain damage. Also from that Wyton crash was Sergeant H Day, who was on the

DI list with a fractured right femur and scapula. His condition improved and he was transferred to the SI list the same day, 17th December, and came off the SI list on 20th December.

Clair Nutting, who had arrived at the hospital in the same ambulance as his dying captain, is not noted in the ORB, having been admitted for observation only. He was to spend about a week at the hospital. His words in a recent letter conjure up the sheer chaos of the scene, after so many patients had been brought in at once due to the terrible series of crashes caused by the fog.

> Though I have a vivid recollection of the last few nights there, I recall nothing of the first part of my stay. It seemed very crowded. In my ward were many burn victims, who were incredibly brave about their terrible injuries, which they made light of by indulging in the black humour of often grotesque jokes that would touch your heart. Other patients were in traction. Still others were psychiatric cases who would wake screaming and try to get away. There must have been, though I was unaware of them at the time, others like myself, who were only under observation and subsequent examination for the effects of concussion.

Joe was in the orthopaedic wards, but some of his fellow patients would also have had burn injuries, such as James Benbow from Joe's own squadron, who had been severely burned in Deverill's crash at Graveley. In addition, in the grounds of the hospital to which all but the sickest were taken out for air, Joe would have seen many other patients who had suffered the most appalling disfigurement, scarring, maiming, and, in the worst cases, blinding. The plight of these unfortunate souls made a permanent impression on him.

The surgeon in charge of fractures at Ely, as indeed he was for the whole of the RAF, was the foremost orthopaedic surgeon in England, a civilian, Reginald Watson-Jones, also Surgeon General to the Royal Household. His contribution was so outstanding that he was later knighted for his wartime services. His influence – indeed the word genius is not too extreme – can be traced through all the RAF centres for the treatment of the wounded, and the rehabilitation centres to which they went after recovery which brought them back to the highest degree of mobility attainable.

During the war, knowledge on how to treat fractures and their associated problems expanded at an exponential rate. In 1943, Watson-Jones brought out a revised version of his January 1940 book, *Fractures and Joint Injuries*, which reflected the enormous changes of the last three years. He wrote in his introduction, 'Much has been learned and scarcely one page of the book remains untouched . . .'. There had been unparalleled opportunities to learn about hitherto rare conditions – he gives as an example the fact that nearly all previous studies of fracture-dislocation of the talus had been based on isolated cases, but in the first two years of the war he personally had reviewed 75. The huge increase in knowledge meant that the 1943 edition of his book was 200 pages longer and published in 2 volumes, with many photographs.

It is a spectacularly gruesome publication. I opened it up at random to come face to face with two pictures of the most sickeningly graphic nature – the left-hand one, mercifully in black and white, showing gangrene of the arm caused by the misuse of a tourniquet, the right-hand one in nightmare technicolour showing the innocuously named 'immersion feet', the feet in question hardly being recognisable as such with their swellings and protrusions of charred necrotic black and whelk-like orange, shiny and unnatural as plastic.

The patient in question was a pilot, who had been adrift in the North Sea in a dinghy for fourteen days. He had no food at all, and was without water to drink for the last six days. Under the picture of his poor gangrenous feet, the caption notes 'His life was saved by a seagull'. Eagerly one turns to the text to read this touching and heartwarming story, only to find that the pilot had in fact eaten the bird which, exhausted, had alighted on his dinghy: 'With relish and no aversion, he ate the bird; he sucked its brains and enjoyed its blood; he ate a small fish in its belly'.

This very vivid telling of the pilot's story is characteristic of Watson-Jones's style, which immediately rivets one's attention. The book is very readable in a way which few medical textbooks can be. It is also outstandingly sympathetic and humane. At a time when doctors were looked upon as little short of gods, Watson-Jones unquestionably sided with the men he was treating. He believed above all in the accountability of doctors and their sacred duty to do their very best by their patients.

Watson-Jones had an absolutely revolutionary attitude to injuries which would formerly have led to amputation or the permanent crippling and disablement of those who had suffered them. His attitude is epitomised by a jaunty picture in his book, which shows two RAF men – their upper parts, necks and heads almost entirely corsetted in plaster – playing cricket, with the caption 'In 1943 it is possible to break your neck and enjoy it'.

Watson-Jones came to Ely Hospital at least once a month. 'W.J.' was a favourite with both patients and staff for his cheerfulness and inspiring optimism. No one who remembers him can speak highly enough of him – 'he was a quiet man, with very nice manners' – 'he was very very nice, an unwinding sort of bloke'. An ex-patient, Leslie Morgan, remembers him as being of medium height, dark-haired, and 'very much the eminent physician or consultant, very smartly dressed with exceptionally nice clothes'. His clothes would have been particularly noticeable in contrast to the uniforms habitually worn by all the medical staff at Ely – even the ward rounds were conducted by the Commanding Officer and Medical Officers in full RAF uniform, which looks very strange to modern eyes.

The Commanding Officer at Ely in early 1944 was Group Captain G P O'Connell. He appears in a photograph of the weekly CO's inspection, a tall man, impressive looking, and immaculately turned out. All the Commanding Officers were chiefly remembered for their once weekly inspection when they went on the ward rounds with a 'terrific entourage, quite a retinue', as Valerie Cornford, then Valerie Blackwell, a sister of Princess Mary's RAF Nursing Service, described it. Everything was supposed to be even more immaculately neat and tidy than it was usually. The obsession with military tidiness extended even to the patients, who if they were up were supposed to stand to attention by the bed, or if bedridden were not supposed to lounge about but lie neatly and quietly whilst the Commanding Officer spoke to them. The men complied with this, though out of earshot of the CO there was much grumbling about it. Valerie Blackwell remembers that one of the chaps said to her one day, 'Sister, if we were all dead in our beds, it would be much tidier'.

Ely was Valerie Blackwell's first posting after she became a fully fledged nursing sister. She found it difficult at first to adjust to being in a military hospital. All the nursing staff were under military discipline. In addition, there was a terrific amount to learn, not least all the RAF jargon and slang which was a closed book to outsiders, and also the exact ranks – 'people would get very huffy if you called them by the wrong rank'.

The head of the nursing staff was Miss J D Jackson, a Squadron Leader. Unlike the sisters who were all in white, she wore a dark blue uniform with magnificent buttons down the front, dark stockings and black shoes. Jack Reynolds, a surgical patient, remembers that Miss Jackson 'seemed a bit of an old crab, but she only appeared that way – she was not really, she was a lovely person'. He recalls the time that she intervened when he and a couple of others, now fairly recuperated, were deputed to push the big electric dinner trolleys at meal times. These dinner trolleys came up in the lifts from the kitchens, and they were extremely heavy. When Miss Jackson discovered what was going on, she immediately put a stop to it – 'I am not having my boys doing that hard work'. It was probably just as well, because the game was to ride the dinner trolley down the spacious corridor which gave ample room for getting up speed. One gave the trolley a bit of a push and, once it had gathered sufficient momentum, jumped up and put one's feet on the bars. There had already been a minor crash, in which some of the plates had fallen off and broken, and something more serious might soon have taken place. Jack Reynolds and his friends, now bursting with youth and health, were always up to mischief and he remembers the punishment being that one had to fold swabs for hours. The swabs came in large squares and one had to fold them into small squares until one's mind was numb with boredom. Another similar punishment was folding blankets.

Miss Jackson, who accompanied the CO on his weekly tour of

inspection, also made her own daily round. On Jack Reynolds' ward, there was a slightly unpopular sister whom they called Dicky Bird. Dicky Bird wanted everything just so – the tiny bedside lockers always had to be arranged in a certain way, with the cigarette ration neatly piled up, the towel folded, the soap in the right place, the blues (RAF uniform) at the bottom with the shirt and tie in their mathematically correct position. Resenting this regimentation, the patients would play tricks on her, 'we used to drive her wild'. A favourite joke was unwinding a toilet roll up and down the ward in between the bed legs just when the Matron's inspection was due. On another occasion, there being no place to hide a cake in those immaculately arranged lockers, they hid it under the wire cage which kept the blanket off one particular patient's injured legs. Unfortunately, when the CO came round, he said 'I want to have a look at this chap's legs', and then the cake was discovered, to the dismay and embarrassment of Dicky Bird.

The Surgeon-in-Charge at Ely, who operated at least twice upon my father, was a fiery-tempered Irishman, Wing Commander Jimmy Armstrong. Armstrong was proverbial for his rages in the theatre, in which he would use the most blood-curdling language and hurl his instruments to the floor. On one occasion he asked a member of the theatre staff for a scalpel, and when she passed him one, flung it away in a fit of rage, 'This bugger's blunt'. All the orderlies wore gym shoes, and the scalpel went through the thin material of one of these and cut the woman's foot. History does not record that Armstrong was particularly repentant.

When Tom Williams went in for an operation on his remaining leg, which was stapled with two pins through the fibula, the anaesthetic mixture was not strong enough and half way through the operation it wore off. Tom Williams came to just as Armstrong was pulling out one of the pins. As soon as Armstrong became aware of this horrific fact, he bawled out, 'Oh for Christ's sake!', hurled his gory instrument on the floor, and shouting 'Give me that bloody syringe!' shot Tom Williams through with dope so that he could feel no more.

Tom Williams bore Armstrong no grudge – 'he was miserable looking but a hell of a nice chap when you got to know him'. Armstrong was small in build, as thin as a rail, with a weasel-like face, and a characteristically pugnacious moustache, the only one of the doctors who wore one. He also never wore an officer's peaked cap, but instead the soft simple cap known as a 'fore-and-aft'. He smoked like a chimney and had duodenal ulcers, a possible cause for his rages. Valerie Blackwell, who worked with him as his Theatre Sister for almost two years, remembers one occasion when he slapped up the latest X-ray of his ulcers and asked if she wanted to see them. 'Not particularly' retorted Valerie. Armstrong turned away, amused, and studying his picture noted with satisfaction, 'It looks as if the rats have been at it'.

Armstrong frequently reduced the girls who worked with him in the operating theatre to tears. David Page, a rehabilitation instructor who worked with the patients, said about him, 'he had a terrible, terrible temper – he was the most marvellous surgeon but he was one terror. It was extraordinary – he was the only one of that type there – the others were all so easy-going.' Armstrong had two assistants, Flight Lieutenant Hughes and Squadron Leader Guest, both of whom were mildness itself compared to him. He also had several regular staff to assist him in the theatre; in particular, there was LAC Karlstaat, 'his favourite, his blue-eyed boy'.

Armstrong had a fearsome reputation altogether. One often repeated hospital story was that he had removed his own appendix by means of a mirror whilst under a local anaesthetic. One of Armstrong's nicknames in the hospital was 'The Maestro'. He probably also had several others a great deal less flattering.

There were two orthopaedic wards at Ely, Ward 2 and Ward 3. Ward 2 was known as the 'clean' ward and Ward 3 as the 'dirty' or 'stinking' ward. Ward 3 had all the cases where fractures had become infected, and at times the smell in there was unbelievably awful, like nothing on earth. Peter Lawler's worst memory was of the unfortunate Peter Harper, who had suffered very serious gunshot wounds in a Lancaster. These wounds became gangrenous, and the stench was so appalling that he was put out in the solarium, the long glassed-in verandah adjoining the ward. Herbert Bailey, whose wound also became gangrenous, remembers how putting such patients in the solarium was common practice in order to give the others in the ward 'a bit of relief'. The stink of such wounds was almost unbearable in hot summer weather. Ely was surrounded by farmland, and he remembered how masses of flies would descend on his sheets – he would give a wave and they would go off in a great cloud, but only for a moment before settling back again.

Ely Hospital, under Watson-Jones's direction, practised the closed plaster treatment for all fractures. This included fractures in which it was hoped to avoid infection, fractures which had already become infected, and even fractures associated with burns – Watson-Jones often advocated such a treatment for burns even when no fracture was involved. On the surface of things it would seem the height of insanity to simply cover up infected wounds in this manner, but it was the best treatment available at the time and gave most strikingly successful results.

The closed plaster treatment called for the most scrupulous care if a wound associated with a fracture was not already infected, and nerves of steel and a skilled hand if it was: 'Be bold; saucerise the wound; a 10-inch wound heals as quickly as a 3-inch wound; leave no pocket or recess . . . lightly pack with vaseline gauze; immobilise in plaster; watch the temperature chart . . .'

The wounds, once thoroughly cleansed and plastered over, continued to make their presence felt. If, regardless of all precautions, they became infected, the plasters surrounding them would become heavily stained and a foul smell might arise. In the worse cases there might be streams of pus running out of the ends of the plaster, and the wound might even become infected with maggots, which contrary to expectation could actually be beneficial.

Such a treatment could only succeed if the closest eye was kept on the patient's condition, with daily monitoring of the pulse and temperature, and a careful watch on the patient's general health. Not only was there the risk of the infection rioting out of control, but there was also the possibility of the much dreaded plaster sore, which could lead to the flesh rotting right back to the bone.

In instances of severe infection, the first plaster put on would be one of several. This is what happened in my father's case because his contaminated leg fracture went septic. Because of the pain involved, such plasters were invariably removed under anaesthetic, the wound redressed whilst the patient was still out, and the plaster replaced before he regained consciousness.

Ward 3 was full of such cases. It is remembered as having a great atmosphere, and that it was far more easy-going than the other wards where the floors always shined twice as brightly, so brightly it seemed that one could shave in them.

'They were mad in Ward 3, but very loyal to the nurses as long as they were not pushed around' said Tom Williams. One sister, who was far too domineering and obsessed with neatness, was got rid of after she had refused to let a man have his breakfast until he had shaved and washed properly – there was a campaign against her and eventually she was sent to the Ultima Thule of Littleport. Because so many of the men were in Ward 3 for months, it was easy to produce the kind of social cohesion which led to the dumping of unpopular staff. The long-stayers were also pretty tough on what they called 'weekend cases', patients with simple straightforward broken legs or arms. When these got dumped in the ward with the hardened cases, woebetide them if they moaned, for 'they were ribbed like heck', teased and taunted unmercifully until they learnt to bear their afflictions with more grace.

But there was also laughter, and crazy games. The ward had access to the grounds of the hospital, and men would wind one another up by referring to the ghost of the headless airgunner, who was said to walk at nights 'over at the back of the garden there'. Ghosts were in fact rather popular. One of the favourites was the phantom who propelled the ward's wheelchairs. All the wheelchairs were lined up neatly down the middle of the ward at night, and those patients who were more mobile would creep out of bed, select a wheelchair and tie cotton threads to it, rigging it up quite carefully, and then at a given moment it would start to roll eerily across the gleaming polished floor, leading to hysterical giggles smothered in the pillows of those who were in the know.

My father came off the SI list on 8th January, which meant that his life was no longer in any danger. He had recovered his general health fairly quickly, and when Monica visited him again in mid-January, she was able to report to Michael, 'Joe is simply wonderful now . . . has a normal colour and fairly happy in spite of [being] in plaster practically from head to toe. He is off the danger list now . . . He still doesn't remember anything about the crash.' His memory was to come back in patches over the course of time.

Altogether, Joe would spend six months at Ely Hospital. During this period, he records in his memoir that he had three blood transfusions, and three operations. At least two of the latter must have been for the purpose of removing a plaster, checking his wounds and replastering. The third was far more serious, because his severely injured left leg had to be re-fractured and reset. My father comments rather tetchily, 'I don't know why [they had to refracture the leg], but I had no choice in the matter because I was not just a patient, but I was also subject to military discipline and I had to obey orders'. After this last setback, he rapidly improved.

Incredibly, there still exists a theatre list for Armstrong's patients, dated 24th January 1944. Armstrong's blue-eyed boy, LAC Karlstaat, was in attendance in the theatre, together with three other orderlies. My father is 9th on the list of patients to be treated, and his notes state 'GSW elbow – replaster (bed)'. '(bed)' means he was taken into the theatre in his bed, because he was in traction and therefore could not be moved on a trolley for obvious reasons. GSW stands for gunshot wound, and is a most astounding piece of information, as no one in my family ever knew before this piece of paper surfaced that my father had been shot in the elbow, and there is every reason to suspect he did not know it himself. Monica referred in her first letter about his injuries only to 'puncture compound fracture of the humerus', but then she had never actually seen the wound as it was covered in plaster on the first night at the Addenbrooke's annexe. Had the bullet gone clean through the arm, as it apparently did, there was no particular reason to mention it afterwards given the severity of his other injuries and the words 'puncture compound' adequately covered it.

Where had he received this wound? There is not the slightest particle of evidence that K-King had run into trouble on the homeward journey, and it seems that the only possible explanation was that Joe was hit shortly after the crash, whilst still unconscious, by one of the bullets set off by the fire. This is therefore the explanation I have given in my account of the crash.

The survival of this theatre list is nothing short of miraculous. The Theatre Sister that night was Valerie Blackwell, who worked with Armstrong in the theatre in 1943-1944. In 1944 Armstrong wrote a book called *Bone Grafting in the Treatment of Fractures*. This was published in 1945, and Valerie Blackwell bought a copy of the book to remind her of her days with him. She still had one of the theatre lists, and she placed it in the book, because it was Armstrong's list and Armstrong's book. The list

remained in the book for 53 years, until Tom Williams told his friend
Margaret Bull that I was looking for information about Ely Hospital, and
Margaret Bull told her friend, now Valerie Cornford. Valerie Cornford
rang me and gave me much valuable information. She also asked me what
my father's name was. And there was my father's name on the one and
only operating theatre list that she had kept. With the greatest generosity
she sent it to me as a present, a frail scrap of yellowing paper, typed in blue
ink with pencil emendations, which had survived against the most far-
fetched of odds.

IV. The Death of Leslie Laver

Around the time that he had this operation on his arm at the end of January,
Joe was visited by the Welfare officer, and 'when I again asked him about
the other members of my crew, he told me that they were all dead'.

They were all dead. Not only those who had died in the crash but also
Leslie Laver, who had helped save his life.

On 14th January, scarcely one month after the crash, on the first
operation he had flown since that night, Leslie had gone missing with his
new crew.

Much later it would become known that five of the crew had died but
two had survived to become PoWs. It was from one of these PoWs, half a
century later, that I learned many details of what had happened that night.

Flight Sergeant Albert C East, always known to his crew as 'Ace'
because of his initials, had been a printer before the war. He had originally
gone into the RAF as a mechanic, but whilst he was on the mechanic's
course the RAF, who had been losing far too many pilots, scrapped the
position of Second Pilot and replaced it with that of Flight Engineer. They
asked for volunteers to retrain and Ace was one of these. After completing
his St Athan's course, he joined the crew of Kenneth Munro Steven as their
seventh and last member at 1656 Conversion Unit, Lindholme, Yorkshire,
on 26th June 1943.

After six weeks at the CU, just as Ted's crew were to do five months
later, Steven's crew became direct entrants to the Pathfinder Force. Having
completed the PFF's standard fortnight training at Upwood, they arrived at
Bourn on 8th August. Between August and January 1944, they flew nearly
thirty operations, over half of the required tour of 45.

Flight Lieutenant Kenneth Munro Steven, known affectionately to his
crew as 'Steve', was a very able pilot who would be posthumously awarded
the DFC. He had worked for a bank in civilian life and at thirty years of age
was older than most wartime pilots. His bomb aimer, Pilot Officer Ridley
Brown, was the only other officer in the crew. Easy going, dark-haired,
with a neat moustache, 'Rid' came from Hexham in the north of England.

Flight Sergeant Samuel Stevenson, the navigator, was a replacement for
their original navigator, Jimmy Rainsford, who had been shot down whilst
replacing a member of another crew on the Nürnberg raid of 27th/28th

August. (Jimmy Rainsford survived and, after walking hundreds of miles, got out through Spain and returned to England, one of the minuscule group of nine men from 97 Squadron who became successful evaders in 1943.) Samuel Stevenson was a quiet and serious young man of 22 years of age. Always known as 'Paddy', he came from Belfast in Northern Ireland. He was to be posthumously awarded the DFM.

Flight Sergeant William Gadsby, 'Bill', was the wireless operator, again fairly old for the RAF, being 27 years of age, and, like most of the crew, married. Clifford Skinner, 'Jack', the mid-upper gunner, was more typical, being only 22, but he too had a wife, Edith.

The crew's usual rear gunner was Sergeant K D Newman – Ken.

The crew had been through some bad times together, but with the commencement of the Battle of Berlin in mid-November, there had begun a period of increasing stress with ever more exhausting demands being made upon them. The crew missed the opening raid of 18th/19th November but flew those which began on 22nd, 23rd, 25th, 26th, and then December 2nd and 3rd. They were fortunate to miss the disastrous night of the 16th/17th, and the raid which followed four days later on 20th/21st, because they were on leave – the bomber crews had seven days leave every six weeks. They returned to ops on 23rd December, and also flew the raid of 29th. In January of the new year, they flew the raids beginning the 1st, the 2nd and the 5th, their penultimate raid.

During these operations, they saw some very dangerous times. Their favourite Lancaster, P-Peter, took a beating on the night of 22nd/23rd November; the ORB reports 'Bomb doors would not close after bombing and the hydraulic system rendered u/s [unusable] by flak'. Steve got the aircraft back but it was badly damaged and had to be taken out of service for repairs. The next raid they flew in a different Lancaster, Q-Queenie. P-Peter was repaired in time for the operation of 25th/26th November, and they flew the three following raids in it until they went on their December leave. Whilst they were away, P-Peter became one of the casualties of Black Thursday; flown by Squadron Leader Deverill, it crashed, out of petrol, into the bomb dump at Graveley, burst into flames, and was completely destroyed. On their return, the crew had to make do with several different aircraft. In one of these, on the Berlin attack of 29th/30th December, they were again severely hit by flak. The outer port engine was damaged and caught fire, and the plane's fuselage was badly holed. Steve got the Lancaster home on three engines, earning a mention for this in the ORB.

Leslie Laver, who had been placed on ground duty on 17th December, the day after K-King's crash, returned to flying duties on the 30th. As was all too often the case, little allowance could be made for any trauma he had suffered in the horrific accident which only he and Joe had survived.

As he had lost his entire crew, Leslie had become a 'spare bod', one who would step in when other crews were short of a rear gunner. But for the first two weeks of January no such occasion arose, and during this period he was probably helping out the station's armourers as they tested guns and gun turrets or loaded the ammunition belts for the aircraft. It must have been a very difficult period of readjustment for him.

The other two lightly injured survivors of the crash night were from Squadron Leader Mackenzie's crew. Flight Sergeant Hunter and Flight Sergeant Lang were transferred back to flying duty on 11th January, but on the 13th Lang once more had to be returned to ground duty. Next to his name in the ORB is that of Ken Newman, the rear gunner of Steven's plane, who is also noted as being taken off flying duties. There had been no operations since 5th/6th January, but in the anticipation that they would begin again shortly Ken Newman was barred from flying by the MO because he had a skin complaint. To such flukes of luck did men owe or lose their lives. Ken Newman could not fly, so Leslie took his place.

As the replacement rear gunner, Leslie had no time to get to know the crew, in fact Albert East does not recall them ever having flown with him before. He does not remember whether Leslie was introduced to them at the briefing, or simply scrambled onto the aircraft at the last minute – he recalls nothing about him, he was 'just a body dressed up', boarding the aircraft in the near-darkness of the winter's evening before settling down in his turret far away from the rest of the crew.

The raid of 14th/15th January, consisting of 496 Lancasters and 2 Halifaxes, was made against the German city of Brunswick. Smaller than Bomber Command's usual targets, Brunswick was also one hundred miles closer to home than Berlin. This signified one hour's less flying over a particularly dangerous section of the Reich, and probably all had breathed a sigh of relief when the destination had been revealed in the afternoon briefing at Bourn. Brunswick was not a prime target, although it was an important transportation centre lying on the direct rail link between Berlin and the Ruhr – the South Marshalling Yard was one of the biggest in Germany. It also contained two Messerschmitt factories. It had never suffered a major raid before, and its ground defences were nothing like as formidable as Berlin's, but, as Air Commodore John Searby later wrote in *The Bomber Battle for Berlin*, 'it lay in an area stiff with nightfighters grouped for the defence of the German capital'.

As twilight deepened, 97 Squadron's 21 planes took off at much the same time as on the Berlin raid one month earlier. Already the days were drawing out a little, and it was lighter than it had been on 16th December – the silhouettes of the departing Lancasters stood out clearly in the darkening sky as a handful of well-wishers waved them off. Steven's plane, S-Sugar, left at 16.46. As this was a very experienced Pathfinder crew, S-Sugar was carrying red, green and yellow PFF flares, as well as the very large 4,000 lb bomb known as a cookie.

The shorter distances involved meant that the squadron's aircraft would be back early in the evening, before ten o'clock for the leaders, the stragglers coming in at intervals for around an hour afterwards.

When 97 Squadron reached Brunswick just after seven o'clock, they found the target cloud-covered. The defences were slight, with the searchlights ineffective and the heavy flak inaccurate, firing well below the height of the aircraft. Charles Owen was still keeping a diary of his operations. His style was always laconic in the extreme, and about this raid he noted on his safe return to Bourn:

> Surprisingly quiet trip and very little opposition. 10/10 cloud at
> the target and markings rather scattered. Long stooge home, but
> quiet except for some heavy flak from Brussels. Pleasant
> change from the City.

He was lucky to have met with so little opposition. The squadron's ORB notes, 'Fighters were very active from coast to target and on the return'. In fact, the Germans picked up the bomber force only 40 miles off the English coast, and entered the stream soon after the German frontier was crossed near Bremen, continuing to shoot down aircraft until the enemy coast was crossed on the return home. The losses this night were the heaviest for six weeks, 38 aircraft altogether, with eleven of the missing planes being Pathfinders.

Unrealised as yet by the RAF, the Luftwaffe were now perfecting their long-term tactical plan to counteract the effects of Window. Known as *Zahme Sau*, Tame Boar, it revolutionised the deployment of the twin-engined night fighters whose radar sets had hitherto been blinded by Window. Using new radar equipment, and a change of tactics, the fighters could now follow the bombers from coast to target and back again, the attacks being continuous due to the stationing of different units at various places along the bomber routes. Long-range Junkers 88s and upward-firing *Schräge Musik* (slanting music) cannons meant that the German fighter defence was becoming ever more deadly. *Schräge Musik* used only dim tracer and was very difficult for other aircraft to spot in the darkness. If the fighter using *Schräge Musik* took advantage of the Lancaster's blind spot and crept up stealthily beneath its belly, the likely ignition of the petrol tanks in an attack would mean the crew would never know what had hit them and neither would any of their fellows flying near by. So apparently unexplained were some of the mid-air explosions being reported by the bomber crews that they were put down as 'scarecrow flares', fired by the Germans to affect the crews' morale. Scarecrow flares were, in fact, almost certainly completely fictitious. Bomber Command Intelligence did not realise what the real danger was for far too long.

The Brunswick raid was not a success. The Pathfinder markers were scattered, no continuous concentration of bombing was achieved, and the aiming was inaccurate. Many bombs fell in the countryside well to the south of Brunswick, and the city report quoted in *The Bomber Command*

War Diaries gives the result as only 10 houses destroyed and 14 people killed. The price of this was some 266 of Bomber Command's best young men. Amongst those who never made it back to England was the crew of Kenneth Steven.

The only other crew missing from those sent from Bourn that night was that of Pilot Officer Hodgson. All his men were sergeants. All but J B Nicol, the bomb aimer, had come from Wigsley on 20th December, just as Leslie's first crew had done one month earlier. Due no doubt to manpower shortages, they were immediately sent out on an operation. They survived that first raid to Berlin on 2nd/3rd January, and the one to Stettin on 5th/6th, but lost their lives on this third trip.

The ORB records the losses of the night in its standard terse but moving format: 'F/Lt Steven and crew, P/O Hodgson and crew are missing, nothing heard since'.

Amongst Charles Owen's papers at The Imperial War Museum is the flight plan for this operation drawn up by his navigator, Bill Shires. It shows the flak areas roughly scribbled over in crayon, including the West Frisian islands at the top of Holland, Hanover, Brunswick itself, Magdeburg, and the huge and lethally dangerous area of the Ruhr marked out by Dusseldorf, Aachen, Koln, Essen, Dortmund, Munster and Duisburg. The return route avoided this black spot, necessitating an extremely long flight back, far longer than the outward journey, crossing Belgium and leaving Belgium territory just above Bruges. Landfall in England was on the Suffolk coast at Southwold – the lighthouse there was a useful navigation point.

What is odd is that Steven's plane, S-Sugar, was not following this, apparently the official route home. Instead, it virtually retraced the path of its outward flight. Albert East did not recall them having had any earlier trouble which might have necessitated a quicker route home, 'we weren't shot up at all'. He could not think of any reason why their route had changed. What was certain, however, was that they had indeed been to the target and were on their way back, for the 4,000 lb cookie was no longer on board.

S-Sugar was hit immediately after crossing the coast of Texel, at about half past eight in the evening. Texel was a notorious hot-spot, and that S-Sugar had ventured near the island at all is another mystery, particularly as the Lancaster was not flying especially high at around 10,000 feet.

Belonging to Holland, Texel had been occupied by the Germans along with the rest of Dutch territory. It was a very prominent feature on the enemy coastline, being the first and largest of the string of West Frisian or Wadden islands. Texel had only one big town, Den Burg, though there were several other settlements and hamlets. Otherwise the place was lightly populated, its inhabitants being mostly fishermen or farmers. It was very beautiful territory with extensive sand flats and salt marshes, and in the interior much rich pastureland reclaimed from the sea, divided up by reed-grown drainage ditches. There was an abundance of birds and wild life. The west side of the island, that which faced the North Sea, was edged by immense white sand beaches and shifting sand dunes bordered by pine trees.

Texel was an extremely important part of Germany's Atlantic Wall. Because of this and its usefulness as a navigation point for the English bomber crews, it was home to German heavy flak installations. Two of the flak installations directly faced the North Sea – the Nordbatterie at the Krimweg in the Eierlandse dunes, and the Sudbatterie at Pompevlak, at the other end of the island. There was a third installation in the centre of the island at Ongeren. Texel was, in fact, so notorious for its fire-power that it was often used as an alternative target for bombers which had to turn back for technical reasons; this was the last scrap of enemy territory which could be bombed before the perilous crossing of the North Sea.

The North Sea – all the crews breathed a sigh of relief when they got clear of the enemy coast, but the Sea itself was implacably dangerous and hostile to a bomber in trouble. Ditching was very tricky in the best of conditions; on a dark cold night in the middle of winter, it was a hellish option. If, despite considerable damage to the aircraft and the huge waves likely at that time of year, the Lancaster managed to come down straight on the water, there were only seconds to get clear before it sank. There would be a mad scramble for the lifeboat, bucking and tossing in the swell in total blackness. Once in the lifeboat, your troubles were only just beginning. It would only be by the greatest good fortune that the survivors would be picked up before the dinghy was overturned by mountainous waves, or they died of exposure. The wireless operator was supposed to transmit the aircraft's position at the last possible moment, but if he left it too late no such message would be sent. Even if he succeeded, a tiny dinghy was virtually impossible to spot even once daylight stole over the endless wastes of grey water. Only a tiny number of such aircrew were saved from the sea by Coastal Command or Air Sea Rescue, or by the enemy themselves. Most died, going down with the plane, parachuting in and drowning, or making it into a dinghy only to perish of exposure. Theirs are amongst the names recorded on the Runnymede Memorial, missing, no known grave.

For the only two survivors of S-Sugar's destruction, it was fortunate indeed that the aircraft did not reach the North Sea before it was attacked. Lieutenant Kurt Matzak, flying a Messerschmitt 110 from the nearby German base at Leeuwarden, was the one who claimed the hit. However, when questioned many years later by Ab A. Jansen, the author of the Dutch book *Wespennest Leeuwarden* (Wasp's Nest Leeuwarden), Kurt Matzak said he thought that the plane had gone down in the waves 60 kilometres from the coast, so it appears he had been mistaken about his victim. According to the German authorities, S-Sugar was the only aircraft shot down in the area that night – Kurt Matzak may have thought he had made a kill when in fact he had not.

Whoever was the attacker – whether it was a nightfighter as Rid Brown was later to testify or a flak installation as Albert East thought at the time – S-Sugar went down so quickly that it never reached the North Sea but crashed in the pine woods which edged the western sand dunes.

At the time of the attack, all the crew were beginning to feel that the worst was over, 'we were thinking we were nearly home', and nobody saw a thing which might have warned them that they were in the gravest danger. In fact, seconds before the catastrophe, Albert East, 'Ace', had been down to the blister in the bomb-aimer's position in the nose to check as best as he could underneath the plane, and had seen nothing – all seemed clear. Neither of the two gunners, Jack or Leslie, noticed anything either. It was as if the attack materialised out of nothing; 'we didn't have a clue what it was, we never dreamed that it was an aircraft underneath shooting up at us'. All they could think of was that the flak had caught them, that somewhere, down in the darkness far below, an unseen gun emplacement or flakship had targeted them.

S-Sugar was almost certainly crossing the east coast of Texel when suddenly, completely without warning, the attack commenced. A burst of something tremendous hitting them, and one of the engines caught fire. Steve called Ace back to feather (shutdown) the engine in question; even as he did so, there was another burst, and a second engine caught fire. Ace feathered that one also, then all at once the situation became critical, with the petrol tanks igniting and the plane catching fire from wing to wing. Steve yelled over the intercom to the crew to abandon the aircraft, 'Parachute, parachute, jump, jump, jump'. An instant later he spoke over the radio to Bourn, transmitting the last message they would ever send, informing base that they were on fire over Texel and that they were abandoning the aircraft in the air.

S-Sugar was losing height rapidly though Steve struggled at the controls to keep it going long enough for the crew to bale out. Leslie's state of mind when he realised that yet another appalling tragedy was imminent, that his second operation was going to end as horrifically as the first, is too dreadful to imagine. One can only hope that things happened so quickly, the need for action was so pressing, that he did not have much time to think. As Ace said, 'We were too busy to be frightened'.

In a controlled bale-out, the bomb-aimer, navigator, flight-engineer, and w/op, would leave by the front hatch in the nose, whilst the two gunners went out through the main door close to the tail. With the automatic pilot in control, the pilot would check that all had gone, and only then would he return to the nose and leave by the front hatch.

This, however, was a dire emergency, in which every fraction of a second counted. In the front of the aircraft, reacting virtually instantaneously, Ace and Rid went through the forward hatch. They were the first to leave the aircraft, and probably the only ones to do so. Someone might also have gone through the rear door – reports are confused – but it seems unlikely that this was Leslie. It would have taken him much longer than Jack to reach the emergency exit – to do so within the few critical seconds left to him, hampered by a heavy and most cumbersome flying suit, he would have had to revolve his turret half-circle, open the doors behind him, extricate himself from the tight embrace of his gun turret, seize his parachute, open the rear fuselage door, and slither as fast as he possibly could up the narrow passageway which led from the tail to the rear door. With the aircraft falling in flames out of the sky, it seems very unlikely that he could have made it.

Leslie's best option would have been to rotate his turret half-circle the opposite direction, open the doors, and fall backwards out of the rear of the plane. There was a hand-turned wheel to operate the turret if the hydraulics had gone. However, first of all he had to get his parachute from where it was stowed in the passageway. This would have consumed several vital seconds.

Paddy, the navigator, who could easily have been out of the forward escape hatch an instant after Ace and Rid, seems to have elected to stay with his pilot, Steve. Perhaps he was waiting with him to be sure that everyone had baled out; perhaps he felt that he just could not leave him. Such a dreadful scenario was played out all too many times during the war.

Still losing power, blazing with the brightest light, the plane sunk down towards the west side of Texel. It approached the sea and the slope of the high wooded dune, Fonteinsnol, half-way between De Koog and Den Hoorn. Eyewitnesses saw it come flying over on fire, the clouds above it shining with the red light of the flames, then suddenly it crashed vertically into the ground after one last explosion had broken it up completely. The wreckage fell onto Fonteinsnol amongst the tall pine trees there and ignited them.

The crash site was very close to a small country lane called Westerslag which led out to the western dunes. The Germans, who had observed parachutes coming down in the searchlights, split into two main groups. One began the search for the parachutists; the other rushed out down Westerslag to the remains of the aircraft, burning fiercely in the pine wood. Amongst the wreckage of the Lancaster, they found the dead body of the pilot, Steve, who like so many pilots before him had carried out his duty to the letter and kept the Lancaster flying as long as possible to give his crew the maximum chance to get out. There were two other bodies with him. The pine woods and sand dunes were combed for the four missing aircrew, but for the time being at least the Germans found no one.

Rid Brown was later told by the Germans of the fate of his five crewmates. He was given some of the information after he left the island, whilst at his final interrogation at Frankfurt. His undated testimony was entered, much later, on the loss card for the aircraft, and was almost certainly given around May-June 1945, once he had returned to England from his Prisoner of War camp.

> I was second to leave the aircraft which was on fire. As far as I
> know the remainder of the crew were alive and uninjured when
> I left. The Germans told me three bodies had been recovered
> from the wreckage and buried on 16th January. The pilot,
> Steven, was identified, not the other two. Later the Germans
> said the other two of the crew had been washed up on the shores
> of the island.

The municipal records of Den Burg confirm the burial of three of the crew
at the Den Burg cemetery – on 15th January – and that two of them were
unknown. The information about the crew members washed up on the
beach appears, however, to be incorrect.

Leslie's remains were buried in the same cemetery 16 days later on 31st
January. Given the area in which Rid and Ace came down and the location
of the crash site, it is not possible that Leslie parachuted out, drifted out
over the sea and was drowned. He may perhaps have baled out but too late
for his parachute to save him – another faint rumour which survives about
the tragedy is that some of the crew baled out too low. Alternatively, he
might have been blown away from the aircraft by the final explosion.
Whatever fate overtook him, he fell somewhere away from the wreck and
his body was not discovered for a fortnight.

His burial, like that of the others, was carried out by the local population
under close German supervision. His surname is recorded in the Dutch
municipal records at Den Burg, but next to it there is the abbreviated word
'Vermoed', suspected to be. There must have been a name tag on his
clothing or some item in his pockets which had given the finders of his
body his distinctive surname. His dog tag was not found, for in place of his
initials there is a question mark and his service number is marked
'Onbekend', unknown.

What remained of the wreckage of S-Sugar was guarded by German
soldiers and the local people were forbidden to go near it. It is thought that
when the Germans came to clear away the wreckage, they found the
remains of the last crew member. No dog tag was found with the body.
Local memory has it that the unknown young man was buried at the crash
site, and during the war the local people cared devotedly for the grave and
often placed wild flowers upon it.

For the two survivors, Ace and Rid, the change from the warm interior of
the Lancaster and the companionship of their friends to a bitterly cold
winter's night in enemy territory, was a profound shock. What is more, they
were on their own, having lost one another in the darkness and confusion.

Ace had hit his head so hard on the edge of the door as he baled out that
he lost consciousness. When he came to, he was lying on the ground, in a

small hard-frozen field of sheep-bitten grass. He was in a bad state, confused by his concussion and severely chilled, having lost his boots which had been ripped off by the wind as he fell. Shivering with cold and shock, he managed to get to his feet and set off to look for help and shelter. After some while, he came across the house of Piet Smit, a sheep farmer who lived in the hamlet of Noord Haffel, just south of Den Burg and some two miles south-east of the final crash site. Smit, who understood no English, took Ace to shelter in one of the sheep huts near his house. In this miniature wooden barn, with slat sides and a small loft, Ace lay down in the hay and tried to sleep and forget.

The following morning, Smit took him tea and some socks for his bare feet. A neighbour had told Smit that a stranger was sitting in one of his sheds, evidently Ridley Brown. The local people were exceedingly cautious, thinking the whole thing might be a trap set by the Germans, and it was not until later that day that Rid and Ace were brought together. They were so ecstatic to see one another, greeting one another so rapturously, that the people were convinced they were genuine.

However, an English-speaking doctor who had come to examine Ace for his concussion, told them that the civilians sheltering them were in the gravest peril, that they were likely to be shot if the fugitives were discovered. Reluctantly, not wishing to put their new friends in such danger, Rid and Ace gave themselves up. They were marched by very aggressive soldiers with fixed bayonets to an interrogation centre at Den Burg, and put through the initial basic interrogation. It was the German policy to move such prisoners off the island as soon as possible, but as there was only one boat a week there was a delay, during which Rid and Ace had plenty of time to worry about what was going to happen to them. When eventually they were taken outside and stood up against a wall, their immediate thought was that they were going to be shot. Instead, to their enormous relief, a bus turned up packed with islanders who were likewise headed for the mainland. Rid and Ace were herded onto it. What happened next would stay with Ace forever. Even though it was in full view of the Germans, all the Dutch people on the bus stood up out of respect for the two captured airmen.

On arrival on the mainland, Rid and Ace were split up and never saw one another again. Ace went to Stalag 4B, at Muhlberg (Elbe). As an officer, Rid was sent to a different camp, Stalag Luft 3, based at Sagan and Belaria.

Back at Bourn, on the 15th January, after it had become obvious that neither Steven nor Hodgson's planes would be returning from operations, an urgent telegram was sent to each of the fourteen families:

PRIORITY . . . DEEPLY REGRET TO INFORM YOU THAT YOUR SON . . . IS REPORTED MISSING FROM OPERATIONS OVER ENEMY TERRITORY STOP PENDING RECEIPT OF WRITTEN NOTIFICATION FROM

THE AIR MINISTRY NO INFORMATION SHOULD BE
GIVEN TO THE PRESS STOP LETTER FOLLOWS – OC
97TH SQUAD BOURN

That same day the Commanding Officer wrote the fourteen letters of
condolence – that to Ace's family is representative:

Dear Mr East
It is with the deepest regret that I must confirm that your son
Acting Flight Sergeant Albert Charles East failed to return from
night operations on the 14th January 1944, and I wish to
express the sympathy of the whole Squadron with you in your
anxiety.

A/F/Sgt East took part in a raid on Brunswick as Flight
Engineer, no news having since been received. We can but hope
that the aircraft was forced to land and that the crew are safe,
even as prisoners of war.

Your son has been with us since the early part of July last
year and has taken part in 24 operations over enemy territory.
He was most conscientious and a very efficient Flight Engineer.
Having been with us so long we shall greatly miss him, and his
loss will be keenly felt by the Squadron.

His kit and personal effects are being carefully checked and
will be sent to the RAF Central Depository, from whom you
will hear in due course.

If any news is received I will communicate with you
immediately, and in the meantime I join with you in hoping we
shall soon hear that your son is safe.

Yours sincerely – Wing Commander E J Carter

Leslie's personal effects were also sent to the RAF Central Depository at
Colnbrook, near Slough. It was by this route that the photograph which he
had been given by his girlfriend Doris came back to his family, rather
creased and battered from Leslie's keeping it by him for so long. It was a
formal portrait of him and Doris, a small plump pretty Catholic girl, the
only girlfriend he had ever had. On the back, with nine crosses for kisses,
she had written 'To my own darling'. It was just one more romance
shattered by the war.

Ace's family did not hear any news for three months. But they were
fortunate compared to the families of the five of the crew who had died.
These did not know the fate of their loved ones for many months.

The usual channel for news about RAF deaths was via the International
Red Cross in Geneva. The Germans issued periodic 'totenliste', death lists,
which covered those known to have been killed; these passed via the
Wehrmacht or Luftwaffe to the Red Cross representatives in Germany.

However, many aircrew deaths were never confirmed. Even by the end of September 1944, Leslie's family still did not know what had happened to him. Leslie's older brother Wally wrote, via the Air Ministry, to Albert East's father:

Dear Sir

I understand, from the Air Ministry, that your son, Flight Sergeant A C East, was one of the Crew of the Lancaster Bomber in which my brother – Sergeant L N J Laver – was Rear-Gunner.

As your son has been reported a Prisoner of War, and as I have not had any news of my Brother, who is still reported missing, 'believed killed', I should be most grateful to you if you would let me have any information, in case your Son may have mentioned him in his letters to you.

I hope that you will not consider this request an imposition on the part of a complete stranger, who, you will appreciate, feels very worried about his Brother. At the same time I would like to offer my sincere sympathy to you in your own trouble about your Son.

Thanking you in anticipation

Yours faithfully – W E Laver

I am not sure how much Albert East's father was able to tell him but it would seem from the correspondence below that it was very little. On June 15th 1945, shortly after his return from the PoW camp in Germany, Rid Brown wrote to Wally who had for some time been in touch with his wife:

. . . My wife has told me, and shown me, your letters in which you enquire for news of your Brother.

No doubt you must be anxious to hear the news of that fatal night but I'm afraid you may be disappointed with my story.

To begin I must state that I did not know your Brother personally as he was just taking our rear gunner's place for that night only and I only met him at briefing and when we went to the aircraft for takeoff.

We were returning from an op on Brunswick and had just crossed the West [almost certainly, in fact, the East] coast of Texel when we were attacked by a fighter, from below. His cannon fire hit us and set on fire the petrol tanks in both wings. The fire spread very rapidly and within a few seconds our captain (F/Lt Steven) gave the order to bale out. Our engineer (W/O East) was the first to leave the aircraft by the front exit and I followed him . . . When I left the a/c all the crew were uninjured.

My shute knocked me out and when I came to I found myself on the ground about two or three hundred yards from a burning a/c. The Germans were heading for the fire so I went off in another direction and the following morning I met W/O East. On the night of Jan 16th we were taken by the Germans and when they got us to their H.Q. we were told that three bodies had been recovered from the a/c. One of them only had been identified and that was our skipper F/Lt Steven. The other two had no identification discs. There were still two members of our crew missing. When on final interrogation at Frankfurt I enquired of our two missing members and was told that two bodies had been washed up on the shores of Texel but had not been identified and they were presumed to be the missing ones from our crew as there was no other a/c shot down in that area that night.

I am afraid that is all I can tell you of the unfortunate affair. If I said more it would only be guesswork. But I do not think there is much chance of your Brother turning up now. I'd rather presume him dead than live on in the hopes that he may still be alive.

I can only offer you and his parents and family my deepest sympathy for your great loss. As I said before I did not know your Brother well but he did seem to me to be keen at his work and was no doubt a good gunner and devoted to his duty . . .

If by chance you think I can help you in any way please let me know and I'll do my best to try.

Wally wrote to thank him, 'I cannot say how much I appreciate your gesture, and I sincerely thank you for your letter.' He went on:

Yes, we have been very anxious indeed, particularly my Mother who has worried over the affair as she has not known whether she could hope for his return . . . For my part, I think it will be better when her mind is at rest about it one way or another, as he was the youngest of the family and she misses him so much . . . I would again thank you for your letter, and also would express the sincere hope that you are in good health, and have at least somewhat recovered from the Prison Camp experience.

It was a very bitter relief to Leslie's mother, Jenny, to know. Before this letter which ended all hope, she used to say to her daughters about Leslie, 'I wish I knew what happened to him, I wish I knew'. In her desperation she had even been to a spiritualist to find out. The medium, holding the dead man's glove, had told her of the moment of Leslie's death, 'he's in a tight cage trying to get out'. The family felt sure this referred to the lethal confines of his gun turret, and their only consolation was that the medium had added that he had not suffered long but had died quickly.

The family were left with nothing but their memories, a few photographs, and a handful of letters. Wally, who worked at Bernard Weatherill's, the exclusive and extremely expensive tailors, would always treasure one of the last letters he ever had from his brother, which ended with a little joke:

> There isn't much more I can say now except keep all your chins up and keep smiling, this damn war can't last forever.
> I remain your Loving Brother – Leslie.
> P.S. Don't forget to keep one of those 15 guinea suits ready for me as soon as I get my D[emob] Papers.

Leslie is buried alongside Bill Gadsby and Jack Skinner, in the General Cemetery at Den Burg. His skipper, Steve, and navigator, Paddy, are in the beginning of the next row.

The last member of the crew, either Bill or Jack, was not buried at Den Burg until 2nd October 1946. At the same time, the four other crew members were exhumed so that their identity could be verified. The injuries of all the dead were then recorded as being consistent with impact with the ground; none are mentioned as having been washed up from the sea.

The work was carried out by the Missing Research and Enquiry Service, the MRES. After the war, the RAF Missing Research teams fanned out over Europe on the herculean task of trying to trace every single aircraft which had been lost during the preceding six years. Their task was to identify, if at all possible, all RAF dead, and they visited every known and reputed RAF crash site. The many thousands of loss cards which they completed recorded the precise details of where each aircraft had crashed, the reason for the crash if known, and the burial sites of the crew. At the same time, scattered bodies were disinterred and re-buried in war cemeteries. In many instances, however, there were no remains. The aircraft had blown up in the air, atomising all evidence of its identity, or had been lost at sea, its crew drowning or surviving only to perish of exposure. 20,345 airmen with no known grave were eventually to be listed on the Runnymede memorial, close to Windsor Great Park, on Cooper's Hill above the Thames.

Once exhumed, confirmation of the identity of S-Sugar's crew was made where possible. Leslie's initial identification in the municipal records was now confirmed, almost certainly by his clothing as he was the only sergeant on the crew. At the same time something was found which suggested, though did not absolutely confirm, Paddy's identity, but there was nothing left to tell who was Jack or who was Bill.

Once the examination was over, the bodies of Steve, Paddy, Jack, Bill and Leslie were reburied side by side in graves 143 to 147. Only now would their relatives be officially informed that there was no hope of their loved ones ever coming home.

The Netherlands War Graves Committee, whose offices were in Amsterdam, arranged pilgrimages for almost thirty years after the war to British and Dominion war graves in the Netherlands. A visit by two of the relatives would be financed, and thus, around 1950, Leslie's mother Jenny went out to Texel to see his grave with her eldest daughter Marjorie. It is Jenny's tribute which appears on her much loved son's tombstone:

> Although you've gone, my Boy,
> I know that some day
> We'll meet again
> In a world of gladness.

Though she lived to be 89, Jenny was never reconciled to the loss of her youngest child. Though her daughter Jessie would gently remind her, 'Mum, so many other boys were killed in the war,' Jenny would reply almost with anger, 'What consolation is that to me?'

Sometimes, in her grief, she believed that Leslie came to visit her. She continued to live on in the old Victorian house in Panmure Road with her invalid daughter, Dorothy, who could not climb the stairs. Upstairs there was still the big sitting room with the piano, in which once the whole family had gathered for parties and singsongs. Jenny had always been strict about having doors shut; she did not like open doors in the house, and in the old days she had forever been telling her children to shut them. Leslie, he was always leaving that dratted door open; he would go upstairs and tinker on the piano and leave the door ajar. One day, years after his death, when Jessie was visiting her mother, Jenny suddenly turned to her and said, 'That front room door's open again upstairs – Leslie must have been in'.

Five

The Sole Survivor

I. Convalescence

Even though Joe must have long suspected that Ted and the others had been killed in the crash, he cannot have expected to hear from the Welfare Officer that Leslie was 'missing, presumed killed'. The news must have been deeply upsetting. Now only he was left out of the crew of seven who had joined the Pathfinders with such high hopes only two months before.

Though he was not an imaginative man, he wondered why he had been spared, why the others had died, and that unanswerable question was to haunt him for many years. Early in their married life, he often showed distress about the crew's deaths to my mother, saying 'Why did I survive? It should have been me that died and the others that lived – I was no good.' He was the one who had never done particularly well in the RAF, and he struggled to understand why he had been spared whilst those who had been so outstanding in their work had gone.

I often wonder whether Leslie, in his last month of life, went to visit my father in hospital. Leave would certainly have been granted by his Commanding Officer, and it would have been surprising if Leslie had not gone – aircrew were bound to one another by deep ties of loyalty, and whatever their personal relationship Leslie had helped to save my father's life. The fact that such a visit was never mentioned by my father certainly does not mean it did not take place. His secretiveness was so intense that he was virtually bound not to mention it; subjects he did not want talked about he always placed off limits, either by concealing the true facts or simply by refusing to discuss them.

Peggy, the mother of Tony Lawrence, visited the hospital and there met up with Joe's mother, Kathleen. In his memoir my father mentions the two mothers meeting, but does not say if he himself met Peggy. Well, of course, he did – what on earth was she doing at the hospital otherwise? – but he does not describe her visit in any way. Peggy must have wished to speak to Tony's friend, to hear why her son had died, and at the same time, in her grief, to show sympathy and affection to the young man who had survived. Yet Peggy features as a mere name and nothing else in the record which my father chose to make of those times.

At the time that Peggy visited Joe at Ely Hospital, she was working in the Land Army. An ebullient independent lively woman, just turned forty, full of good fun, stories and anecdotes, she had never been the sentimental type of mother. Yet apart from Ted's brother, Jim (who as a member of the RAF was able to go to Bourn and actually met Sidney Matthews), Peggy appears to have been the only bereaved relative who had the persistence to discover more about the crash than the absolutely minimal information supplied by the RAF.

Whatever Joe had to tell Peggy about the crash, it cannot have been much. Perhaps he was still too ill to talk, perhaps his memory was still clouded, or perhaps he thought he ought to keep silent. Whatever the reason, the Burroughes family never knew the truth of what had happened to Tony that night, but were left with the vague impression that the aircraft had been damaged by enemy action and that this was the reason for the crash.

Tony's photograph taken in the summer of 1943 before he joined the crew would always be preserved by his family, a copy of it prominently displayed in the homes of both Peggy and her brother Tom. In the picture Tony appears the very personification of the dashing young airman, standing there so tall and slim and straight in his RAF uniform and flying boots. The drama of his image deeply impressed his young cousins, who knew the photograph well. It would help to preserve in their memory the times that, as young children, they had seen the real Tony home on leave, that tall handsome blue-eyed auburn-haired young man whose death would forever seal him in legend, a shadowy, thrilling, almost supernatural figure.

By the end of May 1944, Joe was well on the way to recovery from his crash injuries. To complete his treatment, he was transferred to No 2 Airmen's Convalescent Depot at Hoylake, near Liverpool, where a strenuous but very kindly and benevolent regime aimed to bring such injured airmen back to full mobility and health.

Reginald Watson-Jones had been one of the prime motivators behind the policy of the separate rehabilitation centre. Such a policy had been judged unworkable pre-war, when Watson-Jones and his colleagues had been viewed as 'idealists whose heads were in the clouds'. After the outbreak of hostilities, however, the scheme was implemented on a small-scale, experimentally, and it soon proved so outstandingly and amazingly successful that eventually five rehabilitation centres were created. The pioneer centres had been the Officers' Hospital at Torquay and the Convalescent Depot at Blackpool, and these were followed by Hoylake, Cosford, and lastly Loughborough College.

My father's rehabilitation centre was based at The Leas, which had been a private boys' school before the war. Taken over by the RAF in June 1940, and reopened officially as a rehabilitation centre on August 1st, 1941, The Leas was a commodious and austerely handsome building, with two wings set at right-angles to the main block designed to take advantage of the magnificent seaview. There were three floors, extravagantly gabled, and all the rooms were large and airy.

The building was situated just off a long road, Meols Drive, which led to Hoylake to the north and West Kirby to the south. The landscape was rather flat, with few undulations, and not many trees, but all the same it was a beautiful spot, very close to the long sands of the Dee, scene of Charles Kingsley's famous maudlin poem *Mary on the Banks of the Dee*, about a drowned cattlegirl. On clear summer days, the coast of Wales and the island of Anglesey could be seen. My father found it very much to his liking, calling it 'a most pleasant place', high praise for him. In winter, however, it could be desolate and bitterly cold, with fierce winds roaring up unhindered from the Atlantic. Its proximity to Liverpool was also a mixed blessing because the city suffered from heavy air raids, necessitating the building of a large air-raid shelter in the grounds.

Also in The Leas' grounds were squash and fives courts, a bowling and putting green, a swimming pool, and playing fields large enough for at least three football pitches. The emphasis was very much upon games being played to improve fitness and physical confidence, and the list given by the Chief Medical Officer, Squadron Leader Harold Cantor, included deck-tennis, medicine ball, basket ball, bowls, skittles, squash and fives for the upper limbs and spine, and football, cricket, swimming and cycling for the lower limbs. My father, who was decidedly unathletic, profited from this regime, exclaiming about volleyball, 'I got quite good at it'.

Harold Cantor, who had been a civilian doctor prior to the war, was well known in Merseyside medical circles. Quietly spoken and pleasant, he was reputed to be something of a ladies man. His medical knowledge was first-class, but some of his staff considered him neither forceful nor inspiring enough to be the charismatic leader essential in such a place.

The Commanding Officer, Wing Commander George William Patrick Dawes, DSO, AFC, alias 'Old Dawes' or 'Daddy Dawes', was an entirely different kettle of fish. Many people remember him vividly, whereas they remember very little about Cantor other than that he was kindly and a good doctor.

Daddy Dawes had made his career in the RAF. He had, in fact, been known as Daddy Dawes since 1914, to distinguish him from another pilot in the same squadron, Leonard Dawes, who had received the alternative soubriquet of 'Sonny'. Prior to the First World War, as a Captain in Number 2 Squadron, Royal Flying Corps (Military Wing), Dawes had been one of the stars of the early days of flying, at a time when – only ten years after the Wright brothers' historic flight – aviators were idolised like film stars and huge crowds gathered to see them.

Daddy Dawes was old-school and totally inflexible, a 'real military-looking character, a military type altogether, a diehard, domineering, his Word was Law' as David Page, one of the former Leas instructors told me.

Daddy Dawes confined himself mainly to administrative matters, 'and we didn't see a lot of him – he commanded by remote control, and a lot of people were dead scared of him'. Most people shook in their boots when Dawes was on the warpath, and even Cantor appeared frightened of him.

Dawes was proverbial for his irascibility. An ex-patient, Norman Scullard, recalled arriving at The Leas in April 1944:

> On arrival, the group of you were gathered together in a biggish room, you sat in a semicircle as best as you could, and Dawes went round each of you asking what you were in for and how you had received your injury. He asked the first chap and he said: 'Playing rugby', the second: 'Playing football', the third: 'Playing cricket', and so on – Dawes went on all round the circle and everyone was just the same. At last he got to one poor chap, 'What are you in for?', got the same sort of answer, and Dawes just exploded, got all red in the face and angry – 'Doesn't anyone fly in this bloody Air Force any more?' At last he got to me, glared at me all fiercely. 'And what happened to you?' 'I crashed at Syerston on three engines.' 'Oh,' he said, 'thank the Lord for that!'

Over and over again in connection with Dawes one hears the word 'whisky'. It appears that Daddy Dawes, who seemed positively Methuselan to his young charges, was particularly partial to whisky and always managed to get hold of some despite wartime rationing. The men were allowed a whisky ration and allegedly Dawes kept this ration for himself on the grounds that it was unsuitable for the medically unfit. What he did not drink with his visitors, he sold to the neighbouring golf club. One ex-patient, referring to this, spoke strongly, saying Dawes was 'a crook', and added that he was 'heartily disliked by the overseas people' as he would have all their parcels opened and anything he wanted he would have confiscated.

However, Dawes certainly had his virtues as a CO. Peter Ray, who set up a training school at The Leas in December 1942, remembered that 'whatever Dawes wanted, he got'. At the start of his posting, Ray had written out a long list of supplies for the training school, not really expecting to get any of it. However, when he gave the list to Dawes at their next meeting, Dawes immediately picked up the phone and began ringing various high-up names in the Air Ministry, with all of whom he appeared to be on first name terms. Peter Ray was bedazzled by the dropping of these illustrious names, which were those of Gods, far beyond his own life as a humble wireless operator. And sure enough all the supplies were there within a couple of days.

Amongst those involved with the setting up of this training school was Air Commodore H Osmond Clarke, of CME, London, the Consultant in

Orthopaedics, a figure second only to Watson-Jones himself. Watson-Jones was more the theorist – Osmond Clarke was the one who 'did the mangle work' as the current jargon had it. An extraordinarily kindly and unaffected man, Osmond Clarke regularly visited The Leas, examining as many as 50 patients in one visit and deciding who should carry on with treatment, who should return to flying duties, and who should be hospitalised, temporarily grounded, invalided from the Service, or repatriated.

The instructors at The Leas were a distinguished bunch, all of them adept at some form of physical training and many of them professional sportsmen such as Sergeant Edmund Burke, who had trained the Davis Cup team before the war, or Flight-Sergeant Danny Glidden of Tranmere Rovers.

Exercises were specifically tailored for each patient. The Medical Officer initially spent many hours with the new patient, 'instructing and guiding him, encouraging, sympathising, cajoling or even bullying him' until he began to regain his confidence. Once the patient had a clear idea of what was expected of him, he was placed in the care of a remedial instructor, trained in the art of rehabilitation.

David Page was one of these instructors. Speaking of his patients, he said 'they were such a smashing bunch' – he obviously felt the most tremendous warmth and affection towards them even though at times he had to act the martinet.

> We would be there in the gym, with all these boys in plaster, on crutches, and we would stand at the front bellowing out commands at them, and these boys who had been shot up, they couldn't care less. We would go up close and bellow in their face 'Stand legs apart! With arms raised!' and they would try to do it, and the others would try to help them and then they would all fall over in a heap on the floor. The people who came to visit the place, the dignitaries, the bigwigs, well, you could see their mouths drop open, you could see them thinking, 'This is not a rehabilitation centre, this is a lunatic asylum' – but after a while their attitude would seem to change. I've seen them in tears – the place had that effect – they went away very different people to what they came in.

What the 'Leas Boys' found when they first arrived at the ex-boys' school was indeed something very like school, but school with virtually all the nasty things abolished. Service life had been left far behind – as an ex-patient, John Curwood, said, 'our duties were to get better'. Deliberately, the authorities swept away as many petty restrictions, rules and regulations as possible, intent on counteracting the memory of the hospitals the men had so recently left, and instead creating what Rexford-Welch in his history of RAF medical services calls somewhat over-optimistically 'the atmosphere of a country club'. His Rotarian vision did not take sufficiently into account the sheer exuberance of the youthful patients.

The Leas Boys were forbidden to drink on the premises but that did not prevent them from getting a skinful elsewhere, at the most popular local pubs like The Green Lodge, The Dee, and The Punchbowl, or further afield, at pubs and hotels in New Brighton, Birkenhead and Liverpool.

They were a highly noticeable and dramatic set. At the Adelphi, the big hotel known as the Ritz of Liverpool, an amputee released his hand when a girl reached out to shake it and as the dead thing fell off in her hand she fainted on the spot. A favourite saying of the old lags when rebuking someone innocent, enthusiastic and credulous, was 'Wait until you get some flak up your arse,' and one man used to demonstrate the phrase literally, by taking down his trousers to reveal his backside which had been absolutely peppered with it.

At times, the jokes played were closer to home, as David Page recalled:

> Meols Drive, well it was like Millionaires Row there, and on this particular night when they came back they unscrewed and laid down all the gates. It wasn't malicious, they hadn't damaged them, but every single one was taken off. In the morning you looked down the road and all you could see were all these gates lying on the ground, all the way along.
>
> Those boys were wild, you just couldn't control them.

A similar story was told by Ken Dykes, a mid-upper gunner, who had been with 97 Squadron when they were based at Woodhall Spa before the move to Bourn. He remembered Anzac Day, when the New Zealand contingent got completely plastered. They and their friends, about 16 of them, by brute force shifted the shell of the old Hampden bomber, which was kept for morale-building purposes, out of the grounds and plonked it in the middle of Meols Drive. They just 'melted away afterwards, pretended they were soldiers, nothing to do with The Leas – the local police were very put out'.

Another time they tried to do the same thing with the Link Trainer, a flight simulator, but it was too heavy to be shifted.

A more sedentary passion was gambling. There was mah-jong, at which the Chief Medical Officer, Harold Cantor, excelled, and there were the infamous all-night card sessions. The Canadians, Australians and New Zealanders in particular, being far from home, had little to spend their money on, and in preparation for one of these card sessions would draw out their pay and lose it all by the following morning. One ex-patient, Gerry Turl, remembered Cantor sometimes playing cards with the lads for money, which if he tended to win may partly explain his occasional unpopularity with his patients.

During the day, the Leas Boys could often be seen cycling in groups around the local countryside and villages. They were all in uniform, but that uniform was worn in the most scruffy, casual and disreputable style –

sometimes with trousers, sometimes with shorts, always with gym shoes, the jacket unbuttoned, the sleeves rolled up – these were very individualistic dressers.

John Gittins, then a paper boy of 13 years of age, used to take his papers up to The Leas and he well remembers the Leas Boys and their 'big old solid Raleigh bikes; they would ride along with their limbs in plaster – they might be cased in plaster right up to their necks but they were still riding those bikes'. He was in great awe of these impossibly glamorous figures until one day 'I asked a fighter pilot with a leg in plaster, "What happened to you?" and the pilot said "I got drunk and was knocked down by a taxi", which rather spoiled it for me, as they were all heroes to me'.

Sometimes war injuries were hammed up on purpose. George Hodgson's family lived at Birkenhead and once he took some friends home with him. They went to a dance at the Town Hall.

> The commissionaire on the door could not believe his eyes when he saw one lady and four airmen hobbling along to the dance hall. He hadn't the heart to charge us, so we got in free, and once inside our walking sticks were stacked in a corner and we got on with the serious business of dancing.

At the local pub, The Green Lodge, the leg cases used to walk in and throw all their crutches and sticks in the corner, and if Cantor came in they had to scurry to retrieve them. It was the same at the dances, and as John Curwood said laughing 'they all limped badly, of course' to attract the sympathy of the girls.

The local girls' heads were completely turned by these god-like young men. Mrs Shillcock, then single, used to work in a little insurance company in the old village of West Kirby. Across the road from her office was Miss Cook's Cafe, a tiny restaurant, and all the Leas boys used to go there on their bicycles – they would pile all the bikes up outside and go in to have tea and scones. As soon as she saw they were there, she always went across to have a bite to eat herself. The boys all seemed very dashing and desirable, 'they were super' – and like so many others she couldn't resist them.

Mrs Curwood, who had met her husband John at the Tower Ballroom in New Brighton, said with a hearty laugh that the Leas Boys were:

> quite the ravers locally with the girls – girls used to think they were quite safe as they had been injured, but there were some horrendous stories. There were dancing classes up at The Leas, and all the girls would go rushing up there, practically breaking their necks in their hurry to get there 'to help them with their therapy'. The Leas Boys were the cream as far as the local girls were concerned.

The dancing classes, held on two afternoons a week, took place in the main school hall, a huge room with the most beautiful parquet floor, with the Allied flags hung all around to break up the harshness of the parallel bars and exercise bikes. An article on April 28th, 1944, in the *Liverpool Daily Post*, describes the scene:

> A polished dance floor, a gramophone playing 'Pistol-Packing Momma', a dozen young sergeant pilots, each with an attractive partner – a pleasant scene of social relaxation in short.
> But the dance floor is in an RAF hospital; the airmen, although you would hardly suspect it, have all been wounded; and the dancing is a valuable part of their care – the medical authorities call it remedial dancing . . . It was found that men who were very hesitant about putting their weight on an injured limb, even during the ordinary remedial exercises, would do so readily when dancing. The music and the rhythm of the dance helped, and the presence of attractive partners very naturally tended to make the men forget their injuries.

Everyone who was at The Leas remembers the dancing classes with great gusto, affection and laughter. Many married their instructresses. My father, too, remembered the classes with pleasure in his memoir. There are a great many mentions of girls altogether in his stories about his convalescence – he was certainly a considerable flirt, and must have lapped up all that unconditional feminine indulgence and affection which he attracted as an injured RAF man, a war hero.

In many ways, this period at The Leas was a charmed time for him. He was physically fit in a way he had never been before and would never be again; he was living in a relaxed, cheerful, carefree environment with highly congenial companions. When he and the other Leas boys went out in public, they were smiled upon as heroes by the local people and doted on by the blushing besotted girls. Everyone liked to indulge them, to do them little favours and express their unbounded admiration of what they had done for their country. Amongst numerous other little gifts and benefices, there were free tickets for the local cinemas, The Tudor in West Kirby and The Kingsway at Hoylake, where aisle seats were reserved for those with gammy legs. For the rest of his life, my father would always request an aisle seat when he went to the theatre or opera.

The most striking thing in all the recollections of The Leas and in all the photographs of the patients is what a happy place it was. The faces in the pictures positively beam. As John Curwood said: 'It was an excellent place and the staff were most kind and understanding of the traumas of the crashes and so on – also the locals were very very kind'. And George Hodgson, to whom I remarked on the beaming faces in the photographs, wrote back to me: 'The atmosphere at The Leas was calm and tranquil.

Most of the fellows were recovering from a most traumatic experience and beginning to feel well again. Every reason to look happy.'

The Leas was rightly proud of its achievements. It was much publicised, though for security reasons the name and location were never revealed. The BBC visited and reported on it, and *The Liverpool Daily Post*, *The Daily Mirror*, and many other newspapers wrote ecstatic articles.

A yellowing cutting from an unknown local paper, the date around November 1944, captures the universally favourable response:

RAF MIRACLE
Where Cripples Become Fighters Again
Broken Back Cases Play Football
Men with broken backs playing football, flight-sergeants who stopped a cannon shell over Germany, running, playing squash and handball when in the last war they would have been hopelessly crippled – these miracles are being done daily at an RAF rehabilitation centre on the N.W. Coast where men are fitted out physically, eventually to resume the duties they left . . .

The anonymous reporter was exceedingly impressed, mentioning the 3,000 cases which had passed through the centre since it had opened and how phenomenally high the success rate had been. The article concluded, 'Every relative and friend of RAF men should know the extraordinary care which is lavished on them to make these battered and broken men useful members of society once more'.

One thing is for sure, my father had the very best medical care throughout his convalescence. I have spoken to several people who were at The Leas and a wonderful glow comes to all their voices when they speak of it. Perhaps the last word is best left to one of David Page's patients, Ray Langford, who wrote on the back of a photograph he gave David Page before he went back on ops and they lost touch: 'To my friend and the one who made me fit, worse luck. The best days of my life at The Leas – [stay?] the same now if you please – good luck always, Dave – Ray.'

II. Discharged from the RAF
Even before autumn 1944 when he was discharged from The Leas, Joe was well enough and mobile enough to go home on leave. Some six weeks earlier, in July, he had been at Little Kendals but had apparently missed the Sunday night that the V1 flying bomb nearly hit the family house. 'Although it did not destroy the building it did very heavy damage' as his father, R.J., noted.

The detonation was heard a mile away by those attending a meeting that evening at Christ Church. They heard the plane approaching, then the engines cutting out, followed by the massive explosion. The vicar, Gerald Hawker, said he had better go and see what had happened and gamely jumped on his bike and cycled off.

The bomb had fallen close enough to Watling Street to kill anyone passing by on the road, but fortunately there were no casualties. Little Kendals was not really that far off the point of impact, but it stood at the top of a slight hill, situated just off the brow, which must have protected it from the worst of the blast.

Monica, Joe's sister, wrote to tell her husband Michael about the bomb. Though she did not live at Little Kendals but at her hospital, UCH, she often spent her leisure time there. 'Apart from quite a bit of bomb damage to the house, all is well . . . most of the ceilings are down and all the windows are out. However, the house is liveable in.'

Joe must have seen the damage but was not apparently unduly disturbed by it. I do not know whether he was at home when a second bomb landed nearby – Monica told Michael in early August, 'Little Kendals has been vaguely blasted again and a couple more ceilings down but the family are more or less unperturbed and have moved into another room'. From September the V1s were for the most part superseded by the infinitely more terrible V2s, which were of the most immense size, and travelled too fast and too high to be shot down. Their range was more limited, but all the same 34 fell on Hertfordshire before the launching pads were overrun by the Allied armies.

Because of Joe's connection with the RAF, the family at Little Kendals had adopted a group of American airmen who were based nearby. They often entertained them, and Monica refers in one letter to having ten of the airmen there for breakfast. The airmen themselves sometimes carried their affections for the family so far as to 'buzz' the house, once miscalculating and lopping off the top of a tall tree just outside Monica's bedroom when she was in it.

Joe, when he came home from The Leas, would have been seen as part of this glamorous community of airmen. He was seen by his family as a war hero. Everyone was very proud of him, and very grateful for his wonderful recovery from near death. Nobody had the slightest idea that it had been his first operational flight on which he had crashed; they would not have dreamed of asking him for specific details, and he himself did not volunteer them. Most RAF men did not tell their families very much about what they had been doing, and Joe was also highly secretive and evasive by nature. His family knew full well this trait of his, which had begun in his school days when he would tell funny stories about his school friends but would adamantly refuse to give their names.

He was never to tell his family anything about his crew. 'Tall' – that was the only adjective he ever used to describe any of them, Ted Thackway, his outstanding young skipper, reduced to that single, almost nothing-meaning word. Nor would Joe ever admit to the fact that it had been his very first operation which had ended in tragedy. Instead he would tacitly let it be understood that he had 'flown many missions'.

As for the reason for the crash, none of Joe's family would ever hear from him about the dire situation that night which had affected so many other aircraft and crews. Having spent so long at Ely Hospital, Joe cannot possibly have been ignorant of the other casualties of Black Thursday. Yet it was only ever the story of his crash which was told, isolated and highlighted, one solitary terrible incident.

The inference that the aircraft had been damaged by enemy action and had struggled home bravely, only to crash in dense fog, now became the official explanation for the tragedy. This is certainly the explanation that had been given to Tony's mother, Peggy Lawrence (and many years later would also be given to Joe's children when he told the bedtime story).

In all fairness to Joe, this may well have been the semi-official RAF line at the time. The full implications of what had taken place that night were known to very few, and many aspects of it were shrouded in the most impenetrable secrecy – to take but one example, the landing aid FIDO. In 1944, Joe could not possibly have told Peggy Lawrence, or his own family, what had really happened, even had he been the type of person to make such a disclosure. What is so bizarrely intriguing is why he continued to obscure the matter for the rest of his life, maintaining his silence long after the necessity for secrecy had passed.

Joe's homecoming in the autumn of 1944 was a source of joy and relief to his family. It cannot have come as a disappointment to them when finally, by the end of the year, the RAF said they did not need him back – after all, everyone felt he had done his bit. Yet there is a mystery here. Looking at the brilliant results which The Leas achieved, it is very difficult to understand why Joe was in the small percentage referred to the Medical Board, prior to being invalided out of the RAF.

I am not sure exactly when he left The Leas, as this is one detail not recorded on his service papers, but it must have been in September or October. The Leas' figures show that of the 92 patients discharged in September, 45 went back to full flying duty, 9 to ground duties, and 18 to non-operational flying, 'fully operational in 2/3 months', as opposed to only 11 who were referred to the Medical Board (the remainder went back to hospital for further treatment, were repatriated or invalided out). In October, dramatically reflecting the successful progress of the war in Europe, there was a kind of wholesale clear-out of everyone who could be cleared out, to make room for 'the very high intake of patients with serious injuries and many repatriated ex-Prisoners of War'. Of the 152 patients discharged, 105 went back to full duty, 2 to ground duty, and 19 to non-operational flying – 126 men returned to duty as opposed to the 10 referred to the Medical Board.

In the context of the horrendous injuries suffered by many of his fellow airmen at The Leas, Joe had come off comparatively lightly. It would appear from the scanty contemporary sources that the worst injury, to his left leg, had healed extremely well. Throughout the summer, Monica had continued to write to her husband Michael about Joe's progress, how he had graduated from walking on crutches to using sticks, and how eventually all the injuries had healed perfectly except for the troublesome knee. The knee had restricted movement and he needed further treatment on it at The Leas. In September, Monica wrote: 'Joe home again on leave. Walks without a stick. 45° knee movement. No pain. Both legs same length. They had done a jolly good job on him.' He still did not have sufficient flexion in the knee to go back to operational flying in a Lancaster. However, the concept behind rehabilitation was that the patient should be returned to some form of duty as soon as possible and in most cases this happened before complete recovery.

There seem to be only two possible explanations why Joe was not transferred to ground duty but was given a medical discharge. The first is connected with the success of the Allies. Towards the end of 1944 the tide had so obviously turned in their favour that there may not have been the same drive to get an injured man back to duty. Nonetheless, The Leas discharge figures do not suggest much laxity in that respect.

The only other explanation is that Joe was suffering from some form of post traumatic-stress syndrome, an idea which is based mainly on what his sister Monica said about a distressing incident in 1945, on what my mother said about the early years of their marriage, and an unnerving incident which I myself saw many years later, when a pet dog's leg was hideously broken.

The incident described by Monica appears in a letter written to Michael on 5th December 1945 (Michael returned to England the following year): 'A Hermes-type new civilian aircraft crashed in front of our house whilst on its first test flight. Poor old Joe took this very badly – it was rather a repercussion of his own experience.'

This is surely the first sign that Joe had been permanently emotionally and psychologically scarred by the crash. It was almost exactly two years since it had happened. The words 'Poor old Joe took this very badly' suggest a kind of hysterical breakdown, a temporary but complete loss of control, freezing helplessness, tears and sobbing, the sort of reaction I myself witnessed twenty years later when the pet dog's leg was broken. In this very upsetting incident, two young boys having a game in my father's music room accidentally knocked over some furniture and smashed the dog's leg so badly that the bone protruded forth. I was upstairs when I suddenly heard the dog's piteous yelping, followed by my father's shrieking, a terrible, unnatural, spinechilling sound. Running downstairs, I found him completely distraught, huddled in a corner behind the harpsichord, incapable of either consoling the children or helping the dog.

Whatever the reason why he never returned to flying, by December 1944 Joe was posted permanently in Radlett, at Little Kendals, awaiting his discharge after three and a half years in the RAF. In early February, Monica told Michael that Joe was still at home, forgotten by his Medical Board –

'terribly well except for stiff knee and bored'. This would seem to indicate that Joe was already easing up on the strenuous routine needed to maintain full physical fitness now that he was out of the highly motivated atmosphere of The Leas. Over the years his adamant refusal to keep himself active would cost him dearly, and by the end of his life, in an increasingly poor state of health, this old, long-neglected war injury would make a cripple of him.

Three years after he had resumed being a civilian, Joe got married in December 1948. My mother remembered in the early years of their marriage that he would have terrible nightmares, from which he would awaken himself by screaming. When she asked him what he had been dreaming of, he would tell her it was about the aircrash. It was then that he would ask that terrible rhetorical question, 'Why did I survive?' He said that it was he who should have died and the others been saved. 'I shouldn't have lived – my friends should have lived – I wasn't good enough.' What seemed to particularly prey on his mind was a sense of his own worthlessness, the contrast between the others' great talent for their flying duties and his own comparative failure in the RAF.

Joe's father, R.J., a man of the strictest and most incorruptible integrity, died in autumn 1955. His death removed the counterbalance in Kathleen's affections, and left her free to dote on Joe extravagantly. She had never considered my mother a fit bride for her son, and now took sides with Joe in all his marital difficulties, and later against us children too when we proved so disappointing to him. Kathleen was the one who would make the absolute most of his war, in which 'our little boy' had been such a brave man. It was almost certainly she – rather than he – who first began to exaggerate his war record, though it all happened so diffusely and so obscurely that it is impossible to be sure now. But whoever was responsible, and however intentionally or otherwise the deceit was entered into, there now began the slow insidious transformation of Joe from a rather mediocre but apparently (up until the crash) pretty carefree RAF recruit into a much darker, more dramatic, indeed tragic figure, one who had flown on ops numerous times and had seen many dreadful things, nightmare horrors which must never ever be spoken of.

The exaggeration of what Joe had done in the war had two benefits: firstly it made clear how terrible his experiences had been and that therefore he could not be expected to discuss them; secondly it provided an explanation for his inability to handle traumatic situations, that something in him very close to hysteria which lay just below the surface.

It was never precisely said what had affected him so badly, just that one had to treat him with kid gloves. And certainly by the late 1960s it was obvious that something dreadful was afflicting my father; after the incident with the pet dog, I could never forget that searing glimpse of his emotional vulnerability. Something was not right with him, something very serious was amiss.

Strangely, in his slightly schizophrenic way, at this very same period my father was entering consciously and deliberately into another deceit about his war record, this one so distasteful to me that I still have not managed to forgive him for it. In 1968, in order to impress the stuffy and ultra-Establishment people he met through his socialising with City livery companies, he began to put 'DFM', for the Distinguished Flying Medal, after his name. He actually went so far as to purchase and to wear a miniature of the medal (together with the four ordinary campaign medals which he *was* entitled to wear) at the City livery banquets. As he never took my mother to these banquets, there was no problem in keeping the matter a secret from her. He did not mention the fact that he had a DFM to his natal family either until after he and my mother had separated and the danger of a disillusioned wife questioning this surprising award was over. The startling lapse of twenty-eight years between Joe's supposed award of the medal around March 1944, and the June 1972 revelation that he had won it, was then put down by his natal family (who always implicitly believed everything he said) to Joe's innate modesty.

There is no evidence whatsoever – in fact completely the reverse – to support my father's claim to have won the DFM, and there is no record of his name on the official MOD list of those who were awarded it.

The DFM was a very special medal. The award of it to William Darby Coates, the twenty year old pilot who had been at Silverstone, Wigsley and Upwood with Joe, and had arrived at Bourn on the same day, shows what feats of courage and endurance were demanded before the DFM was awarded. Coates brought back his severely crippled plane on the night of 16th/17th December and landed it safely at Downham Market after more than eight and a half hours in the air, a feat about which everyone on the squadron would have known. Joe must have learned about it whilst in Ely Hospital – he may even have been visited by Coates or one of his crew, as much in memory of Ted and the others who had died as anything else. I only realised how interconnected the crews were comparatively recently, when I suddenly spotted Coates's name in the ORB for Silverstone, checked the records and realised that the two crews had trained together for five months. Now, with acquired cynicism, I begin to wonder if the old bedtime story, with its inference that my father's plane had come back crippled, limping, doomed, carried echoes of Coates's outstanding feat of flying.

Had the award of the DFM to Coates stuck bitterly in Joe's memory, that glowing heroic deed which juxtaposed so painfully with his own strange record in the RAF? Or had he forgotten all that stuff by 1968 – the real friends, the real heroes – and only thought of the medal as something which in a particular social circle would bring him respect, admiration and kudos, the sweets of a distinguished war record? I guess I'll never know.

Writing about my father's falsification of his war record is very difficult. Hard to know what to put in, what to leave out, but to ignore it altogether would seem like a further falsification of the facts. He was very deeply affected by the crash, and if some of the results of this were less than praiseworthy they are nonetheless a vital aspect of this story.

Unfortunately the deeply tragic circumstances mean that his crewmates, recalled half a century later by friends and relatives who still deeply mourn their loss, perforce appear saintly and angelic by contrast. My father looks the villain of the piece, but then he was the only one who would live on to face the tangled and multifarious difficulties of maturity. As Jill, Ted's last girlfriend, once said to me, 'Who knows how Ted would have turned out?' The sheer youth of the crew gives their deaths an unbearable poignancy. All save Jack died between the ages of 20 and 23, and Jack was only 31.

The family legends about Joe's war service grew ever more preposterous as the years went on. They were eventually enshrined officially in his 1994 obituary in *Standard Bearer*, the in-house magazine for the Standard Commercial Tobacco group, the last company my father worked for after the family firm had been sold to that conglomerate. It was apparently Dad's sister who tendered the relevant information though it is a Colin Hose whose name is under the headline, 'Peter Mack Remembered by Friends' (my father's baptismal name, of course, was Peter):

> Peter was a RAF Pathfinder during World War II and was awarded the Distinguished Flying Medal (DFM). He kept this news very quiet and it was twenty years after the event that his family learned about the award. Apparently Peter was flying over France dropping agents when a flare became lodged in its exit shute. He had 15 seconds to defuse the flare which he succeeded in doing, with total disregard for his own life, thus avoiding certain disaster.

It is perhaps a bit literal-minded to point out that it can't have been 'total disregard for his own life' which led him to defuse something which going to blow him to smithereens anyway. As for the idea that he might have won the DFM for this action, well, making sure that the photoflash (as my father himself names it in his memoir when describing the Boulogne flight from Silverstone) had dropped correctly was a standard part of the w/op's job. No one got medals for performing their ordinary duty – it would have been a complete absurdity. Nor would anyone dropping agents be setting off photoflashes, which burned with the most dazzling phosphorescent light, having been specifically designed to light up a landscape from 18-20,000 feet up in the air.

Ah, but those 'agents', meaning, of course, secret agents . . .

Somehow this ludicrous Boys' Own flourish had also become part of Joe's distinguished war record. The nebulous lies, the exaggerations which never got entangled in specifics, the hints, the heavy meaningful silences, the deliberate obfuscation of the facts by Joe himself, had in the end borne this last, ridiculous, malformed fruit. All the facts of his service record, and those of his six crewmates, completely contradict such cloak-and-dagger stuff. Also, sadly for the legend, agent-dropping was the provenance of the SOE, and so far as Bomber Command was concerned only the two Special Duties Squadrons were involved, neither of which Joe had the teeniest thing to do with.

I have occasionally seen it mentioned (though never verified by the official histories or reputable witnesses) that agents were dropped by ordinary bomber crews on the way to a raid, the raid itself acting as cover for such clandestine activities. However, had such missions indeed taken place, no commanding officer would ever have entrusted such a dangerous and tricky job to an untested junior crew on their first operation.

I can only think that my father hinted at the stuff about the agents (he would never have given hostages to fortune by talking about it in a concrete, factual sort of way) and awarded himself the glittering honour of the DFM to make up for some very sad interior sense of worthlessness and failure. These unworthy impostures must have considerably exacerbated the problems he had in old age in facing up to what had happened to him in the RAF. What seems so very sad and pointless about all the lies is that the plain unvarnished truth of life in Bomber Command is the very stuff of Legend itself.

There was a further difficulty for him, as there was for all the surviving bomber crews, and that is that History has taken a most critical and hostile view of the bombing campaign. The continuation of the bombing of German cities after the Normandy landings, culminating in February 1945 with the appalling firestorm at Dresden, has come to be seen as representative of the whole campaign, as a savage act of vengeance against helpless, innocent civilians. What has been forgotten is the very different nature of the air war from February 1942 to March 1944, when the RAF was the only force which could take on a seemingly invincible enemy on its home territory. It was hoped then that bombing alone could win the war. Though this hope turned out to be false, the aircrew of Bomber Command showed superhuman courage, endurance and bravery in attempting to make 'the bomber dream' come true. It is one of the bitterest quirks of History that the few who survived that annihilating campaign would discover, in the long years of peace, that their country had become ashamed of what they had done.

Joe's crew had been representative of the dozens of novice crews which were lost, often in the most horrendous circumstances, before they could make much impact on the conflict.

And just as representative were the crew of DFM-winner Bill Coates. Coates would get his crew – navigator Stanley Nuttall, Canadian bomb aimer John Moody Baldwin, w/op William Chapman, flight engineer Bertram Horace Nicholas, and gunners Frank Thompson and William Lambert York – through the many horrendous weeks of operations which followed Black Thursday, when the most dreadful toll was being exacted of Bomber Command. They were a good close team, and must have at last begun to hope that they might be one of the lucky crews who would finish their tour. But the losses grew ever more appalling. The last two raids of the winter-long campaign, against Berlin and Nuremberg, were the bloodiest of all. The crew's luck finally ran out on Saturday, 25th March 1944. Their aircraft was shot down on the homeward journey from Berlin, at about half past twelve at night, near Luyksgestel, 12 miles from Eindhoven and close to the Dutch/Belgium border. The crash was so violent that it was impossible to identify individual remains, and the crew were buried together in a common grave at Woensel General Cemetery.

The aircraft's identity would only be confirmed in August 1946 by the Missing Research and Enquiry Service, basing their findings on the meagre evidence surviving – a number on the starboard fin and a single signet ring which had belonged to a member of the crew. The Air Ministry breaking this dreadful news to Coates's parents (they had lost their oldest son, Gordon, at sea in October 1943 when his ship HMS *Charybdis* was torpedoed) wrote, 'It is hoped that the knowledge of your son's resting place and that he lies in friendly soil may be of some comfort to you in your great loss'.

Joe was the only survivor of fourteen young airmen, those with whom he had been most closely associated in the RAF. The bitter irony is that the crash on that foggy December's night had saved his life.

He had been phenomenally lucky. In First World War parlance, he had got a Blighty one, an injury which took you out of the conflict with no discredit, yet without permanently damaging your health. He had been most fortunate but it was a very tainted kind of luck, unnerving, inexplicable, and discomforting. Perhaps even as early as his time in Ely Hospital, he had felt confused and ashamed of his survival, experiencing a deep sense of guilt about it which he was quite unable to come to terms with. This guilt may have been irrational but it was far too strong to be conquered.

He had spent two and a half years being expensively trained by the RAF, to fly just once with his squadron. Through no fault of his own, he was the sole survivor of his crew, and the rest of his war was spent well out of danger. To make his bizarre survival justifiable, he must be worthy of it. But he felt that he was not – he felt that he was a failure. He had never achieved the officer's rank marked out for him, and can have been only too well aware how little he approached the calibre of his skipper, Ted, or Jack, the meticulous and intelligent older man who had beaten him to the coveted navigator's badge.

That his memories were a trauma to him is undoubtable. Because he would not speak about anything which might stir up emotions he couldn't control, it can never be precisely known what he saw on that foggy December night. Perhaps he remembered the most dreadful things – the dead mutilated bodies of his friends – and yet somehow managed to put them out of his mind as he told the bedtime story like an adventure story, something marvellous and dramatic rather than terrible. Or perhaps he actually remembered very little about it all, only the salient facts of his own incredible rescue.

What he certainly had to live with was survivor's guilt, the bewildered incredulous astonishment that he had been the only one to be spared. He mourned his crewmates, especially Tony. But if one can make any judgements at all about what he felt from the very little information which he imparted over the years, it seems to have been less the deaths of his own crew which were a grief to him than the remembrance of the many severely wounded men whom he came across afterwards during the long months in hospital. He did not write anything about these particular men, or about those who survived with terrible disabilities or deformities, yet these memories evidently remained with him over the years and towards the end of his life became increasingly a source of anguish to him. My sister Kristine had a momentary glimpse of the pent-up grief which lay just below the surface on the day before Remembrance Sunday nine months before he died, when she was alone with him at his house.

> He made a reference to a phone call which hadn't come. Anyway, something prompted me to say 'Well, I'll ring you tomorrow.' He said, 'You've seen me today, we'll have nothing to talk about.' This was a friendly comment. I said, 'I've always made a point of telephoning you on Remembrance Sunday. I expect you'd not realised that.' It was then that he started to open up a bit. He didn't talk directly about himself but talked of the people he had come into contact with, who had been injured. He talked generally about them and their injuries, mentioning no names. It appeared that these were people he had come across in hospital. He started to show small signs of suppressed emotion. Then he burst out quite loudly saying (as far as I can remember) 'It was the blind ones – I couldn't bear that – to see the ones who had been blinded – it was terrible – I still can't bear it – anything but that.' He burst into tears and sobbed violently.

It was a totally uncharacteristic outburst. He struggled to regain control of himself, and once he had managed to do so turned grumpy, as he always did when he was on the defensive, and said he did not wish to talk about it any more. Kristine covered it over – as we always did with our Dad – and went to make a cup of tea to cheer him up.

Six

The Day Of All Days

When I think about my father and his crew now I chiefly see them as they are about to take off for their first and last operation. They are in their Lanc, and hardly able to suppress their nerves and excitement as they run through the long series of preflight checks. And then at last the call comes and all around the vast airfield the powerful Merlins roar into life.

K-King moves from its dispersal point slowly along the perimeter track and up to the end of the runway. The green Aldis lamp flashes to show that they are cleared for take-off. Ted releases the brakes and the Lancaster's engines roar up to full power. All on board know that they are about to leave. Their pulses are racing, the palms of their hands are damp. They are keen and committed and ridiculously young; they believe they are going to kick Hitler; they have had no time to get heartsick of it all.

They start to move, faster and faster; they can hardly breathe; the moment has come when they are about to put into practice all those months and months of training. The plane is racked with shattering vibrations, they feel the rumble and thunder all through their bodies, the plane shaking and rushing with insane speed as if trying to burst the bonds of earth, and then suddenly – quite suddenly – it does; there is that incredible sensation when it becomes alive with power, springs with a whoosh of exhilaration into the air, and leaves the ground far behind it.

They are off.

They take their last look at England as they climb away from the airfield, and through the patchy mist and twilight they see the church at Hardwick and the track which leads out behind it to a huge ploughed field. Eight hours later that is where they will come to land, in fog and darkness, fire and blood.

It is always difficult to extricate the first version of a story from its subsequent encrusting layers. Once I had read my father's very short written account of the crash, already the old bedtime tale had become hidden, existing behind the replacement version like a star no longer visible because the sun is out. And yet that star is still there; I can still faintly hear and see the tale I heard in childhood – the plane coming in low, the sound of the crash, the flames leaping up in the darkness, the solitary rescuer

155

throwing aside his bike – I can still see the violence and hear the sound of that action, and see the silhouetted figure running towards the burning wreck.

The plane had come back limping, crippled, doomed, the pilot and crew courageous to the last. The sound of the plane as it came low overhead was odd – that was how the man on the bike knew something was wrong, and so did I, the child standing invisibly beside him.

My father was not telling the tale to shock or upset, but to enthral, and perhaps also to relieve some pressure somewhere deep down inside himself. It was never precisely said what had happened to his friends, just that they were dead, all six of them. There was to be no mention of the brief respite for Leslie. I did not even know his name. I did not know the names of the others. My father did not specify how they died. I think he may well have believed that all save Ted were burned to death, trapped in the aircraft unable to free themselves – time simply ran out and the plane exploded.

Or perhaps this was our interpretation, made because no alternative explanation was given. Such a fate, of the most intense horror, gave all the more drama and vividness to the scene. His rescue was miraculous – astounding – incredible – and he so clearly felt it to be so himself that he could not help wanting to relive it.

So the tale shrank, contracted and hardened round that central core, became emblematic, almost a parable, simple and elemental, stripped of all baggage but the stark juxtaposition of elements: the white fog, the dense night, the crimson fire, the noble rescuers, the wounded hero. Coldness, dampness, and darkness met their antithesis – flame; my father met his saviours, who dragged him clear. He lay on the cold ground and saw the plane burn like a gigantic funeral pyre. For the rest of his life he would remember that scene, 'the Day of all Days, the Fateful Day'.

Appendix

The Evidence Concerning K-King

There has inevitably been an element of guesswork in writing this story, but I have always based my conclusions on solid evidence, even if it has sometimes been tantalisingly small and fragmented.

In trying to create as accurate an account as possible of what happened to K-King that night, I have of course used a number of different written and oral sources. However, my centre point has always been the bedtime story, which more than thirty years after I had last heard it I was to rediscover in a slightly different version in my father's memoir about his life.

The bedtime story was never told as factual history; it was told to enthral and entertain, and that aim it achieved brilliantly. Dry facts were secondary to the thrill of the narrative, and as a child I never noticed the lack of them. My father did not supply the date, or the place, or the squadron he was flying with, or the names of any of his crew, or the name of the man on the bike, or the reason why the plane had crashed (though there was that romantic inference that it had been damaged by enemy action and had struggled home bravely, against impossible odds).

In the story six men had died, perhaps killed in the impact, perhaps burned alive, too injured to save themselves. One other man, it seems, may perhaps have survived, but only for a very short while. Perhaps it was implied – perhaps I just assumed – that he was dragged as an unconscious figure from the wreck, but I clearly remember in one imaginary recreation of the scene that I saw not just one figure but two, prone upon the lush grass in front of the hedgerow, lit by the eerie glow of the burning plane.

My brother and sister had also heard the story on many separate occasions. The basic framework was one on which we could all easily agree, but we did recall slight shifts of emphasis, probably remembered from some particular evening when Dad had been in the mood for more spin and drama. My brother, for example, did not recall one other man being rescued – for him, it was only ever my father who had been saved from the burning plane. But because I remember my dream-like recreation, I am convinced that my father hinted to me at least once that not all his six companions were killed outright.

What my brother, sister and I were all equally and absolutely certain about was that the rescued man did not survive. The paramount, never-changing feature of the legend was that Dad was the sole survivor, the only man left out of the unlucky crew of seven. As a child, the magic of his escape enchanted me and I never considered in any detail the fate of the others. They were shadowy figures, undefined; my father was the true hero of the drama.

It would only be in his memoir, written in old age, that my father would for the first time state without equivocation that Leslie had also survived the crash. I never had any opportunity to ask my father about this because I did not see the memoir until after he was dead.

In the very strange events surrounding his death it was an amazing piece of luck that the memoir turned up at all. When it did, it was in a very unfinished state. Only the first part had been carefully corrected, and this was about his early childhood. The critical parts about the war were in the most ramshackle form, but though there was scarcely 2,000 words about his time in the RAF up until the crash (and about the same amount again about his convalescence), even that little was invaluable.

His account of the crash almost entirely concerns what happened once the aircraft was down. My father suffered from partial amnesia after the accident and remembered virtually nothing of the events leading up to it. In the memoir he makes no further suggestion that the aircraft was damaged by enemy action but instead gives an entirely new reason: 'There was . . . a very thick fog, which doubtless caused the bad landing, coupled with the fact that the altimeters were very primitive and had to be set according to the atmosphere pressure'. Altimeters were set to the airfield's barometric pressure, the reading being transmitted by Flying Control to each returning aircraft as it joined the stack at Bourn. In fact, an incorrect altimeter reading seems to have had little or no bearing on the loss of K-King, and my father is probably just repeating a rumour which became current in the RAF after the crashes, that incorrect altimeter settings had caused the multiple disasters.

There are several other details which were certainly not in the bedtime story. Yet just as in the oral version, the written account spares not a single word on his crewmates; Ted, Sandy, George, Jack and Tony remain as they always had been – anonymous shadowy figures, cyphers, enigmas, not real flesh-and-blood.

Nor is Leslie described in any way, and only the most laconic mention is made of his eventual fate.

> As for Leslie Laver, he was the Tail Gunner of our aeroplane, and was unhurt in the wreck, which often happened to Tail Gunners because they were nowhere near the point of impact. After the rescue he went back to flying with another crew, but eventually lost his life in a subsequent raid. So that only leaves me out of a total of seven young men in that aircrew.

And that is just about all my father says about the man who helped to save his life.

Though I know my father was excessively secretive, it still staggers me that he never personally described Leslie, either in the story or in the memoir, and that he never showed the least signs of gratitude to him or paid even the smallest debt of honour to his memory. Why was he left such a shadowy figure, this man to whom my father was so supremely indebted, who had been his working companion for the previous five months? This obliteration of Leslie is almost impossible to understand, and can only have been made for the most bizarre psychological motives.

The second man who rescued my father was, of course, the South African flight mechanic, Sidney Matthews. After the war Sidney returned to his own country, which is where my father met up with him again, in Johannesburg, probably around 1960. It is a virtual certainty that they also had a degree of contact soon after the crash; Sidney probably visited Joe in hospital and then told him some of the facts of the story which my father would not have known otherwise.

In his memoir, in order to get around the need to mention Leslie directly, my father never makes it clear which of his two rescuers is playing what part. Though he states elsewhere that it was Leslie and Sidney who were helping him, he never associates them with their actions, does not call them by their names – plain Leslie and Sidney – but instead refers to them in the most convoluted manner as 'my chief rescuer' or 'one of the people who rescued me'. He may actually not have remembered very well. He had been knocked unconscious by the impact and must still have been very woozy when he came round; in addition, it was dark, and he was in a profound state of shock. It is just about possible that he was confused as to the identities of those who had helped him, but I personally don't in the least believe that – I think he knew perfectly well which man had played what part.

Despite his rather half-hearted efforts at concealment, it is actually surprisingly easy to work out who 'my chief rescuer' was – it was Leslie. Straightforward common sense tells one that, knowing the very different roles into which Leslie and Sidney would have been forced by their respective relationship to Joe. Leslie as aircrew would have had some training in the treatment of shock and it would have been he who had knowledge of how to give a morphine injection to his crewmate. There is also the indisputable fact that only Sidney – who had not just dropped in the most horrible way out of the night sky but had been cycling placidly back to base – would have known exactly where they were. Reasoning back from this, I have ascribed direct actions to Sidney and Leslie in my account rather than emulating my father's vagueness.

One small tragic fact I gleaned from Ted's family, and that was that a heroic attempt had been made to rescue Ted. Sadly, Ted's brother, Jim, died three months before I traced the family, but his grandson had completed a school project on the war and with his grandfather's assistance had written briefly about his long-lost great-uncle and the crash which had killed him.

The story which Jim had told his grandson was that Ted's plane had crashed at the base, with the ground crew standing by. Though this was obviously incorrect, it was an inference naturally drawn from the fact that Sidney Matthews, K-King's flight mechanic, had been involved. Jim did not name Sidney, but said that an engineer had bravely pulled Ted out of the burning plane but he died soon afterwards in his rescuer's arms. The engineer was later awarded a medal for bravery. I have checked with RAF Innsworth but there is no record of any such award. Sidney Matthews may well have been recommended for such a medal but did not receive it, probably because he had been breaking Standing Orders at the time of the rescue.

The small tragic detail that Ted had survived the crash, only to die soon afterwards, gave credence to the faint memory I had always retained that there had been two men lying by the hedgerow, their prone bodies lit by the light of the burning plane. In his typical way, my father had muddled and obscured what had happened – Ted had been rescued but had died; Leslie had survived with only a scratch, but had died in another incident sometime afterwards. Their fates had intermingled in the bedtime story, perhaps because the real truth was so very dreadful that my father did not want to speak of it.

Apart from my father's memoir and the above account from Jim, the most critical information in describing the loss of K-King has come from discovering the actual crash site. This at first seemed to me an utterly remote possibility. Though the official notation on the MOD accident card gives the location as one and a half miles east of Bourn, in between Caldecote and Hardwick, there is no map reference and no explanation of what reference point was used, i.e. whether they meant Bourn village or RAF Station Bourn, the latter well over a mile across.

At first locating the site seemed impossible, but then the possibilities began to whittle down, and eventually, thanks to Michael Bowyer, the writer on aviation, I was put in touch with Ken Basham, on whose farm it was said that a Lancaster had gone down in mid-December 1943, long before he himself had moved to Hardwick.

To confuse matters, however, I had by then heard several local reports about the plane crash and all appeared to be mutually contradictory. Two people said that the Lancaster had not gone down upon Ken Basham's farm at all but upon another one closer to Toft. Michael Bowyer's original information was that the crash site was indeed on Ken Basham's farm, but in an orchard, one of those modern orchards of dwarf trees planted in a very tight grid, a location which would have made it totally impossible to find any traces of my father's plane. However, when I asked Ken Basham about this on the telephone, he replied that there was no such orchard anywhere near the site that he himself was thinking of. He added that, of course, I should realise that more than one bomber had crashed in the vicinity of Hardwick during the war, something which made me feel even more alarmed. Even if by a fluke I did locate the place, how could I ever be certain that it was the right one? The RAF cleared up their wartime crash sites efficiently, and it seemed highly unlikely that anything would remain which would confirm the plane's identity more than half a century later.

The confusing testimonies made me lose my faith that a trip to Hardwick would accomplish very much. But at least I would get to see what was left of RAF Station Bourn, and absorb something of the feel of the surrounding countryside. And so, without any great hopes, I went.

Thus it was that we came to be travelling down that long farm track which I described at the very beginning of this book, until the landrover stopped opposite that immense flat empty field above which the solitary skylark hung, singing.

'This is the place,' said Ken Basham, 'Most of the bits of the aircraft were found roughly in the middle there. The tractor boys used to pick them up.'

He spoke of the planes which he had been told had come down on the farm during the war. It was a very large farm, and close to two or three wartime airfields. The most memorable crash had occurred behind his own farmhouse, when a Stirling had gone down, narrowly missing the house and taking a section off a tree very close by it. A Spitfire had gone down at another site on the way out of Hardwick. But local reports had always been that this was the site of 'the plane which had gone down in the fog'. Pieces of aeroplane used at one time to turn up, 'even in my time, in fact'. The tractor boys kept an eye out for them, and took the best bits home.

I felt very annoyed with those darned tractor boys. They had probably taken any vestige which remained of the aircraft. I was too late. Fifteen or twenty years ago, perhaps, the men would just have ignored the bits of wreckage, and the field would still have carried its bizarre crop. For many years after the war, such fragments and shards would have been looked upon as nothing more than bits of old rubbish, perhaps briefly picked up and admired by romantic-minded schoolboys, then tossed aside. As time had gone by, however, they had gradually assumed the status of relics, touchstones, a link to an impossible mythic past, as stirring as fragments of weapons on a Civil War battlefield.

Ken Basham unrolled a huge farm map on the black bonnet of his landrover, and he and the others grouped around, discussing the likelihood of my father's plane having crashed here. I stood a little way apart, unable to overcome an acute feeling of disappointment. It was not implausible that this was the place where K-King had crashed even if I found it hard to reconcile the locale with the bedtime story. After all, we were a mile and a half from the airfield, and if this was not the exact place, then it could not be very far off. I should be pleased that I had got this far. But I was not. It was not just the bareness of the field and the location, with nothing left to mark that night, but the thin, watery and insubstantial nature of my feelings – I had expected an electrical charge from this place, some incredibly powerful sense of contact, but instead it was as if I was divorced from the whole thing, isolated, disembodied, disengaged.

For a moment it almost felt like 'Is that all?'

I desperately longed to walk out into the field and see if I could find even one remaining fragment of the aircraft, but Ken Basham had been so kind that I did not want to impose on him, particularly as the crop was just sprouting.

The others were still talking, and I wandered away from them, took some photographs, and then followed the ditch edge for a few yards. The grass was green, rich and coarse. I had already noticed, from where we stood at the end of the farm track, a round disk of rusted metal and I was drawn to it as if by magnetism, with the preposterous hope that it might turn out to be a bit of a Lancaster. I picked it up – it was heavy and rust-red. Then my eye fell on something just a little further on, a tangled intertwined bit of metal, caked in dry mud, but still unusual enough to attract notice. It was metal skin, with small rivets stamped along its side, the whole much twisted and coiled violently back upon itself. I picked that up too and went back to the land rover.

Holding out the rusty disk, I asked tentatively, 'Could this be something?' In a very amiable and kindly way, both Michael Bowyer and Ken Basham started laughing at my optimism and foolishness. Ken Basham said 'I know exactly what that is . . .' and named some piece of farm machinery. But I did not hear the end of his sentence as I could see the change in the expression of Michael Bowyer who had taken the other piece of metal. He was picking off the mud and examining it. Ken Basham went over to him. They had both become very serious all in a moment as they turned over the piece of apparent junk. Ken Basham said emphatically, 'That is not agricultural'. Michael Bowyer said, 'You may have something there'.

As further dirt came away, it became obvious that there was black paint on the metal, fine matt black paint almost silky to the touch. It was to prove to be the paint that they used on the bombers to dim the reflection of the German searchlights, to make the plane merge more efficiently into the night sky. The black finish was known as Night, more prosaically as Matt Black. Earlier paint had been thick and rough to the touch, almost like sandpaper, and though it was very efficient in cloaking the outline of the plane, it cut speed by a significant amount. The new paint, which came in during the autumn of 1942, was smoother, thinner and slightly more glossy, like the paint on this coiled scrap which had such a silken feeling under my fingers.

Everyone was very excited by the discovery. It appeared we definitely had a bit of warplane, though what type of plane it was and who had flown in it were still mysteries as deep as ever.

Ken Basham had to leave for a meeting, but with great kindness he said we could stay there and walk over the field in search of more fragments. We stayed half an hour more and went away loaded – it was unbelievable – in my wildest dreams I had hoped for just one piece, but as my husband Jon said jokingly 'we are going away with half the aircraft'. The recent torrential rain had washed the dust off everything, and the fragments lay on the surface, quite plain to the eye. We found perspex from the cockpit and the gunturrets, cloudy and scratched in places but still transparent. The best piece of perspex was a double-pad from the bomb-aimer's window in the nose, the very window through which Sandy might once have gazed down on Berlin. Once glued to one of the attachment points to give extra strength, the pad was marked with two terrific chips and a very deep scratch as if it had been gouged with claws. Even after fifty years, you could still see the tiny bubbles in the glue between the two layers which surrounded the broken attachment point. The four screws at the corners were still there, their black washers perfect, neat and trim, but the screws themselves had long ago rusted to a blob. I thought of the moment that someone had put those screws in, tightening them up, as they had tightened up hundreds of similar parts on aircraft, never realising in what strange circumstances their handiwork would be seen again.

Many pieces of aircraft skin were also found, all with the characteristic silky black paint. Some of the skin was even attached to parts of the plane's skeleton, and all trimmed up the side with multitudes of tiny rivets. All the metal bore mute witness to the extreme violence of the crash, with pieces bent and contorted into themselves in the most incredible manner.

Audrey, Michael Bowyer's wife, found a bullet from one of the Browning machine guns. Later when I cleaned that bullet off, I found stamped on it the manufacturing details and the date, '43'.

Michael Bowyer had the most significant find of all. It was nothing to look at in itself, a totally undistinguished piece of silvery metal, quite thick, bent over on itself as so many of the pieces of metal were. It bore on its surface, in black paint grown a little watery with age, 97 Squadron's code, 'OF'. It may perhaps have been part of the camera casing, marked, as all such removable items on the aircraft were marked, with the squadron code followed by the individual letter of the aircraft. It was hugely frustrating that the fragment had been broken off short of any identifying letter, but all the same it was a miracle find; the chances of picking up a piece of such significance seemed to veer into the realms of the utterly fantastical. Here at last was concrete evidence that the aircraft in the field had belonged to 97 Squadron. The squadron had been in Bourn for one year, from April 1943, and by that period of the war were only flying Lancasters. Therefore this had to be a Lancaster.

The only remaining question was the exact ID of the plane. Later, when I got home, I would check the records and find that there did not appear to be any other 97 Squadron crashes in 1943 or early 1944 which bore any similarity to this one. In the absence of any alternative 97 Squadron aircraft, it had to be K-King which had been destroyed on the Hay.

In hearing what local tradition said about the bomber which had 'gone down in the fog' (and there were only three people alive in Hardwick in 1997 who might have first-hand knowledge of what had happened in December 1943, one of them an old lady who was senile), I was to owe much to Ken Basham, who became interested in the search, asked around, and forwarded on all traces of what had once been said or could now be remembered, together with the phone numbers of Jack Marshall and Bob Plane, the only possible remaining first-hand witnesses.

Ken Basham and I also discussed the likelihood – or not – of this being my father's aircraft. One of the reasons why he had found it so hard to credit the idea when it had first been mooted was that the local report was very much that everyone had died, and I was too young to be the daughter of a man killed in 1943.

The main problem with reconciling the opposing local stories is precisely this fact – that they all insist that everyone died. No one seems to have realised that my father was taken away in an ambulance, nor indeed that Leslie had also survived the impact. But then, as Ken Basham said after reflecting upon the anomaly, 'How could they have known?' It was in the middle of the night, very foggy; the fog did not clear until ten o'clock the following night, and by then a guard had been on the wreck for some twenty hours. After the RAF arrived at the crash site, there would have been several vehicles coming and going. All would have used the farm track which ran down past St Mary's Church. Though Ken Basham's farmhouse and one or two other houses were close to the church, the fog and the darkness would have made it next to impossible to identify the vehicles. The station's ambulance would simply have been part of the confusion.

As Ken Basham remarked, 'You have to remember it was a very small village at that time, there were very few people, and all the men had gone to war'. The later accounts of the crash were, it seems, the result of exaggerated gossip on a par with the 'they lost half the squadron that night' story. Such amplification and distortion is partly the human love of drama, and partly the need to express properly the enormity of the loss, which hard dry facts simply don't seem to convey.

An old farmworker, now dead, sometimes talked about the crash to Ken Basham – 'he would tell you all the gory details but I didn't want to know'. He said that the bodies of the crew were strewn up the field, horribly mangled, all the way along.

Another version was that the plane had clipped a hedge before it came down and one or two of the crew's bodies were left hanging in the hedge. This was according to Ken Turner, a local historian, also now dead, but apparently a very reliable man though that did not necessarily vouchsafe for the reliability of his original witnesses. Ken Turner had never seen the aftermath of the crash but had only been told about it. Knowing what I did about the night in question, I felt highly dubious that anyone in the village could have seen the actual bodies, but naturally they could have seen the damage done to the hedge, which would have been in plain view for months or even years afterwards. How the macabre elaborations then accumulated was anybody's guess.

There was one often repeated detail about the Hay crash – that the plane had made a forced landing and had ploughed its way across the field, it had 'made a very long mess' as it moved across the muddy furrows and had travelled some distance along the ground before it came to a halt.

For some time there was still a little residual confusion about the other crash sites round Hardwick – could those have been the place instead? Jack Marshall had been at the other crash on Ken Basham's farm which had involved a heavy bomber, and to a certain extent the stories of that bomber and the one on the Hay had got confused over the years, with people no longer being sure exactly which was which. That crash had also happened in December, but Ken Basham managed to establish that it was in the year before my father's crash. Jack Marshall was working on the farm at the time and immediately after that he went away into the army, so there could be no confusion about the dating.

A very serious problem in comparing the Hay site to what my father had said about that night had actually been cleared up on my first visit there. I had initially been very puzzled, indeed dismayed, to find out that the crash site was nowhere near any roads or lanes upon which the man on the bike, Sidney Matthews, might have been travelling. The closest byway was the farm track itself, which in 1943 was considerably shorter than it is today and truncated very abruptly about half-way across the Hay, leaving no easy route for a bicycle to cross the acres of muddy furrows beyond it.

I had muttered something of my disquiet to Ken Basham. And strangely it appeared that once there had indeed been a track across this otherwise featureless waste. It had been made by village folk taking the short cut to the doctor's surgery which had formerly been in the vicinity of Highfields, though no one could remember exactly where now. The track had been ploughed up many years before, not a vestige of it now remained, but Ken Basham thought it had run straight across the Hay to Highfields and the eastern perimeter of the airfield.

What still bothered me a great deal was why Sidney had been out in that bizarre place in the middle of the night. There was no direct access onto the land other than the farm track, and the proper roads were much too far away for him to have been travelling along one of them when the Lancaster went down. The fog was so thick that the plane, even once it had caught fire, would only have been traceable by someone in the very near vicinity. Had Sidney gone by the main Cambridge-St Neots road, which would have been by far the quickest and most convenient way to get back to the camp, he would have heard nothing of the crash other than a distant, indeterminate, muffled thump. Nor had the bedtime story ever indicated he had searched for it, rather that the Lancaster had come down virtually over his head.

And then I learned about the illicit holes cut in the perimeter fence of the camp, and how those holes linked up with the local footpaths, and everything began to fall into place. I remembered that Sidney *had* to get back into the camp unseen, because he was out without a pass, and that he could not go home by the quickest and most convenient way without being stopped by the Service Police, always on guard at the checkpoint by Great Common Farm, who would have put him on a charge immediately. Capture by an SP whilst you were AWL, Absent Without Leave, meant you would be on a 252, the Charge Sheet for breaches of discipline and a very grave matter.

My father always delighted in the part of the bedtime story which recounted that his rescuer had 'gone awol' – in fact, this was the first piece of RAF slang that I ever knew. Using the word always made Dad giggle slightly; it was a key point of the story, Sidney's misdemeanour.

It had always been incredible, even in the original story, that Sidney had been there at all, but the extraordinary nature of his presence became even more apparent when the likeliest explanation turned out to be that he had been sneaking in the back way to RAF Station Bourn. Only this could sufficiently explain why he was using a very muddy and uncomfortable short-cut, the old track to the doctor's surgery near Highfields, leading to the eastern perimeter of Bourn airfield and no doubt to a hole in the barbed wire. Without his necessity to sneak in quietly, there would have been no 'man on the bike', no second rescuer. Though Leslie might have succeeded in getting my father out of the plane on his own, what happened after the rescue was equally critical. Without Sidney's presence, his knowledge of the area, and his mobility, Leslie might have spent fruitless hours trying to find help and my father would certainly have died from shock and blood loss. As it was, he was only just taken to hospital in time.

Sidney Matthews is thought to have died over twenty years ago, and due to the ubiquity of his name I have been unable to trace his family. However, I thought I might perhaps glean something about the crash night from other ex-RAF servicemen. Unfortunately, though I advertised in the RAF, Aircrew and Pathfinder magazines, no one responding had any direct recollection of the loss of K-King. There was only one possibility of a memory. One of the old ground crew at Bourn remembered the Mackenzie crash by the St Neots to Cambridge road – many people did, for the burnt-out wreck was so obvious by the side of the main road. However, he also recalled that another plane had crashed near Bourn that same night, but not the names of the pilot or the crew. It is possible that he could have meant Kirkwood's plane which crashed at Gransden Lodge, but it is infinitely more likely to have been Ted's aircraft that he was referring to. He said that he had been told that the pilot had made a perfect landing, but unfortunately it was in a ploughed field and when the plane touched down it just cartwheeled and broke up. I asked him how they had known that the pilot had made a perfect landing, and he gave a little hollow laugh on the other end of the phone and admitted that he did not know. Then suddenly he came out with the oddest little remark, 'Because he [the pilot] had a smile on his face'.

I found this idea of the smiling corpse of Ted difficult to believe and also strangely disconcerting and repulsive. But the saying about the perfect landing was an odd one, as was the fact that it was in a ploughed field. The cartwheeling of the plane I had to discount. Perhaps the wrecking and breaking up of the Hay plane had ended in much the same visual effect. Had the plane really cartwheeled, it cannot have been my father's aircraft, because it is impossible to believe that anyone could have survived apart from Leslie – just as the rear gunner, Clair Nutting, had survived the flipping over of D-Donald in the crash near Graveley. My father, in the centre of the plane, would have been subjected to the most tremendous battering about the head as the extremely heavy Lancaster turned over. Yet in contemporary family correspondence he is recorded specifically by his sister, a doctor, as having no head or chest injuries. It was the injuries to his legs which were the most serious, which would seem entirely consonant with the idea that the plane, once it came down, slid along the ground unimpeded, not meeting any obstruction like the ditch which had proved so fatal to McLennan's crew at Ingles Farm.

The Lancaster was an all-metal aircraft, and its construction is a vital factor in determining what happened in K-King's crash.

The plane's basic structural framework was exactly like a cage, a skeletal body of risers, formers and ribs, over which the skin of the aircraft was stretched, fastened by thousands of meticulously spaced rivets. The remaining pieces of K-King's skin appear very thin and delicate – the aluminium alloy is a mere millimetre in thickness and you can bend it with your fingers without exerting any particularly brutal force, though it has a 'give' in it and immediately springs back once released. However, the serrated edges of these broken pieces are sharp enough and strong enough to cause the most appalling injuries to the human body.

In a crash like K-King's, the most dangerous place to be was in the nose of the aircraft. The bomb-aimer's window, the huge domed chin of the Lancaster, was almost entirely composed of perspex and gave virtually nil protection in the event of a crash landing. Though it was very securely bolted on with anti-vibration mountings, it simply did not have the same strength as the metal framework. For this reason it was standing orders for the bomb aimer to vacate the nose section before a crash landing, though as has been seen in the case of Y-York the bomb aimers were staying in position that night in order to give directions to their pilots.

The adjoining section of the Lancaster was known as the front centre section, and it contained the cockpit and the positions of the pilot, the flight engineer, the navigator and the w/op. Though it was the purest fluke of chance who lived and who died, on the night in question Joe's metal cubicle was the safest place to be. Behind the w/op's position was the strongest component of the entire aircraft, the main spar, and underneath it the reinforced bomb bay. The seat faced forward and was neatly tucked in behind the desk – this and the wall in front of it prevented Joe from being hurled violently forward on impact, and he was fortunate enough not to strike his head against the wall-mounted instruments directly in front of him.

The gunners were some considerable way back from the five crew at the front. The mid-upper gunner sat with his head and shoulders just above the top of the plane. He could be flung through the perspex of his turret in a crash, particularly one which involved the aircraft bucking. If the aircraft cartwheeled, he was crushed.

The rear section of the aircraft was known as the tailplane. At the very end of this, beyond the tail, the rear gunner's turret sat like a bubble on a platform, the least integrated part of the whole structure. Looking at the construction drawings of the Lancaster or walking round an actual plane, it is very easy to see how this turret could shear off during a crash landing, and bounce away like a metal and perspex ball. Either that or the whole tail section might break off. Rear gunners could escape, virtually unscathed, horrendous crashes which killed the rest of the crew – it was a tiny compensation for their terrible vulnerability in the air. Leslie and Clair Nutting emerged with scarcely a scratch from the crashes which killed their comrades at the Hay and Ingles Farm.

The person who told me most about the Ingles Farm crash was Colin Stocker, who as a boy had seen the wreckage of D-Donald and ever afterwards kept an eye out for fragments of the aircraft. He remembered vividly how the RAF had cleared the site, how the larger sections of the wrecked plane had been taken away on the low-loading lorries known as Queen Marys whilst the smaller pieces were diligently picked up by the salvage crew, who did their job thoroughly, apparently far more thoroughly than those who cleared the site of the Hay. Colin Stocker said to me wistfully when I told him about the squadron mark and the bullet, 'I've never found anything like that'. But perhaps the truth of the matter is that the job the salvage crews had to do was much more difficult at the Hay, because the combination of the immense weight of the aircraft and the damp muddy ground would have buried many, many pieces immediately, and they could only have been recovered by digging up the entire site. The salvage crew cleared it as best as they could, but the difficulties were immense. The earth in that field is peculiarly clinging – it holds the damp and adheres to your shoes, so that after a few minutes of walking in it, it is as if you are wearing galoshes. The soil is sticky, and clogs everything. Fifty years back, it would have been even damper, because the drainage system was not so well advanced and the weather was far wetter than we have had in recent years. As Bob Plane said of the wartime Hay, 'it was heavy soil – when it got wet, it stayed wet; I can easily imagine how the plane would have slid a long way on that surface'. An object which went under the earth was not easily turned up again. It would have sunk deeper over subsequent years, gone further and further down, until by some strange alchemy it rose once again to the surface and was thrown out by the plough.

Several other sites on the farm had turned up crash fragments, but as Ken Basham said 'none more so than on that field'. There was such abundance of pieces there that the tractor boys would keep picking them up and bringing them back to the farmyard. Eventually, a year or two before I got there, they cleared out the workshop and chucked all the stuff in a skip. This was the worse possible news, but at least I had the date on the bullet, '43', and the squadron code, 'OF'.

I was as certain as I could be that I had the right place, but there was still a nagging element of doubt. I did not want to build any theories upon an illusion, and would have preferred something really concrete.

Ken Basham had said that I could go back, with an aircraft recovery group, once the linseed crop was harvested, and finally on 18th September the crop was taken off and on the 19th, after five months of thinking about little else, I arrived back at that immense, empty field. My companions this time were Dave Stubley and Ian Blackamore of the Lincolnshire Aircraft Recovery Group.

There are supposedly 55,000 different component parts in a Lancaster. We certainly found a very wide variety of these – pieces and fragments, some marked with part codes, some not – together with aircraft skin, perspex, black bakelite from smashed instruments, wiring and gadgetry probably from the radio and wireless sets.

Whilst Dave and Ian scoured the earth with metal detectors for these tell-tale fragments, I wandered away on my own, seeking firstly the place where Sidney Matthews had crossed the field, and secondly verification of the story that the Lancaster had clipped a hedge as it came in. Neither the western nor the northern boundary hedges were particularly high; both were composed of insubstantial hawthorns, with the heavy thickened joints on their lower limbs indicating they had been clipped to a much lower level at one stage. The only way such a hedge could have destroyed a Lancaster, the cockpit of which stood twelve feet high on its undercarriage, was if the aircraft had either been running along the ground or was just on the verge of touching down. Given the location of the main area of debris, the first theory was out of the question. In the case of the second, one would expect to find debris close by, leading in a trail up to the main area. But though I spent at least two hours searching for pieces, I found absolutely nothing, and neither did Ian later with his metal detector, save for one tiny scrap which could easily have been moved there by the plough.

As for the gate over which Sidney Matthews had vaulted, hurling his bike aside, I could find not the least remnant of a gate or gatepost. However, there was an old established gap in the western boundary hedge in exactly the right place for the old track to the doctor's surgery at Highfields, and it seemed very likely that this must have been the spot.

Wandering about in the Hay, even though I was missing the direct confirmation for which I had hoped, at least accomplished perhaps the most important thing of all – it satisfied the raging hunger I had felt for months to get the feel of just what this place was like. In the five hours that I was there on that September day, I realised for sure in just what wastes of solitude it *felt* that it lay. The air was buzzing with the noise of that modern curse, the motorcar, rushing by on the St Neots-Cambridge road, but other than that you would indeed feel that you were 'miles away from the base, and nowhere near the runway, and nowhere near any road' as my father had written in his memoir. It was perfectly clear now why there had been no sound, other than the fire, to be heard in the field that night, smothered as it had been by the dense fog. The nearest building then as now was Highfield Farm, almost half a mile to the north-east. The crash site is approximately equidistant between Highfields and Hardwick, the first to the west, the second to the east, both being just over half a mile away. On that September afternoon, I could see Highfield Farm but neither of the two settlements. The leaves were still on the trees, as they would not be in December, but still both places seemed a mighty long way off.

No one could have found the plane in those weather conditions had they not been virtually on top of it. Some folk at Hardwick did in fact hear the sound of the crash. Bob Plane, the 14 year old lad who lived near St Mary's Church, heard it – 'a thump, and a scrape, and "What was that?"'. The fog was so thick that it muffled and confused all sound and direction – people had no idea where the noise had come from.

The local story was that the plane had hit the hedge (now a double hedge – a row of conifers had been planted in front of it) at the northern boundary of the farm, then crashed and ploughed its way along, coming to rest almost exactly in the centre of the modern field. As on my earlier visit, we found huge quantities of debris in that central spot, but Dave and Ian also located another very large area about 300 yards further to the south. What now became certain was that this was the very spot where the aircraft had burned out. Dozens of small corrugated nuggets of 'molten' surfaced, indicating that the fire had burned very fiercely for a considerable time. The aluminium skin of the aircraft had been heated to such a fearful extent in the fire that it had melted into red-hot liquid and had dripped down onto the earth to form the nuggets. Puddles of liquid metal had also run down and collected on a flat surface. Two incredible fragments were found, flat as pennies, with scalloped rounded edges. The first was rather billowy in shape like a malformed cloud, the other was lighter and shaped almost like a tiny fan. Both tapered off to a point where the molten aluminium, beginning to overflow the flat surface on which it had collected, oozed downwards under the force of gravity. When the fire died down, the drip hardened and solidified. More than half a century of being kicked around in the field had broken off the bulb-like end of the drip but the narrowing feed into it could still be seen.

Given the location of the two main areas of debris, it looked certain that the aircraft had come in over the hedge which formed the western boundary of the farm, rather than over the northern boundary as local memory said. However, the aircraft must have come in so close to the corner between the two hedges that it was easy to imagine how they might have been confused over the years.

Hitting the hedge had not caused the destruction of K-King. Either the aircraft had landed close to the hedge and had run along some way before the undercarriage collapsed, or it had made a belly landing. Various factors made the latter an unlikely scenario, and besides other Lancasters landing in dire circumstances that night had flown with their undercarriage down, for example McLennan's aircraft and Y-York in its one attempt to land.

So why did K-King crash? That is the question which gave me no rest.

For a long time after I had begun researching this book, there was a persistent worry at the back of my mind that the plane herself had contributed to the disaster, a fear that could be traced back to the bedtime story when it seemed that there had been something dreadfully wrong with the aircraft. I wondered whether K-King had been a rogue Lancaster, the sort that no one had wanted to fly and which thus had ended up as a reserve, to be taken out by unfortunate junior crews. I wondered whether she was sluggish, unresponsive, with quirks which made her yaw to port or starboard, or whether she was dogged by a spate of malfunctions, with always something going wrong and causing irritation, discomfort or danger to the crew. One comes across these rogue aircraft in wartime memoirs – they were much hated and heartily abused and cursed. But it would seem that K-King had not been of this pernicious type. When first delivered to Bourn, she had been the favourite aircraft for six operations of the very high-ranking crew of Squadron Leader S P Daniels. It was only after this crew temporarily left the squadron that she became one of the reserve aircraft. It would also appear from the little evidence available that she only once suffered battle damage, of a fairly moderate sort, in her penultimate trip flown by Charles Owen.

So if the aircraft herself was not implicated, what other possibilities were there?

There is no evidence to suggest navigational errors, that Jack and Sandy had got their location completely wrong and their mistake was not discovered until it was too late to correct it and K-King was coming down not on a runway but in a field. PFF navigators and bomb aimers were of very high calibre, and in any case their navigational aid, Gee, would have helped position the aircraft within one hundred yards of the runway.

The more I learned about the circumstances of that night, the more glaringly obvious it became that K-King – like several others – had been forced down by petrol shortage. My visit to Hay only served to confirm this. It would seem that Ted had indeed made the 'perfect landing' remembered by one of Bourn's old ground crew, but the difficulties were too great, the terrain too rough, and the resulting wrecking of the aircraft killed nearly everyone. Though there cannot be total certainty, such an explanation accords best with the known facts. It is tribute indeed to Ted's skill as a pilot, and to the others on board who also made such a landing possible, that Joe and Leslie survived what was an exceedingly dangerous last-ditch solution.

In the main area of debris in the centre of the field we found parts of the casings of the engines, which were formed of extremely strong and heavy metal. They were insignificant in themselves, but they spoke all too plainly of the terrific force with which the aircraft had hit the earth, probably because the undercarriage had given way, and how the propellers must have hacked up the soil as it did so.

One of these fragments of engine casing had a part number on it, which Dave said he would look up when he got home.

We had had a very good haul altogether, and were pleased, but behind it there was a shade of disappointment that we had not found any relic truly dramatic or conclusive.

They dropped me at Cambridge station and went on their way back to East Kirkby with the muddy bag of remnants.

Then, on Saturday afternoon, Dave Stubley left an ecstatic message on my answerphone. 'Ring me as soon as you can – I've got some exciting news.' I did not get the message until the following morning, then rang him back at once. It was not a part number on the engine casing – it was the actual registration number of the Lancaster's Merlin engine. The engine numbers can be checked against K-King's accident card – the second engine down, the port inner, is listed as '327002', exactly the same number as on the fragment. A shard of black metal, against the most incalculable of far-fetched odds, had survived 54 years to establish the plane's identity. The Hay was indeed the place where my father's plane had crashed. At last I had the irrefutable proof.

Bibliography

The Augsburg Raid by Jack Currie DFC. Goodall Publications Ltd, 1987 edition.

Action Stations I Wartime Military Airfield of East Anglia 1939-1945 by Michael J F Bowyer. Patrick Stephens Ltd, 1980 edition.

The AVRO Lancaster by Francis K Mason. Aston Publications Ltd, 1989 edition.

AVRO Lancaster The Definitive Record by Harry Holmes. Airlife Publishing Ltd, 1997 edition.

The Battle Of Hamburg The Firestorm Rage by Martin Middlebrook. Penguin, 1984 edition.

Battle Under The Moon by Jack Currie. Air Data Publications, 1995 edition.

Bennett And The Pathfinders by John Maynard. Arms and Armour Press, 1996 edition.

The Berlin Raids RAF Bomber Command Winter 1943-44 by Martin Middlebrook. Penguin, 1990 edition.

The Bomber Battle For Berlin by John Searby. Airlife Publishing Ltd, 1991 edition.

Bomber Command by Max Hastings. Papermac,1993 edition.

Bomber Command 1939-45 by Richard Overy. Harper Collins Publishers, 1997 edition.

The Bomber Command Handbook 1939-1945 by Jonathan Falconer. Sutton Publishing Ltd, 1998 edition.

The Bomber Command War Diaries by Martin Middlebrook/Chris Everitt. Penguin, 1990 edition.

Bomber Offensive by Sir Arthur Harris, Marshal of the RAF. Greenhill Books, 1990 edition.

Bomber Squadron At War by Andrew Brookes. Ian Allan Ltd, 1983 edition.

The Distinguished Flying Medal A Record Of Courage 1918-1982 by I T Tavender. J B Hayward & Son, 1990 edition.

Enemy Coast Ahead by Wing Commander Guy Gibson VC, DSO, DFC. Michael Joseph Ltd, 1946 edition.

Flying Bombs Over England by H E Bates. Froglets Publications Ltd, 1994 edition.

Flying Through Fire FIDO The Fogbuster Of World War II Freeing the RAF's Airfields from the Fog Menace by Geoffrey Williams. Alan Sutton Publishing Ltd, 1995 edition.

Fractures and Joint Injuries by Reginald Watson-Jones. Williams & Wilkins, 1943 version.

The Hardest Victory RAF Bomber Command In The Second World War by Denis Richards. Coronet Books, 1995 edition.

History At War by Noble Frankland. Giles de la Mare Publishers Ltd, 1998 edition.

Hitler On The Doorstep Operation Sea Lion: The German Plan To Invade Britain, 1940 by Egbert Kieser (translated by Helmut Bögler). Arms and Armour Press, 1997 edition.

Lancaster At War 2 by Mike Garbett/Brian Goulding. Ian Allan Ltd, 1985 edition.

Lancaster At War 4 Pathfinder Squadron by Alex Thorne. Ian Allan Ltd, 1995 edition.

Lancaster RAF Heavy Bomber by Dan Patterson/Air Vice Marshal Ron Dick. Airlife Publishing Ltd, 1996 edition.

Lancaster Target by Jack Currie. Goodall Publications Ltd, 1997 edition.

Lancaster to Berlin by Walter Thompson DFC. Crécy Publishing Ltd, 1997 edition.

London At War 1939-1945 by Philip Ziegler. Mandarin Paperbacks, 1995 edition.

The Night Blitz 1940-1941 by John Ray. Arms and Armour Press, 1996 edition.

No Moon Tonight by Don Charlwood. Goodall Publications Ltd, 1995 edition.

The Nuremberg Raid 30-31 March 1944 by Martin Middlebrook. Penguin, 1986 edition.

One WAAF's War by Joan Beech. D J Costello (Publishers) Ltd, 1989 edition.

Owen, Charles – Operations Diary – unpublished manuscript, held at Imperial War Museum, London.

Pathfinder Force A History of 8 Group by Gordon Musgrove. Crécy Books Ltd, 1992 edition.

Pathfinder Wartime Memoirs by Air Vice Marshal D C T Bennett CB, CBE, DSO. Frederick Muller Ltd, 1958 edition.

The Peenemünde Raid 17/18th August 1943 by Martin Middlebrook. Penguin, 1988 edition.

The RAF In Camera 1939-1945 Archive Photographs from the Public Record Office and the Ministry of Defence by Roy Conyers Nesbit. Sutton Publishing Ltd, 1997 edition.

The RAF Medical Services by S C Rexford-Welch – HMSO, 1954 edition.

Raiding The Reich The Allied Strategic Bombing Offensive in Europe by
   Roger A Freeman. Arms and Armour Press, 1997 edition.
Rear Gunner Pathfinders by Ron Smith DFC. Goodall Publications Ltd,
   1987 edition.
The Right Of The Line The Royal Air Force in the European War 1939-
   1945 by John Terraine. Hodder & Stoughton, 1985.
Royal Air Force Bomber Command Losses of the Second World War
   1943 by W R Chorley. Midland Counties Publications, 1996 edition.
Royal Air Force Bomber Command Losses of the Second World War
   1944 by W R Chorley. Midland Counties Publications, 1997 edition.
The Royal Air Force In Cambridgeshire Part I by John F Hamlin.
The Second World War by Winston S Churchill. Cassell & Co.
Tail Gunner 98 Raids in World War II by Chan Chandler. Airlife
   Publishing Ltd, 1999 edition.
A WAAF in Bomber Command by Pip Beck. Goodall Publications Ltd,
   1989 edition.
Wespennest Leeuwarden (Wasp's Nest Leeuwarden) by Ab.A Jansen.

Index

The index is arranged alphabetically on a word-by-word basis, except for the subheadings under the names of K-King crew members, which are arranged chronologically.